The Transcendental Masque

An Essay on Milton's *Comus*

The Transcendental Masque

IIIIIIIIIIIIIIIIIIIIIIIIIIIIIIIIIIIIIIIIIIIIIIIIIIIII

An Essay on Milton's *Comus*

by ANGUS FLETCHER

CORNELL UNIVERSITY PRESS Ithaca and London

First published 1971 by Cornell University Press.
Published in the United Kingdom by
Cornell University Press Ltd.,
2–4 Brook Street, London W1Y 1AA.

International Standard Book Number 0-8014-0620-x
Library of Congress Catalog Card Number 78-148019

Printed in the United States of America by Vail-Ballou Press, Inc.

To my dear mother

Contents

Preface

In 1632, John Milton, then twenty-four, left Cambridge
and retired to live at Horton, in Buckinghamshire. In his
Second Defence of the People of England he describes a
studious existence: "At my father's house in the country,
to which he had gone to pass his old age, I gave myself up
with the most complete leisure to reading through the Greek
and Latin writers; with this proviso, however, that I occasionally exchanged the country for the town, for the sake of
buying books or of learning something new in mathematics or
music, in which I then delighted." Book learning, mathematic
forms, and music, which so pleased him, were to be vital in-
gredients in his second dramatic work.

On Michaelmas Night of 1634, in the Great Hall at Ludlow Castle, near the border of Wales—"this tract that fronts
the falling sun"—Milton's *Comus* was played before the
Earl of Bridgewater, on the occasion of his installation as
Lord President of Wales. Henry Lawes, who instructed the
Earl's children in music, wrote the songs for *Comus* and himself played the part of the Attendant Spirit. Lady Alice, then
fifteen, played the part of the Lady; John, eleven, played
the Elder Brother; while Thomas, nine, played the Younger

Brother. We do not know who played the part of Comus. *Comus, A Maske, presented at Ludlow Castle* has preserved its enigmatic façade, which, over time, has elicited much learned commentary. My book is not a commentary but an essay in criticism. It tries to do several things, moving ever closer to the intimate center of the work, while gradually approaching the life of the poet. This essay describes the mimetic character and magic symbolism of the masque, and while setting forth some major principles of transcendental form in poetry, analyzes structural properties of *Comus* to show the transcendental form of that particular masque. Finally I try to draw more general conclusions about the significance of *Comus* for Milton's nascent epic career.

These various aims are not easily differentiable, since they all involve the iconography of music in Milton's thought. Numerous critics have drawn attention to this matter. Discussing *Comus* in *The Return of Eden* (1965), Northrop Frye says that the harmony of the "starry choir," in which the Attendant Spirit and Sabrina have a part, "is more philosophical than genuinely musical: it is harmony in the sense of stable and unchanging relationships, which in terms of music is 'perfect diapason,' an everlasting sounding of something like a C Major chord." The role of music in Milton's works is further complicated by the presence of a declamatory, rhetorical element. Music may represent an ideal stability, and the *ars nova* of the High Renaissance had almost realized this stillness; but during the seventeenth century new emphasis fell on the power of music to "move the very affections of men's souls . . . and raise the spirits," as George Wither said, "to that excessive height, as the soule is almost ravished, and in an ecstasie." Before him, Richard Hooker held that music "carrieth as it were into ecstasies, filling the mind with an heavenly joy and for the time in a manner severing it from the body." Such musical rhetoric is stabilized by the fact that poets balance their emotive rhetoric with themes of spiritual stillness. Thus Hooker could say, "The very harmony of sounds being framed in due sort and carried from the ear to the spiritual faculties of our souls, is by a native puissance and efficacy greatly available to bring to a perfect temper whatsoever is there troubled." In such a vein Herrick could write *To music, to Becalm His Fever*. That sort of lyric makes the role of music simply affective, but in the larger works of the period, music never loses its intellectual values, and they complicate the picture. The best accounts of this complexity are to be found in John Hollander's *The Untuning of the Sky: Ideas of Music in English Poetry, 1500–1700* (Princeton, 1961) and Jerome Mazzaro's *Transformations in the Renaissance English Lyric* (Ithaca, N.Y., 1970).

Musical rhetoric is one source of inevitable overlapping in the problems one has to deal with in reading *Comus*. More serious is the thematic nature of that work. By taking its "device" from the twin mysteries of chastity and virginity, Milton is able to broach the Christian problem of the origin of evil. Chastity is a relatively simple affair. But virginity turns out to be a riddle, and Milton makes the most of it, as he made the most of God's "badness," in the Empsonian sense, in *Paradise Lost*. Having read *Comus* a number of times, one is left with a curious aftertaste; one senses a lingering affinity between the Lady's virginity and the power of God. One purpose of this book is to suggest where the affinity really lies. Clearly, to begin with, both deity and virginity are absolutes.

Although this statement appears a bleak entrance into the warm and luminous world of *Comus*, virginity involves the problem of ultimate goodness and badness, and the *Maske at Ludlow* retains a metaphysical cast. In a word, as he was later to do more grandly in *Paradise Lost, Samson Agonistes,* and *Paradise Regained,* here the young Milton laid himself open to all the contradictions of his received religious knowledge. Later he was to suffer his knowledge of everything, but here it was sufficient unto the evening of September 29, 1634, that chastity and virginity were as problematic as any two virtues that the perverse mind of a metaphysician could conjure up. Much has been made in recent years of the problem of consistency in Milton, which my final chapter treats rather in the manner of *Milton's God* (London, 1961). There William Empson quoted a remark of T. S. Eliot: "To complain, because we first find the arch-fiend 'chain'd on the burning lake,' and in a minute or two see him making his way to the shore, is to expect a kind of consistency which the world to which Milton has introduced us does not require." Empson continued: "Imagism seems to me such nonsense that I cannot guess what may be decided by its rules, but Milton tells us at once that God deliberately released Satan from his chains. The first words of God in the poem, however, which come in Book III, imply that he didn't; and the only way to explain this later passage is to regard it as one of God's blood-curdling jokes." I suspect that *Comus* is full of such jokes, though keyed in a more pastoral tone.

From this angle it may be well worth re-examining R. M. Adams' view, in *Milton and the Modern Critics* (1966), that *Comus* presents "a clear story, a simple allegory, and a graceful compliment." This may be true. Sometimes we wish it were true, for, as Adams says, "Perhaps when the critics have learned a little temperance in the application of their Byzantine ingenuities, we shall be able to enjoy without apology the simple beauties of obvious commonplaces set in musical language." Unfortunately, there may be poetic advantages, in the search for metaphysical truth, in seizing upon the "obvious commonplace." I hope I am not Byzantine. I have tried to remember Samuel Johnson's delicately ironic praise of *Comus:* "A work more truly poetical is rarely found; allusions, images, and descriptive epithets, embellish almost every period with lavish decoration. As a series of lines, therefore, it may be considered as worthy of all the admiration with which the votaries have received it."

A work so often commented upon as *Comus* may seem to demand no further critique. I have tried therefore to stress the ways in which it goes beyond other masques and to stress a fact that has always been known but not often pondered: the central action of *Comus* is the overthrow of one magician by another. *Comus* shows the ways in which magic can imprison and set free. The themes of chastity and virginity give structure to that concern with freedom. Freedom remains Milton's superordinate problem, in this work as in others.

My thanks go to several friends and colleagues who helped in the making of this essay. John Hollander advised me on musical matters; Edward Snow suggested the important problem of interiority in *Comus;* Mark Zorn reminded me of its notable silences; reading the manuscript at various stages of its growth, Jerome Mazzaro and Joseph Summers sought to clarify its intent. A first exercise on the theme of transcendental form appeared, under the editorship of Dante della Terza, in *Strumenti Critici* (June 1969), as "Aspetti della forma trascendentale." Professor della Terza's introductory remarks in *Strumenti Critici* guided the development of that first attempt. As always, I am deeply grateful to Howard Flock for his help in every aspect of my work, particularly in the area of visual perception. Finally, Linda Thurston is the muse of this essay; she inspired me to write it and encouraged me when the task seemed most difficult.

The Museum of Fine Arts, Boston, has kindly permitted

me to reproduce the eight Blake illustrations for *Comus* which are in the Prints Collection of the museum. The Henry E. Huntington Library and Art Gallery has permitted reproduction of Blake's earlier illustrations for *Comus*. To both institutions I express my sincere thanks, not least for their willingness to assume some of the photographic costs involved. Diane Christian was my chief Blakean adviser, and I am happy to acknowledge her very large part in the preparation of "A Note on Blake's Illustrations for *Comus*."

A grant-in-aid from the Faculty of Arts and Letters of the State University of New York at Buffalo has made it possible to print both sets of illustrations in color. The Research Foundation of the State University of New York awarded a grant which gave me leisure to revise and rework. I thank both agencies of the State University for their generous support.

Milton's poetry is quoted from *The Complete Poetical Works of John Milton*, edited by Douglas Bush (Boston, 1965).

Angus Fletcher

London
August 1971

The Transcendental Masque

An Essay on Milton's *Comus*

Drink waters from thine own well.

—Proverbs 5:15

The rites
In which Loves beauteous Empresse most delites
Are banquets, Dorick musicke, midnight-revell,
Plaies, maskes, and all that stern age counteth evill.
Thee as a holy Idiot doth she scorne,
For thou in vowing chastitie hast sworne
To rob her name and honour, and thereby
Commit'st a sinne far worse than perjurie,
Even sacrilege against her Deitie,
Through regular and formall puritie.

—LEANDER in Marlowe's *Hero and Leander*

Certain things are no longer possible.

—THE DEVIL in Thomas Mann's *Doctor Faustus*

Be silent then, for danger is in words.

—FAUSTUS in Marlowe's *The Tragicall History of
the Life & Death of Doctor Faustus*

All art constantly aspires toward the condition of music.

—WALTER PATER in *The Renaissance*

1 *Opulent Optatives*

To the extent that modern Renaissance studies derive from the pioneer work of Jacob Burckhardt, they tend to emphasize the spirit of that period and the cultural products of "the discovery of the world and of men." Burckhardt described an expansion of consciousness that gave to men's lives greater complexity than had been possible during the Middle Ages. *The Civilization of the Renaissance in Italy* (1860) thus reads like an epic of creation, a cosmogony, with new gods, new men, new beliefs, new pains and pleasures. Johan Huizinga, in *The Waning of the Middle Ages* (1924), portrayed the era of transition into Burckhardt's "Renaissance." From both authors we acquire a vision of life as presented in cultural products and processes. These may range in type from the construction of great palaces, through the making of monumental statues, to the pleasures and exercise of conversation and linguistic games and even practical jokes. This is not to say that the approach via Burckhardt must necessarily eschew political and economic issues; but it must employ those materials only, in the last analysis, in order to portray the inner life of Renaissance man. A theory of humanistic culture leads to the history of consciousness, which in turn gives

Burckhardt's masterpiece its overt structure: it must, given his bias toward cultural history, end with the chapter on the "General Disintegration of Belief," which itself depends upon the penultimate chapter, "Mixture of Ancient and Modern Superstition." [1] When Burckhardt forced his account of the period down a road toward the problem of belief, he was following the internal logic of cultural history, whose frame is always—from the humanist point of view of man as

[1] S. G. C. Middlemore, tr. (New York, 1958). For the theoretical problem of a renaissance, see "Beginnings," by Edward Said, in *Salmagundi*, II, No. 4 (1968), 36–55. In his *Renaissance Thought, II: Papers on Humanism and the Arts* (New York, 1965), 3, P. O. Kristeller notes, with some reservations, "I am inclined to endorse the core of Burckhardt's view, and to defend the statement that a number of important cultural developments of the Renaissance originate in Italy and spread to the rest of Europe through Italian influence. The evidence for this statement is overwhelming in the visual arts, and it is equally striking in Renaissance humanism." On the general subject of a discrimination of a "Renaissance period," see W. K. Ferguson, *The Renaissance in Historical Thought: Five Centuries of Interpretation* (Boston, 1948); Ferguson, ed., *Facets of the Renaissance: Essays by Wallace K. Ferguson, Garrett Mattingly, E. Harris Harbison, Myron P. Gilmore, Paul Oskar Kristeller* (New York, 1959, 1963). Erwin Panofsky, in *Renaissance and Renascences in Western Art* (2d. ed; Stockholm, 1965; repr. London, 1970), 36–40 and *passim*, shows that there is a distinctive self-consciousness of thought and art during the Renaissance period: "Thus the very self-awareness of the Renaissance would have to be accepted as an objective and distinctive 'innovation' even if it could be shown to have been a kind of self-deception." Panofsky gives a brief bibliography on this general subject (p. 9, no. 1) and stresses the work of Herbert Weisinger in "The Self-Awareness of the Renaissance as a Criterion of the Renaissance," *Papers of the Michigan Academy of Science, Arts, and Literature*, XIX (1944), 661 ff., and other papers. See also Thomas Greene, "The Flexibility of the Self in Renaissance Literature," in *The Disciplines of Criticism: Essays in Literary Theory, Interpretation, and History*, ed. Peter Demetz, Thomas Greene, and Lowry Nelson, Jr. (New Haven, 1968), 241–264.

a heroic individual, that is, of Renaissance man—an ideology. By contrast, for example, the logic of modern determinism is removed from the realm of ideas (insofar as it is *men* who have ideas) and is given over instead to various mechanistic analogies between men and the engines of reason or force. No such analogies were yet possible during the Renaissance, although alchemy and the psychology of humors did proffer them. This was still a time when it made sense to believe in the "dignity of man," which meant, among other things, to believe in man's powers of decision and motion and creation.

Renaissance thinkers were obsessed by the mysterious relations of nature and art, and through this obsession they attempted to solve the problem of their newly discovered sense of human autonomy. For in many ways they could not fully subscribe to the fiction that man was free; they remained haunted by specters of actual death, disease, plague, war, faction, slander, and corruption, nor was there any relief from the theology of original sin, which retained its easy hold over all reflections upon the human condition. But through the varied responses we can record, by which artists and thinkers formulated the love-hate relationship of nature and art, in both the imaginative and the philosophic realms, we can discern one determining concern of all and sundry: a concern with problems of mutability. During the Renaissance these problems were raised to a new level of complexity, for although they had always preoccupied Western man, notions of mutability entered more painfully into the consciousness of the Renaissance period than into that of any prior period. With great humanistic achievements went corresponding doubts. Burckhardt is right to harp on the nature of the spirit of the Renaissance, for he is getting at what made that period so powerful in its cultural endeavors. True, there had to be money to pay for the sumptuous productions of the theatre, opera, and masque, while power struggles—"the many breaches and ever unsure, never faithful, friendship of the nobles"—were inevitable, but through these troubled times ran the spiritual need to deploy economic and political resources in wildly flamboyant displays, by which we recognize the style of the period. The Hegelian problem of spirit remains a central and useful critical issue, though elusive. It reminds us that we can always ask, Where did the energy to create come from, and how was it directed toward such style and consciousness of style?

The discovery of man in all his variety followed, according to Burckhardt, from his discovery of his place in the cosmos. Leaving aside our doubts about the once supposed liberation through Copernican cosmology, we can perhaps agree that inasmuch as man thought or imagined that he could discover the universal boundaries of his knowledge, he felt himself liberated by that discovery. He imagined that he was standing some*where*, some*how*, and it would not be long before a Descartes told him more exactly the limits imposed upon his knowing intelligence as a consequence of his having supposed a locus of the self. In the meantime, however, before any Cartesian limits were imposed upon human knowledge, there was a momentary playful belief in freedom and expansion through space and time which was to lead to the great creative efforts of the period, such as those Spenser proclaimed in the proem to Book II of *The Faerie Queene*.

In seeking the forms in which Renaissance exuberance expressed itself, we can take many routes. The one I propose is to consider one dialect of the dramatic language of this expanded consciousness and to suggest that masques employed a set of magic terms: magic provided an uncanny vocabulary called forth by the poet whenever he wished to register and reinforce belief in his own humanistic autonomy. Philosophies and theologies he indeed might hold or might doubt; but at all costs he had to assert that somehow, as a man, he possessed the daemonic powers of creativity which, while not precisely godlike, flowed from the godhead and gave him that power which he needed in order to command his symbolic universe. Today many scientists would associate magic with mental abnormalities, with superstition, and would consider magic either a type of debased religious belief or a pseudoscience. Against this modern anthropological prejudice the Renaissance would have made no rebuttal, for magic then penetrated every sphere of intellectual activity.[2] Our first caution should be to accept the excitement of knowledge, as thinkers of the Renaissance conceived knowledge—to be wise in their terms meant to be inspired, if any but the lowest levels of common sense were to be transcended. Before Hobbes an almost general lack of interest in materialist psychology implied an equally broad acceptance of the bond between wisdom and magic lore. This link in turn implied a peculiarly strong and intense belief that "knowledge is power," although we shall find it hard, even with our technocratic pride, to imagine the degree to which this belief was capable of mythic generalization.[3] For the artist every corner of the universe, every range

[2] See Burckhardt on Agrippa of Nettesheim: "We might think that a great mind must be thoroughly ruined before it surrendered itself to such influences; but the violence of hope and desire led even vigorous and original men of all classes to have recourse to the magician, and the belief that the thing was feasible at all weakened to some extent the faith, even of those who kept at a distance, in the moral order of the world" (*Civilization*, II, 504).

[3] See Ernst Cassirer's discussion of Nicholas of Cusa, in *The Individual and the Cosmos in Renaissance Philosophy* (New York, 1964). "Cusanus says that all true love is based on an act of knowledge" (52). Cf. also Robert Ellrodt, *Neoplatonism in the Poetry of Spenser* (Geneva, 1960); and D. P. Walker, *Spiritual and Demonic Magic from Ficino to Campanella* (London, 1958).

of social and political order, every degree of cosmic hierarchy was informed by mysterious daemonic influences. These are assumed in the art of the masque, and it will be useful to explore their dramatistic implications.

Occasion

In principle the performance of a play in a theatre like the Globe would fall on no particular occasion, nor would a good play be performed only once. Conversely, the court masque was almost certain to coincide with a specific state occasion and would only rarely be repeated. The typical happy moment would be the celebration of a princely accession to power, a noble marriage, a Christmas, New Year's, Twelfth Night festivity, a *joyeuse entrée*,[4] a royal visitation, or some similar festive occasion. Bacon's essay is significantly entitled "Of Masques and Triumphs," and the triumphal note is never far from the center of the genre. A triumph signals the end (and therefore also the beginning) of a great period or action. Burckhardt's vision of the Renaissance makes these moments the defining emblems of the era, and it is worth observing that while the primacy of triumphal festivity accompanies a fresh sense of man in history, or man as the maker of history, this new atmosphere carries with it an ambiguity of values. On the one hand, the occasion celebrated is a moment when heroes raise fame's enduring monument; on the other, the very fact that the masque of celebration is a one-time affair suggests that fame is beautiful, but fugitive, a "sudden blaze." Only the element of ritual keeps the occasional nature of masque from being a depressant. Ritual at least holds the

---

[4] For typical *entrées* see Jean Jacquot, ed., *Les Fêtes de la renaissance* (Paris, 1956), I. The English *entrées* were assembled in two classic collections by John Nichols: *The Progresses and Public Processions of Queen Elizabeth* (1823) and *The Progresses, Processions, and Magnificent Festivities of King James the First* (1828); the titles indicate the political aspect of royal "entrances."

promise of repetition, the guarantee that "life will go on." Revelry expresses this guarantee, and the mixed dancing of the spectators and the maskers, besides being a delight in itself, shows faith in the political, social, and personal continuity of the state.

There is a dimension of wonder in the mere fact that an event such as a masque will occur only once, on one special occasion, for the tonality of such ephemera is risk, danger, daring. To put all one's hopes in one moment of dramatic expression—this is artistically refined and aesthetically hazardous. The occasional poem displays a certain uncanniness, in this sense: it pretends to serve the purposes of a moment that comes, and is gone, whereas the poetic act itself calls the impermanence of that moment into question. There is a pathos in the occasional; by commemorating the moment, the poet insists on its loss. Every occasional poem is a tomb.

A corollary of the one-time performance is conspicuous consumption. Most masques at court were costly, some unbelievably so. Jonson's *Oberon*, for example, cost over two thousand pounds. Lord Bacon undertook to pay about two thousand pounds for the Gray's Inn production of *The Masque of Flowers*, a work celebrating the scandalous marriage of Robert Carr, Earl of Somerset, and Lady Frances Howard. By 1634, the year of *Comus*, costs appear to have gone up: Bulstrode Whitelock, in charge of music, said that James Shirley's *Triumph of Peace* and the festivities connected with it cost more than twenty-one thousand pounds. If, as a modern scholar holds, *The Triumph* was intended to refute William Prynne's *Histriomastix*, it made its point in pure gold.[5] Nothing more sharply differentiates the court

[5] See the Introduction, by E. A. J. Honigmann, to *The Masque of Flowers*, in *A Book of Masques*, ed. T. J. B. Spencer and Stanley Wells (Cambridge, 1967), 151–157; also the Introduction to *Triumph*, 277–280; and Murray Lefkowitz, *William Lawes* (London, 1960), 211.

masque from the plays of the public theatre than this economic aspect, which reverses the role of the poet. The public
poet aimed at profit, the court poet at loss. To see therefore
what paradoxical advantage was gained by the masque makers,
we shall have to recall their poetics.

Vision

Old-fashioned as it seems when placed beside the Jonsonian
masque, Samuel Daniel's *Vision of the Twelve Goddesses*
correctly names the main characteristic of the masque: it always presents a vision. The degree of allegorical abstraction
may vary from case to case, and in some works, such as
Jonson's *The Gypsies Metamorphosed*, we may leave the
realm of allegory while antimasque elements take over the
dominant role. Even so, there is scarcely any possibility of a
proper court masque without its central emblematic device,
its hinge, its "hieroglyphic," to use Daniel's term. Allegory always involves a certain amount of riddling and enigma-
breaking, which is no less true in the masque than elsewhere.
But the allegory of the masque at its best is always epiphanic,
and the form of masque may, from this perspective, be described as "visionary ritual." [6] There is nothing crabbed about
the visions. They are splendid. They dazzle in theatrical fact
as well as hieroglyphic fiction. Frequently the device requires
a scene of transformation, and this is a visionary experience.
Such a moment may be announced, as in *The Masque of
Flowers*, by lines like these:

> Song.   Give place, you ancient powers,
> That turned men to flowers;
> For never writer's pen
> Yet told of flowers re-turned to men.

[6] As outlined in my *Allegory: The Theory of a Symbolic Mode*
(Ithaca, N.Y., 1964), 346–359. The contrast is with "defensive rituals."

    Chorus.   But miracles of new event
               Follow the great Sun of our firmament.

Vision is the direct experience of the miraculous. The idea
of vision is itself so rich that in a way it covers the whole
range of the aesthetic of masque, but above all it suggests the
strongly teleological bias of this genre. Masque addresses itself to the court or to the prince, and that regal presence is
its final cause. Stephen Orgel has shown how the court masque
not only honors the monarch, but draws him into the fiction
as muse: "The muse, the inspiration of the work, is literally
present." [7] Were these spectacles simple flattery, they would
not employ the internal complication of displaying the muse
within the work.

This ambiguity of audience, author, and actor helps the
masque to become a vision instead of a propagandistic puff.
The literal presence of the muse *authorizes* the feeling of hope
which always attaches to a festive occasion; the vision is
manifestly not an empty ritual. The royal presence makes
sense of the fiction. Insofar as the festive moment is itself
redolent of high hopes, there is a perfect coincidence between
the daring wish, the hope, the will to a communal happiness
which is the target of the device, and the brute fact that the
anchor of hope—the prince—reinforces the device by attend-
ing its enactment. In the lower reaches of vision man simply
looks out at a distant world and records his impression of
things. In this higher vision his landscape is a hall of mirrors
and monadic windows. The iconography of masque thus
finally levels off at the fourth, highest, anagogical stage of
traditional allegory.

Vision in the metaphysical sense still carries with it the
burden of physical sight, that sense mediated by the eye, and

---

[7] *Jonsonian Masque* (Cambridge, Mass., 1965), 46.

it is through the transcendence of this visual medium that the masque plays such a dominant role in Renaissance poetry. We should insist at once on the dominance, since it does not always appear in boldface type; the fact is that both Spenser and Shakespeare center their greatest works around and in a visionary *templum* which is the scenic focus of the typical court masque. C. S. Lewis argued that Spenser makes an ultimate poetry out of the "verbalization of pageant" whenever he produces the "mythical core" of any book of *The Faerie Queene*.[8] A masking, disguising, personating vision is the typical Spenserian style, and the practice of masque in late Shakespeare suggests the same poetic outlook. Technically, as we shall be constantly reminded, the court masque employs a combination of aesthetic media—sight, sound, bodily movement, touch, and even smell—so that the quasi-mystical origin in the medium of sight is crucial.[9] We can put it briefly: whatever the multiple means employed, the end is a reduction of these means, or their guidance down a unifying track, into the single modality of the visual.

This is a "visual" in quotation marks, an anagogical "visual." For the moment we need only observe that ideas of sight were among the most transient during the Renaissance. As perspective was increasingly understood, the creation of a uni-

---

[8] *Spenser's Images of Life* (Cambridge, 1967), ed. Alastair Fowler, Introduction, 3–7, where Lewis remarks that "the iconography of masques could be extremely sophisticated. In fact, much of the effort in writing them must have gone into subtle finessing on the well-known iconographical types, into progressively lightening the touch in pursuit of the ideal of *multum in parvo*." This last remark is in accord with Jonson's explanations of his own masques, on which see M.-T. Jones-Davies, *Inigo Jones, Ben Jonson et le masque* (Paris, 1967), ch. ii. See also below, Ch. 2, n. 15.

[9] This tradition is pseudo-Dionysian. Rosemond Tuve commented on the imagery of light in her essay "Image, Form, and Theme in *A Mask*," in John S. Diekhoff, ed., *A Maske at Ludlow: Essays on Milton's "Comus"* (Cleveland, 1968), 152–158.

form geometric space altered the conditions of literary vision. It was no longer possible to achieve the pure surrealistic "isolation" of the typical medieval emblem. Now surrealism, a de facto symbolic mode predating the modern Surrealist school, was understood to be a function of optical distortion; anamorphosis could no longer be free of its naturalistic causes, a fact that complicated the use of allegorical symbols. Now the symbol had to coexist with the natural objects of perspective space, and this coexistence forced a genuine confusion upon Renaissance mythmakers. For the first time vision as metaphysic and vision as physical reality had to live together. Poets were forced to contain the confusion of the two kinds of sight, and in our ensuing account of the masque in general and *Comus* in particular, we shall be watching this containment, since it produces the most brilliant methods of poetical transcendence.[10] The masque plays a central role largely because it is the home of poetical diplomacy, in every sense. By "diplomacy" I do not intend an analogy: I mean that the masque maker had to adjust the claims of rival aesthetic media and that the price of failure would be the annihilation of all secondary media by the primary medium of vision. That Inigo Jones and Ben Jonson quarreled and Milton later reconciled their rival claims is one part of my argument.

Representation

On the plane of representation a contrast with public theatre is again useful. The norm for performance in a public theatre would be the convertibility of the actor; that is, an

10 Cf. Lawrence Michel, *The Thing Contained* (Bloomington, Ind., 1970), which analyzes the "containing" force of tragic expression. Jean Rousset, *La Littérature de l'âge baroque en France: Circe et le paon* (Paris, 1954), argues for the necessary streaming, the lack of containment, in baroque works, on which see also Jacques Blondel, *Le "Comus" de John Milton: Masque neptunien* (Paris, 1964).

actor might be called upon to play any role within reason. Even though it is clear that Elizabethan and Jacobean playwrights wrote parts with specific actors in mind (Burbage, as well as Hamlet, being "fat and scant of breath"), it is also clear that the principle of convertibility ruled. We can imagine that a special "doubling" magic occurred when there was a strong sense that Role X was being played by favorite Actor Y, but this was always the magic of the masque; such magic doubling (though it can be popular) is antithetical to the principles of repertory acting, where, as experiments with Euripides' *The Bacchae* have shown, the ideal communal performance is a rotating one, with each part being taken every night by a different actor in the company, and with each actor playing every part in the course of the play's run. Such convertibility of roles implies a neutral stance toward the action; it is not "privileged" in any way. The best actor is the one who can be most convincing. Nothing of this method really pertains to the masque, except in the antimasque, where a custom gradually developed out of physical necessity, which led to the antic dances being performed by professionals who could manage the acrobatics and grotesquerie. (But even this professional role-playing is not neutral, since the antic behavior of the antimasque dancers inevitably suggested that those who could take such parts could not *be* courtiers; if they were, they could never manage such studied disorder. Milder antimasques, of course, might well lie within the courtier's acting range.) We have entered the field of political mystery, and although that field lies outside the purview of the present study, a few words about it are necessary.

To begin with, any self-conscious mode of representation is inherently a commentary on politics, if, as Bacon's *Novum Organum* argued, it projects a covering theory of "idols" to explain why men are persuaded to act as they do in social and political ways. The sixteenth and seventeenth centuries are a time of emerging political self-consciousness, betokened by the Baconian theory of the four idols, but even more graphically and troublingly by the Hobbesian theory of "person." For it was bound to happen that at the moment when new ideologies of group action were about to dethrone, decapitate, the king and his absolutist kingship, a theoretical account would attempt to explain the crisis (if not the outcome). Such is Hobbes's *Leviathan*. The masque is the archetypal case for Hobbes, since it dramatizes absolute royal power and, more important, royal charisma. Each courtly actor in the masque takes a role which is "his" in a privileged sense; no courtly actor is neutral. The masque, like any other play, represents the real court through an ideal court. But whereas the repertory actor might play a king in a theatrical fiction convincingly and with passion, here the monarch or his queen or his princely son or a noble lord from within the court would play at being himself.

To play what one is is a metaphysical game. This *jeu d'esprit* underlies all masque dramaturgy. Here, for convenience, I am oversimplifying the matter. In many cases the device does not allot the central royal place to a literal king. The ruler of the scene may be Orpheus or Jupiter or Juno or Prometheus or Entheus. It is nonetheless true that typically the masque is acted by courtiers and assumes an immediate parallel to an actual princely court—that is what defines it as a court masque.

Hobbes came upon the problem of persona in the course of his analysis of authority, since a person is one who acts by authority. In *Leviathan* the final chapter of Book I, "Of Man," concerns itself with "Persons, Authors, and things Personated," and ties up the whole preceding argument by showing how man's nature is made capable of the contractual, political organization which it requires, particularly to control the desire for power on the one hand and peace on the other. Men may order their political lives, as this chapter shows, because they have a capacity for representing their individual selves through the personating fiction of "a representative." Hobbes describes this represented-representer relationship mainly in terms of person and author. For example: "Of Persons Artificiall, some have their words and actions *Owned* by those whom they represent. And then the Person is the *Actor;* and he that owneth his words and actions, is the AUTHOR: In which case the Actor acteth by authority" (I. 16). There exists another aspect of person, in the Hobbesian sense, and this he calls "natural," in which he includes the actions that a man performs for himself—"on his own," as we say. All complexities aside, it can be held that both sorts of persons are acting; that is, both are living off the force of a given authority, either their own, or a delegated authority in the case of "a Feigned or Artificiall person." Acting, therefore, leads us back to the deeper structure of authority, and if we wish to speak of acting and impersonating in either a real or a theatrical sense, we shall have to recognize not only that authors create dramatis personae, but that various mutual responsibilities of the author and his persons will finally yield, in theatrical life, a rather complete equivalent of the larger political situation in which men (including kings) have their representatives, acting in various complex or simple relations to the ultimate brute fact of authority—or perhaps, in relations to what we call ultimate authority. In a monarchy, the king is the beginning of life—the *arche*—as in the theatre the poet or his theatrical colleague the director-producer is the originator of the actions of the dramatis personae.

This image of action does not reduce politics to theatre,

but it does makes politics "dramatistic," as Kenneth Burke would say, and indeed we find that the realities of political life mainly conform to such an image. Men of the early seventeenth century would have found it quite natural for Marvell to use theatrical imagery in his *Horatian Ode*. When Satan directs a political rally in hell, he is directing a diabolic interlude in the grand revolt from God as supreme author. Whether in any particular case the analogy occurred to a writer or not, in the background of most political or dramatistic scenes during this yet strongly Christian period, the highest drama of all—God's creation and providential ordering of history, his Son's birth, crucifixion, resurrection, and ascension, man's *felix culpa* and his redemption by the sacrifice of the Son, and the promise of universal coherence effected by the Holy Ghost—this drama was the ultimate model for impersonations.

The uncanny theological construct of the Trinity (as Augustine and Calvin, for example, had argued) enables the Christian faith to enter the world with an adequate dramatis personae. Divinity had to be divided, or subdivided, into at least three persons for there to be a family romance within the theological framework. Much this sort of subdivision is the requirement imposed upon the authors of masques, for whom the authority of the king, if it is to be "enacted" (actually in laws, theatrically in significant gestures), must subdivide itself and reach out to include a large and variegated people. For there has never been a successful king who did not at once understand that his power lay in the numbers of people he could get to accept him as an authority. Such problems of political scope tend to be a prime concern of political leaders. It is therefore important to observe that the political theory of person (and whatever theatrical adjuncts it may have) must give some attention, finally, to the philosophical problem: Is it *true* that I represent these people? Is it *true* that I "act for" these people? Does the king represent his people, or do they represent him? Have we an honest covenant? (A modern philosopher-king would have the extra burden of asking himself, Is my covenant with the people "in good faith"?) All such quandaries lead, properly, to existential questions, or in Hobbesian terms, to the two cardinal issues of power and peace. Unfortunately, the mere entrance into such issues will lead to others of more taxing difficulty. To give only one example, which applies whenever we are talking about plays and masques and the like, what is the meaning of "I," when the king or anyone else says "I represent so and so?" This *I* is a perplexing entity, if not, in fact, the only real puzzle that concerns philosophy after Descartes. The *cogito* is Pandora's box, and the philosopher has been given the task of closing it. For theatrical and political purposes, Hobbes himself posed the initial problem of honesty, namely, that *persona* "signifies the *disguise,* or *outward appearance* of a man, counterfeited on the Stage; and sometimes more particularly that part of it, which disguiseth the face, as a Mask or Visard." Hobbes was aware, as Hannah Pitkin reminds us, that the actor is a kind of fraud, but that, as artifice, the theatrical venture is a deliberate deception—it is not necessarily "in bad faith." [11] Human nature and human affairs require fraud of this kind; they need this kind of impersonation; and when men fail to grasp this necessity, as Wilde understood, there will have been a "decay of lying."

Intricacies choke this realm of political philosophy, and I

[11] Hannah Pitkin, *The Concept of Representation* (Berkeley, 1967), 24. Cf. William Shakespeare, *Troilus and Cressida,* I, iii, 83: "Degree being vizarded, /The unworthiest shows as fairly in the mask." "Vizard" occurs six times in Act V of *Love's Labour's Lost;* "masked and vizarded" go together—cf. the preparations for Falstaff's final undoing, *The Merry Wives of Windsor,* IV, vi, 40.

have no desire or capacity to free them here. On the other hand, it seems that a hidden drive organizes the masker's art of representation. It is true that behind each mask, on the stage, there is in one sense a single represented being. One man, one vote. And the prince may "act" himself. But the drive of the representative ethos is to *contain multiple beings* within the person of a single ruler. This is no less true in so-called representative commonwealths than in absolute monarchies—all forms of government, save utopian anarchy, tend to the annihilation of individual differences through the device of representation. Pitkin has outlined a series of ingenious theories by which this annihilation is rationalized, and in the literary field Kenneth Burke has for many years concerned himself with the processes of "mystification" which permit the enclosure of the individual within the embrace of the regal persona.[12] For my present purpose it is enough to suggest that the court masque assumes the validity of the impersonating act, plays with it according to the strictly defined principles of absolutist monarchic polity, and permits the ruler figure to subsume the wholeness and plenitude of a variegated people, a people that at the very moment it gave its full-blooded allegiance to the royal house and to the principles of all such houses, could insist on its ancient yeoman rights of individual difference—the "god's plenty" of a Chaucerian pilgrimage. It is no accident that the masque grew up with Elizabeth, but flourished during the reign of the first two Stuart kings of England. Their reign marked a transition to modern complexity in the political sphere, and it also marked a period of the most subtle attitudes toward theatrical impersonation. If by nature the masque limits individual differences, while

[12] Chiefly in *A Rhetoric of Motives* (New York, 1955), but also in *The Philosophy of Literary Form: Studies in Symbolic Action* (New York, 1957), and in *Attitudes toward History* (Boston, 1961), 75–91.

enhancing differences in status, it becomes a remarkable medium for a poet like Milton, who is devoted to individual differences. Leaving *Arcades* aside, however, it is clear that the choice of subject in *Comus* leaves the poet free to lift or cut away the masks of his players. The earl's children could act their ages, given the rather biographical fable of their return home, which starts the action of *Comus*. Milton plays with the idea that "disguisings" are never complete. His scenario is rather more domestic and has always been thought more naturalistic, more "dramatic" than the usual masque, which is to say that in it the masking principle is held within strict limits, so that its personae are suspended almost equally between the "natural" and the "artificial." There is much less sense of regal or princely power in *Comus* than in any masque of comparable stature, and this is the result of a nascent Miltonic libertarianism, which will not permit the act, the process, the dramaturgy of masking to assimilate all individual differences into the oneness of the princely person. Among other things, Milton here shows his characteristic ambivalence toward the mystification of political conformity.

Expression

Printed versions of the masque sometimes use the term "express" to mean the figuring-forth of the device. The term covers a range of theatrical effects, and at first does not imply anything like our modern "expressionism," which suggests the anguished utterance of a deeply buried emotion. On the other hand "expression" has always implied utterance, and the masque, formal and stately as it is, must share in this function. The same ambiguities that characterize representation in the masque also pertain to its expression. If the masque must idealize the court by a deliberately mystifying format, it does possess a counterweight in the area of utterance. Perhaps we have to stress the example of Jonson, though in lesser ways the same point can be made about other poets, notably Campion, Chapman, and Browne, all of whom are interested in projecting their own poetic processes through the public occasion. Although the masque tends officially to ascribe generative power within the state (which includes the masque itself) to the monarch or his surrogate,[13] the typical Jonsonian masque introduces an alternative monarch of wit, a Proteus—a surrogate for the poet himself. The poet adjusts mythos so that the device will permit a second level of princedom. At the top of the ladder is the king. Under him, besides his courtiers, there is the courtier par excellence, the masque maker, and he is the true prince. Jonson projects this secondary princedom through a variety of mythic figures, who act as vehicles for the personal utterance of the poet as maker. Their presence in so many works indicates that the masque transcends the representing process through an expressive process. Self-awareness and self-command mean self-expression. This is the goal perfectly achieved by Milton in *Comus*. Thus we need to see how much of the groundwork was prepared by his predecessor.

In *The Jonsonian Masque*, Orgel has shown that basic to the genre one finds a demiurgic persona, the Proteus of

[13] W. T. Furniss, "Ben Jonson's Masques," in *Three Studies in the Renaissance: Sidney, Jonson, Milton* (New Haven, 1958), 169–176. Orgel, *Jonsonian Masque*, 108, quotes Jonas Barish, *Ben Jonson and the Language of Prose Comedy* (Cambridge, Mass., 1960), 244: "To eulogize the king is to congratulate the society, of which the king is figurehead, for the communal virtues symbolized in him. To the extent that the actuality falls short of the ideal, the masque may be taken as a kind of mimetic magic on a sophisticated level, the attempt to secure social health and tranquillity for the realm by miming it in front of its chief figure. The frequency of prayer as a rhetorical mode in the masques is hence not accidental."

Francis Davison's *The Mask of Proteus and the Adamantine Rock* (1595). Orgel quotes Lucian's dialogue, "Of Pantomime," where we learn that "the Egyptian Proteus of ancient legend is no other than a dancer whose mimetic skill enables him to adapt himself to every character: in the activity of his movements, he is liquid as water, rapid as fire; he is the raging lion, the savage panther, the trembling bough; he is what he will. The legend takes these data, and gives them a supernatural turn,—for mimicry substituting metamorphosis. Our modern pantomimes have the same gift, and Proteus himself sometimes appears as the subject of their rapid transformations." Because this Proteus embodies all the varied theatrical powers of shape-shifting, "he is, in a sense, the spirit of the masque, the embodiment of the idea of disguising." We are therefore instructed to learn, by contrary motion, that "to the Elizabethan, he is also the great enemy Mutability, threatening the establishment of order and denying the value of permanence. Davison therefore makes Proteus both the center of his masque world and its archvillain. The work is built around him, but its action is his defeat and submission." This could be a description of Comus, a latter-day Proteus. Orgel shows that "Proteus is, then, an embryonic antimasque character"—one closer to the Miltonic invention. Furthermore, the defeat of Davison's Proteus results from his excessive literalism—"his faith is founded on a rock, his vision bounded by the properties of his world, which are after all only stage properties. He is helpless before a figure [the Esquire] who can step outside that world and who can see the properties of the rock as metaphorical rather than physical —a figure, in short, who knows that he is an actor in a masque and is conscious of the presence and significance of the audience." [14] Again the description fits *Comus*, where the failure

[14] *Jonsonian Masque*, 10, 13–14.

of the villain results from his literalist belief in amulets, talismans and other idolatrous charms—a belief, finally, in demonic magic. According to this formula, the spiritualization of magic that occurs in Milton (and before him in all the best masques) is carried out through the enhancement of dramatic self-awareness. The Attendant Spirit can spiritualize the magic that must govern the world of the Lady because he knows the illusionistic conditions of the action itself; he knows that the masque is analogical to the deceitful world of appearances that men and women really inhabit, and therefore must come to terms with illusion through imaginative veiling and unveiling.

Yet the mystic overtones of the Protean archetype carry over in other directions as well. A Dionysian Lord of Misrule in opposition to the Apollo of the "main masque," with its ordered geometric choreography—is Dionysus not the most complicating sort of persona the masque maker could place at the center of his works? Why must a shape-shifter be the center? The general answer is only too obvious: because without Dionysian metamorphoses no artful and controlled music of Apollo would be possible, since the primitive precedes the artificial and constrained. The more specific answer is more difficult: because in the masque, with its royal focus, misrule has to be fully contained, before Apollonian law can take root in a living political ground. Dionysus gets into the late masques with almost neurotic frenzy, in a cancerous proliferation of antimasque dances—but for good reason, since politics outside the court is getting closer to the court, and misrule is becoming a genuine political threat to the protected sacred space, the *coelum britannicum*.

At the same time the masque seems to have more positive virtues. Partly because of its ritual function, whereby it represents festivals of political or social augury, marriages, coronations, Christmas, Twelfth Night, and the like, the masque always tends to explore the conditions of rebirth within the community. It is a triumph of peace and love, and thus the ideas of peace and love dominate the iconography in work after work. Given this context, the masque can *contain* the conflict of the two gods who met at Delphi in mysterious union. Apollo and Dionysus must share these oracular entertainments.

The striking thing about almost every Jonsonian masque is that it includes a Proteus figure. From the various forms taken by him, we can perhaps arrive at a Miltonic summation. Proteus is equivocal and mutable and fearsome, the Lord of Misrule; but he is also "genius." Jonson sometimes spreads the role of genial spirit over several subcharacters, sometimes embodies it in a single person. The classic case is in *Hymenaei*, where the part of Comus is played by Opinion, of Thyrsis by Truth; yet prior to their altercation Reason has already prepared the grounds for the epithalamion, and we may therefore locate the resolution of truth and opinion in the arts of Reason, who herself provides the larger perfect circle of order within which the marriage celebrations can take place. Reason controls the orgia.[15] In *The Haddington Masque*, another epithalamic festivity, the circle-making function is performed by Vulcan, who forms the perfect model of wedded love

> in due proportion to the *spheare* of heaven,
> With all his *lines*, and *circles;* that compose

[15] See C. H. Herford and Percy and Evelyn Simpson, eds., *Ben Jonson* (Oxford, 1941), VII, 214. (This work is hereafter referred to as H. and S.) The character Reason, explaining "these mysterious rites" and their "mysticke sense" in *Hymenaei*, uses the terms "orgies" and, later, "solemne *Orgies*," to which Jonson attaches a learned gloss on the Greek term *orgia*—which he defines as sacred ceremonies which have gradually come to be associated with Bacchic rituals.

The perfect'st forme, and aptly doe disclose
The *heaven of marriage:* which I title it.

Here the irony that keeps Vulcan a somewhat ambiguous
creator may be felt in the fact that Venus would reward his
creative act by returning to heaven, vowing that the lamp
will henceforth burn with "pure and chastest fire." She
swears her love will "never shine / But when it mixeth with
thy *spheare,* and mine."

The Masque of Queenes (1609) seems more complicated.
Here Fame plays the Daedalian part, and we are exposed to
her power through the vision of the House of Fame rather
than through anything she, as dramatic agent, actually says.
The spectators were doubtless aware, without being instructed, of the creative power of Fame, since she expressed
the most fashionable idea of artistic monumentality. Her role
was to enlist the nobility in an eternal company, a heroic
consort whose deeds were memorable, famous, illustrious. A
variation of this heroic fiction is the vision of the prophet
Merlin, who appears in *Prince Henries Barries* (1616) and
forecasts the heroic, Herculean achievements of the Prince,
associating him with the virtues of St. George, who had
guarded Britain's martial destiny in the past.

Love Freed from Ignorance and Folly (1611) predictably
seeks to canonize the powers of Love, but it does so, having
presented the conflict between Love and the "cruel," "mon-
ster" Sphinx, by declaiming a more purely poetical energy. At
the moment when Love is about to be taken away to its
cruel doom—"to the cliffe," says the Sphinx, "where I wil
teare him / Peace-meale"—we get the stage direction *The
Muses Priests: their number twelve: their song, to a measure.*
The Priests decide in favor of the victim of hate, relying
upon the beneficent influence of the Graces, and a marginalian
gloss tells us that "here is understood the power of wisdome

in the *Muses* ministers, by which name al that have the spirit of prophesie are stil'd, and such they are that need to encounter Ignorance, and Folly: and are ever readie to assist *Love* in any action of honor, and vertue, and inspire him with their owne soule." [16] Pallas directly invokes "the poets" in *The Golden Age Restor'd* (1615), who remind us that during the Golden Age "language melted in the eare, / Yet all without a blush might heare." Yet in *The Golden Age Restor'd* it is really Pallas Athene who possesses the Protean powers; as the Poets say, "Our best of fire / Is that which Pallas doth inspire."

Much more powerfully visionary is the Prometheus of *Mercurie Vindicated from the Alchemists at Court* (1616), largely because his prophetic alliance with Nature allows him to "vindicate" one of the great Protean personae of the masque, Mercury himself. The Hermetic principle has to be sublimed above the mere machinery, technology, and alchemy of Vulcan, who is the villain of this masque. We begin to discern a major formal principle of masque drama—that the contest of good and evil powers may take place on two or more analogical levels: Mercury and Vulcan disputing the true form of alchemy, Prometheus and Nature resolving the lower dispute. The action has built into it a transcendental movement from imitation into revelation, phenomenon into epiphenomenon, the visual into the visionary. This is an "upward" tendency, from material to spiritual realms. Sometimes, of course, there is no change of dramatis personae to convey this upward movement, and in both *Christmas his Masque* (1616) and *Lovers Made Men* (1617) the demiurgic principals, Christmas and Mercury, continue untransformed from the beginning right through to the end.

Perhaps the most delicate interchange of protean powers

16 H. and S., VII, 367.

and claims occurs in *The Vision of Delight* (Christmas, 1617), where the device allows Jonson to pit Wonder against its chimerical equivalence, Phantsie. This exquisite masque defines the visionary role of *meraviglia*, the marvelous or wondrous, within the tradition, which it presents as seeking the triumph of perfect harmonious motion and song, a triumph that coincides with the rebirth of life, with the song and dance of nature—the "severall musicke" on every bough, "The treasure that great Nature's worth." Here, quite simply, we have a masque about masques. The obvious aesthetic fact is that the reflexive quality of the piece seems entirely spontaneous and natural to the genre. A similar self-conscious purpose governs *The Masque of Augures* (1622), where a sequence of seers—Linus, Orpheus, Branchus, Idmon, Apollo and his Chorus—wrests the art of true prophecy from "Vangoose a rare *Artist*."

To a degree unequaled elsewhere, Jonson here exploits the prophetic implications of the genre, and his marginalia help us to appreciate the mannered method proper to it. Tradition had presented Apollo as guardian of the oracle at Delphi. One reason for the choice of a prophetic device was the fact that this masque was the first to be performed in Inigo Jones's great Banqueting Hall—in short, in the latest and most magnificent English architectural masterpiece. Nicolas Lanier, who reputedly introduced recitative style into the English theatre, and Alfonso Ferrabosco wrote the music, while Jonson added a footnote to the published quarto: "For the expression of this, I must stand; The invention was divided betwixt Mr. Jones, and mee. The scene, which your eye judges, was wholly his, and worthy his place of the Kings Surveyour, and Architect, full of noble observation of Antiquitie, and high Presentment." [17] There was a time when

[17] *Ibid.*, 625.

the two men got along together, it appears. More curious is the use of the word "expression," which here suggests that between scene and text there was an expressive gap, as "expression" results from the uttering *of* a scene. Even here, in the figure of Van-goose, there is an incipient attack on the scenarist, since this "rare artist" "speakes all languages in ill English" and is "a Projector of Masques" and the butt of an in-group joke among the creators of the court masques.

The most explicit treatment of the poet's role in making the entertainment occurs in *Neptune's Triumph* (1624), where the nature of imaginative creativity is debated in the opening comic dialogue between the Poet and the Cook. Drawing on Rabelais, Jonson here plays with the union of Bacchus and Apollo. The Cook develops a whole theory of culinary fiction: "For there is a palate of the Understanding, as well as of the Senses. The Taste is taken with good relishes, the Sight with faire objects, the Hearing with delicate sounds, the Smelling with pure sents, the Feeling with soft and plump bodies, but the Understanding with all these: for all which you must begin at the Kitchin. There, the *Art of Poetry* was learnd, and found out, or no where: and the same day, with the *Art of Cookery*." To which the Poet replies: "I should have giv'n it rather to the Cellar, if my suffrage had bin askt." And the Cook: "O, you are for the *Oracle of the Bottle*, I see; Hogshead *Trismegistus:* He is your *Pegasus*." [18] Toward the end of this masque Proteus plays a major part, but essentially the protean role has already been taken over by the more complicated Poet. The Poet, who suppresses the "extemporall dinne of balladry," brings the sea-god onto the scene. Meanwhile there is cooperation between the Cook and the Poet; material and spiritual are harmonized in a parody of transcendence.

[18] *Ibid.*, 684.

The harmonizing of Apollo and Misrule need not, of course, obtrude forcefully into the masque, if the monarch is given a dramaturgic role. An instance occurs in the late *Loves Triumph through Callipolis* (1630), where the "heroic love" of the King and Queen, twice noted in the script, makes very short shrift of the antimasquers—"certain Sectaries, or depraved Lovers." These Furies are readily dispersed, after their dance, and *Loves Triumph* shows very little of the complicated *resolving* form which characterizes the most interesting masques. The same impoverished dramatic form rather spoils the *Chloridia* of 1630. Here also, although there are figures of poetic power and antimasque fury, they never engage in an action that binds the whole work into a continuous fiction. But by this time the partnership of Jonson and Jones had withered somewhat, and not much could be expected from their disgruntled collaboration. Jonson's usual lyric finesse appears in fine songs given to Zephyrus, Spring, the Rivers and Fountains, but no strong mechanism of masque-antimasque rivalry ever starts working, and therefore the epiphany of the Queen does not tolerate much ambiguity; it does not reveal the assumption, as *The King's Entertainment at Welbeck* later put it, that the king is "the GENIUS of this State." That assumption had governed the forming of all the great masques at court and needed to be validated in each case by a fresh examination of the idea of genius and creativity.

The Jonsonian masque most nearly related to *Comus* is one in which Comus, though a very different character, a mere belly-god, a Silenus, is leader of the antimasque. *Pleasure Reconciled to Virtue* resembles *Comus* in its device, a variant of the "Choice of Hercules," which is parallel to the temptation of the Lady. Its more interesting parallel with the later work is, however, in the Protean figure of Daedalus. Orgel has analyzed the movement of the work, showing that through Daedalus, the dance becomes a complete image of the various harmonies which must rule, since "one, and chief, of whom/ Of the bright race of Hesperus is come." [19] This "one" is Prince Charles, the chief masquer, and the aim of the masque, as triumph, is to produce the epiphany of what Jonson calls a "royal education." This epiphany occurs with the opening of Atlas, "the hill of knowledge." The masquers sing a hymn, which explicates the Hesperidean garden as a "mysterious map" of love, beauty, and complete learning:

> Ope, aged Atlas, open then thy lap,
> And from thy beamy bosom strike a light,
> That men may read in thy mysterious map
> All lines
> And signs
> Of royal education, and the right.
> See how they come, and show,
> That are but born to know;
> Descend,
> Descend,
> Though Pleasure lead,
> Fear not to follow;
> They who are bred
> Within the hill
> Of skill
> May safely tread
> What path they will;
> No ground of good is hollow.

[19] *Jonsonian Masque*, 150–185. Orgel's account contains an important discussion of the differences between Jonson's and Milton's Comus. Commenting on the phrase "the whole Musique," Orgel observes that "music is integral to the form—and if to the form, then to the scene also. Music is what turns verse to song and song to dance; it is the groundwork of the revels; and this is the masque above all others in which Jonson has made the revels integral to his text" (164).

Pleasure, then, with all the appetitive force of sense and delight, will lead to learned wisdom. The masque needs now only to elaborate its epiphany, which it does through the song given to the master craftsman, the magical creator of artifacts, Daedalus. His lines, divided into three long stanzas, each followed by a dance, celebrate the theoretical, musical form of the dance itself. They represent one of the finest defenses of art in the Renaissance which we possess, and their overall effect is to show that when art (here that of the dance) is most sinuous, intricate, labyrinthine, mazelike, it most perfectly presents the "map" of the human condition and all that its penalties and hopes may include. Daedalus defends the Daedalian complexities of art, their seemingly dangerous twistings and turnings, as the image of a world which needs to be known and overcome by means of "royal education." [20] Daedalus, by defending art, is uttering the *poet's* wish.

Vocation

Throughout the corpus of Jonson's masques the persona of the poet-god permits an expressive attitude. This attitude in turn can embody what might be called the "spirit" of the poet's life, his vocation, or calling. Thus in *Pleasure Reconciled*, Daedalus praises the virtues of wisdom, reverence, gentleness, and so on, but the final effect of his three songs is to define his own calling as daemon, or genius, of high poetry. The Proteus-Daedalus figure breaks out through his

[20] John Demaray, *Milton and the Masque Tradition: The Early Poems, "Arcades," and "Comus"* (Cambridge, Mass., 1958), 128, quotes W. T. Furniss, *Three Studies in the Renaissance*, 158–159, to the effect that with Jonson "in most of the masques music is not mentioned at all. . . . Jonson subordinates dancing to the poetry of the masques almost as thoroughly as he does music." But see, on the contrasting case of *Pleasure Reconciled*, Orgel, *Jonsonian Masque*, 180–181, where the phrase "a newer ground" (l. 284) is glossed as a pun on its musical meaning.

own utterance into a larger expression whose range, with a paradoxical eloquence, expands at the very moment his persona seems most egocentric. T. S. Eliot's formula of the "three voices of poetry" will clarify this process. The first voice, Eliot argues, is "the voice of the poet talking to himself —or to nobody. The second is the voice of the poet addressing an audience, whether large or small. The third is the voice of the poet when he attempts to create a dramatic character speaking in verse; when he is saying, not what he would say in his own person, but only what he can say within the limits of one imaginary character addressing another imaginary character." Eliot is thinking here in terms of dramatic utterance as opposed to dramatic reference. In particular the distinction between the first and second voices "points to the problem of poetic communication." [21] Eliot is led to discuss the more subtle varieties of voice which are possible within each type, and to conclude that the third voice often subsumes the other two. One perhaps can make a general rule about this tendency: given Eliot's scheme, poetry moves toward the dramatic third voice by a process of vocal

---

[21] *On Poetry and Poets* (New York, 1964), 96. The distinction, if not from Nietzsche, is from James Joyce, *A Portrait of the Artist as a Young Man* (New York, 1965), 214–215. Joyce's work appeared in 1916; his division is "the lyrical form, the form wherein the artist presents his image in immediate relation to himself; the epical form, the form wherein he presents his image in mediate relation to himself and to others; the dramatic form, the form wherein he presents his image in immediate relation to others." I am grateful to Jerome Mazzaro for drawing my attention to Stephen Dedalus' remarks. Stephen Dedalus continues: "The simplest epical form is seen emerging out of lyrical literature when the artist prolongs and broods upon himself as the centre of an epical event and this form progresses till the centre of emotional gravity is equidistant from the artist himself and from others. The narrative is no longer purely personal. The personality of the artist passes into the narration itself, flowing round and round the persons and the action like a vital sea."

accretion, each voice adding itself to the "higher" order of address, until in poetic drama there is to be heard the personal voice of the poet, together with the vocative utterance of Voice Two and the overheard utterance of Voice Three. Notice that as we proceed from One to Three, the poet does more and more listening, less and less expressing of his own mind. Silence itself becomes expressive as one moves closer to the third voice.

As distinct from the poetic drama Eliot aligns with the third voice, masque belongs to the realm of the second. This seems odd, and certainly problematic. Masque, as drama, would at first glance appear to be written in the third voice, with the poet creating characters who address each other. Yet reports of the masques suggest the contrary: they do not in fact have "one imaginary character addressing another imaginary character"—at least not in the sense Eliot intended. The "imaginary" element of the equation is certainly present in the masque. But is "character"? Sometimes undoubtedly yes —most often in the opening scenes where the genre recalls *commedia dell' arte* or pantomime and there are farcical discussions of current events. But such farce permits only the most limited notion of character, and pretense at realism quickly drops, in favor of mythopoeic stylization and allegory. Like most allegorical fictions, the masque tends to have a personal, ruminative center—usually defined, it must be said, by the presence of the prince—and this rumination gives rise to a need for the expressive persona, the author's mask. At the heart of each masque there is an arcanum, a secret, something to be veiled and revealed, a tabooed power. By contrast, the mimetic drama uses the third voice, exploring whatever action the characters of the dramatis personae logically and psychologically imply, given certain political or social conditions. The mimetic drama is a macrocosmic, the masque a microcosmic modality. Being microcosmic, the masque works within much tighter bounds, like a controlled chemical process. The poet speaks rather directly to his audience, screened from their critical eyes only by the varied devices of illusion which are the machinery of the genre. The masquer who, in modern fiction, most closely approximates the masquer of the Renaissance pageant is the speaker in a dramatic monologue. Eliot shows that this speaker does not really divide the loyalty of the poet who is making him speak. The dramatic monologue is the form taken by an ideal ventriloquism, and Eliot describes this genre and its poetic from the creator's point of view.

The fact that a number of characters in a play have claims upon the author, for their allotment of poetic speech, compels him to extract the poetry from the character, rather than impose his poetry upon it. Now, in the dramatic monologue we have no such check. The author is just as likely to identify the character with himself, as himself with the character: for the check is missing that will prevent him from doing so—and that check is the necessity for identifying himself with some other character replying to the first. What we normally hear, in fact, in the dramatic monologue, is the voice of the poet, who has put on the costume and make-up either of some historical character, or of one out of fiction. His personage must be identified to us—as an individual, or at least as a type—before he begins to speak. If, as frequently with Browning, the poet is speaking in the role of an historical personage, like Lippo Lippi, or in the role of a known character of fiction, like Caliban, he has taken possession of that character. And the difference is most evident in his "Caliban upon Setebos." In *The Tempest*, it is Caliban who speaks; in "Caliban upon Setebos," it is Browning's voice that we hear, Browning talking aloud through Caliban. It was Browning's greatest disciple, Ezra Pound, who adopted the term "persona" to indicate the several historical characters through whom he spoke: and the term is just.

Eliot seems to have wanted to insist on persona, because he says, "I risk the generalization also, which may indeed be far too sweeping, that dramatic monologue cannot create any character. For character is created and made real only in an action, a communication between imaginary people." On the other hand, although generally "when we listen to a play by Shakespeare, we listen not to Shakespeare but to his characters," we also seek, like Eliot himself, a double author of "To-morrow, and to-morrow, and to-morrow"; "is not the perpetual shock and surprise of these hackneyed lines evidence that Shakespeare and Macbeth are uttering the words in unison, though perhaps with somewhat different meaning?" There are even more elusive passages (Eliot instances "Ripeness is all" and "Simply the thing I am / Shall make me live"), where "we hear a more impersonal voice still than that of either the character or the author." [22]

Several things can be said about the use of the second voice in masque. According to Eliot's notion, the masque permits a direct address of the author to an audience—one feels this very strongly in *Comus*. Then, since the voice speaks author-to-audience, all sorts of questions can be raised about the nature of both authors and audiences. The masque can play with the parallel between the poet and the prince, between "I-Ben Jonson" and "thou-King James," through the inter-mediating persona—so frequently in the masques that he constitutes almost their presiding figure—of the Daedalian, protean genius of a Prospero. One can ask, Is the real creator of "variety and state" the poet or the king? Perhaps the king and the poet create the conditions of each other's utterance. One can ask, furthermore, Who are the real audience? The masquers who dance to each other in complex antiphonal choreography or the enthroned, seated spectators? Who, really, witness the magical revelation of the princely power,

[22] *On Poetry and Poets*, 103–104, 110.

those who stand within the magical circle or those outside it? Or, even, can someone outside the circle know what the circle is? Or those inside it, are they better placed? Perhaps these are the deeper problems inherent in the crossover of masquers and spectators in the revels, where the spectators are allowed to glimpse, touch, experience a mystery into which the former are the initiates. But then, a mystery revealed is not a mystery. What then is the difference between spectators who have been subjected to the almost psychedelic experience of the synesthetic feast and those who, standing in the pit at the Globe, were half in and half out of the public playwright's more narrowly verbal illusion? Since these questions permit no easy answer, the Shakespearean masque calls out for close study, a critical emergency similar to that evoked by the Jonsonian masque. Meanwhile we notice that through its use of persona and the second voice, the masque, whether Shakespearean or Jonsonian, allows the poet a special freedom of utterance, not possible to him in the objective mimesis of the third voice. He can express his authorial consciousness without entirely giving up the dramatic medium.

Finally, the second is an originating voice, a self-consciously creative voice. In keeping with the courtly ambience of the masque, the mode of masque speech insists on the idea of genius and generation. Both king and poet analogously create, if not *ab ovo*, at least *de novo*. The superordered style of masque self-consciously projects creative rigor; the poet is like a structuralist critic who has been asked to design the perfect dramatic action and has insisted on the primacy of order itself as the creative principle. The superordered style is intensely musical, and if we rightly resist the notion that such artificial works represent the whole dramaturgic genius of the English Renaissance, we should remember that their music unites the two controlling principles of restraint and liberty in the highest possible degree. And music is pure voice, the art that cannot help expressing a vocation. The Orphic poet who speaks through the masque, the *actual* Campion, the *actual* Chapman, speaks with an authority coming from his possessing, in this genre, the authority of his delegated, second voice. He can utter *for* himself, *through* the masking device. This he could only limitedly do through the third voice of poetical drama or the undelegated lyric first voice. But in the masque, through elegant ventriloquism, the poet enjoys a rare mandate, a rare freedom of speech, in that his verses appropriately imitate music itself, and without seeming to do so, his verses can speak for him. As Proteus, the poet is set free. Prosodic freedom seems hard enough to define, "freedom of speech" even harder. But if such lyrical poets as Spenser, Herrick, or Marvell were instanced, beside the maskers Jonson and Shakespeare, we would ally their appearance of freedom with their extreme prosodic artifice in the use of conventions which control the expressive voice. Perhaps the masque, as a genre, seeks the alliance of nature and art in the extremes of its procedures—in posing masque versus antimasque, for example—in order that, as a genre, the masque may project the idea of a royal, genial creativity. If so, it is important that in this Apollonian form, where representation limits individual differences, the expressive use of music finally raises the problem of rhetoric.

Persuasion

Although all works of art and literature are under some pressure to persuade, this requirement is deadly serious in the case of the masque, owing once again to its occasional performance. Probably the Jonsonian antimasque met this demand that the poet avoid all "dull and phlegmatic inventions."

Antimasques could reverse the anesthesia that went with the didacticism of the occasion. Imagine, for example, the effect of the witches' dance in *The Masque of Queenes* (1609): "With a strange and sodayne Musique, they fell into a *magicall daunce*, full of preposterous change, and gesticulation, but most applying to their property: who, at theyr meetings, do all things contrary to the custome of Men, dauncing, back to back, hip to hip, theyr hands Joyn'd and making theyr *circles* backward, to the left hand, with strange phantastique motions of theyr heads, and bodies." [23] It made little difference that such motions and such "hollow and infernall musique" were authorized, along with "vipers, snakes bones, herbes, rootes, and other ensigns of theyr Magick," by the "antient, & late *Writers*." The didactic gloss fails to obscure the main effect of such antimasque dancing: the shock and momentary delight caused by a sudden grotesquerie.

Generally, masques, as we reconstruct them from their printed scenarios, seem to have permitted, despite their literal brevity, the utmost range in rhetorical methods. Each introduction of a fresh medium, and the sense of shift from one medium to another, would enhance the persuasive force of the whole, since that whole aimed, as Francis Bacon put it, at refreshment and recreation. Especially when staging was unobtrusive the spectacle would achieve this aim: "the alterations of scenes, so it be quietly and without noise [can] feed and relieve the eye. . . . Some sweet odours suddenly coming forth, without any drops falling, are, in such a company as there is steam and heat, things of great pleasure and refreshment." [24] If such effects had power, geometrically ordered

[23] H. and S., VII, 301. Of this episode in *The Masque of Queenes*, Orgel says, "This performance [of the antic dance] parallels the revels of the masque" (*Jonsonian Masque*, 137).

[24] "Of Masques and Triumphs," *The Essays*, A. W. Pollard, ed. (London, 1900), 95–96.

dances were even more striking; the sight of twelve masked dancers performing complex arabesques would captivate the court, for as Bacon said, "Dancing to song is a thing of great state and pleasure." Songs punctuated the evening's entertainment. There was, in short, no lack of rhetorical means. What partly distinguishes the masque from other dramatic forms is not its rhetorical means, as such, but an intense baroque concentration. Public plays had songs and dances, for example. They depended more than is often realized upon the art of costume and scenic effect. But such theatrical means were always subordinated to the larger curve of an action carried by the unifying medium of blank verse. Not even the more elaborate staging made possible by indoor theatres was as focused and ornamentally enriched as that of the average court masque. Here rhetorical appeal is by design excessive.

In *The Rhetoric of Motives*, Kenneth Burke has set forth the problem of such excessive rhetorical appeals, which more often than not occur in a context of "courtship." Burke's theory of courtship is firmly based on the documents of Renaissance court life, chief among them *The Courtier* of Castiglione. The "principle of courtship" is the Burkean label for "the use of suasive devices for the transcending of social estrangement," and it covers a variety of "mysteries" by which (according to the Marxist analysis) terms of mystical incorporation are used to make men feel at one with each other even though material forces keep them apart.[25] The political myth of the state or of "the king's two bodies" or of any glamorous social unity falls under the principle of courtship. On the broadest possible plane ideology may be mys-

[25] *Rhetoric of Motives*, 208. Burke draws reinforcement from William Empson's *Some Versions of Pastoral* (New York, 1960)— whose account of Lewis Carroll's *Alice* bears indirectly on the treatment of the child-parent relationship in *Comus*.

terious, insofar as it is a fiction intended to unify political men in spite of real individual differences. This makes rhetoric and the science of courtship a single discipline, since the aim of the rhetorician is, roughly speaking, to unify his audience into singleness of response and thus to "court" that audience.

Burke holds that

much analysis of political exhortation comes to look simply like a survival of primitive magic, whereas it should be handled in its own terms, as an aspect of what it really is: rhetoric. The approach to rhetoric in terms of "word magic" gets the whole subject turned backwards. Originally, the magical use of symbolism to affect natural processes by rituals and incantations was a mistaken transference of a proper linguistic function to an area for which it was not fit. The realistic use of addressed language to *induce action in people* became the magical use of addressed language to *induce motion in things* (things by nature alien to purely linguistic orders of motivation). If we then begin by treating this *erroneous* and *derived* magical use as *primary*, we are invited to treat a *proper* use of language (for instance, political persuasion) simply as a vestige of benightedly prescientific magic.[26]

Burke's correction of this theory of origins need not concern us here. We are carried forward by the link of rhetoric and magic, no matter which has priority and is "proper."

It is thus evident that when rhetorical appeals express the "heightened consciousness" of the masque, we are dealing at the very least with a synergy of magic and rhetoric, and magic has no primitive connotations whenever it is colored by Neoplatonic speculation. For this period magic may often be the arcane science of transcendental powers, and there is no modern anthropologist's embarrassment over degrees of tribal backwardness, or the like. Magic here is an intellectual

[26] *Rhetoric of Motives*, 42.

structure. It is, however, deeply implicated in the rhetoric of the masque, and indeed when we come to analyze the overall dynamics of this genre, we find that most of its methods can be subsumed under the category of magic. For that reason the ultimate triumph of masque-making, the creation of *Comus*, hinges upon a drama of conflicting magics, not, as is commonly said, upon a moral debate. Before we can look closely at *Comus*, however, we shall need to examine the typically magical methods of other prior works, in order to establish the weight of this extreme rhetoric.

2 *Festal Magic in Renaissance Masking*

Every mode of thought or feeling may be assumed to have its lower levels, its basement or foundations over which rise the cloud-capped towers of its fancy, and in English dramatic history one imaginative bottom is the tragic lore of ghosts, another the comic lore of fairies, whose monarch is a "spirit of no common rate," as Titania calls herself.[1] Since comedy seems close to the masque, we may begin by noting that in England the "festive comedies," whether Shakespearean or other, purvey a special magic which is of the most basic sort. C. L. Barber has described this spellbinding art precisely as adherence to a *form* or set of *forms*. Noting that Shakespeare draws on the ritual idea of the sacred holiday, Barber continues:

We can get hold of the spirit of Elizabethan holidays because they had form. "Merry England" was merry chiefly by virtue of

---

[1] On the *longaevi* see C. S. Lewis, *The Discarded Image* (Cambridge, 1964), 122–138. K. M. Briggs, *The Anatomy of Puck* (London, 1959), 86–92, discusses fairy lore in *Comus*. The Welsh setting of the Earl of Bridgewater's mandate might have encouraged this vein of folklore.

40

its community observances of periodic sports and feast days. Mirth took form in morris-dances, sword-dances, wassailings, mock ceremonies of summer kings and queens and of lords of misrule, mummings, disguisings, masques—and a bewildering variety of sports, games, shows, and pageants improvised on traditional models. . . . Custom prescribed, more or less definitely, some ways of making merry at each occasion. The seasonal feasts were not, as now, rare curiosities to be observed by folklorists in remote villages, but landmarks framing the cycle of the year, observed with varying degrees of sophistication by most elements in the society.

Among the numerous insights this ritual purview of festivity makes possible, two are of cardinal importance to our understanding of the masque. First, Barber is able to show in what sense the Shakespearean comic forms themselves are influenced by the "framing" of the traditional holiday forms, and thereby why the comedies possess such enormous ritual energy when their climaxes assert the principle of social re-creation. We may say that Barber's comment on Oberon has general force throughout the festive comedies: "In making Oberon, prince of faeries, into the May king, Shakespeare urbanely plays with the notion of a supernatural power at work in holiday: he presents the common May game presided over by an aristocratic garden god." [2] The poet makes a connection in the drama between the most elegant and the most primitive, and festivity gives the natural context for this union. Dionysian presences liberate forces of social coherence. The aim of festive comedy is to structure these forces.

Barber can, in the second place, show why a play like *A Midsummer Night's Dream* possesses strong elements of the pageant, why it recalls the sort of magical encounters represented by the Elvetham entertainment of 1591 and the better

[2] *Shakespeare's Festive Comedy* (Princeton, N.J., 1959), 5–6, 119.

known entertainment at Kenilworth in 1575. An outdoor atmosphere hung over such a play and in a sense over all the festive comedies, because it was outdoors where the fairies lived, and where, during the gentle summer evenings, they sported abroad.[3]

The humor of the play relates superstition, magic and passionate delusion as "fancy's images." The actual title emphasizes a skeptical attitude by calling the comedy a "dream." It seems unlikely that the title's characterization of the dream, a "midsummer night's dream," implies association with the specific customs of Midsummer Eve, the shortest night of the year, except as "midsummer night" would carry suggestions of a magic time.

This magical temporality structures the festive world for Shakespeare.

His fairies are produced by a complex fusion of pageantry and popular game, as well as popular fancy. Moreover, as we shall see, they are not serious in the menacing way in which the people's fairies are serious. Instead they are serious in a very different way, as embodiments of the Maygame experience of eros in men and women and trees and flowers, while any superstitious tendency to believe in their literal reality is mocked. The whole night's action is presented as a release of shaping fantasy which brings clarification about the tricks of strong imagination.[4]

[3] See Enid Welsford, *The Court Masque: A Study in the Relationship between Poetry and the Revels* (Cambridge, 1927), 318 and 334, on the outdoor atmosphere of certain masques and plays, the influence of pageants performed outdoors, and the errors in reading *Comus* which have resulted from responding to this mood. Welsford, and more recently John Demaray, *Milton and the Masque Tradition*, 97–122, have shown that *Comus* was staged indoors, doubtless in the Great Hall at Ludlow Castle, a thirty-by-sixty-foot space, large enough and especially *long* enough to provide an excellent acoustical chamber for the work. See also Willa M. Evans, *Henry Lawes, Musician and Friend of Poets* (New York, 1941), 86–95, on the original production of *Comus*.

[4] Barber, *Shakespeare's Festive Comedy*, 123, 124; see also 139–148.

This description of the dream-festivity puts the emphasis where, with Shakespeare certainly, it should fall, on the workings of imagination. A corollary would be the observation that with the chief Lord of Misrule in Shakespeare, namely Falstaff, the oracular wit of the great clown enables him to stage dramatic interludes, as in *Henry IV, Part I.* Falstaff stages plays within plays and sums up in his person all the Dionysian energies of appetite and mimetic art. With such heroes there is always a double level of creativity, the erotic and the imaginative; the festive clowns and their cohorts in holiday-making are devoted to the principle that art is always a means of rebirth. Insofar as the idea of festivity controls the Shakespearean comedies, it leads to ritual. Festivity exploits that "magic time" of periodic social and natural rebirth, first generally made known to modern readers through what Barber has called "the eclectic pages" of *The Golden Bough.*

Ritual in the public theatre appears, then, to be one understructure of Elizabethan dramatic art, and as festivity it is popular. The magic accompanying ritual is likewise popular, and quite like the pagan mysteries of the Renaissance may be associated with rather primitive levels of folk belief, with Burckhardt's "mixture of ancient and modern superstition." In John Fletcher's defense of his *Faithful Shepherdess* in the quarto of 1609, we can see the degree to which this popularity is implicit in the holiday form of drama. Arguing that he has created a new type of drama, he tells his reader in his preface that this play must compete with stereotyped notions of what an outdoor comedy should be, namely a festive comedy: "It is a pastoral tragi-comedy, which the people seeing when it was played, having ever had a singular gift in defining, concluded to be a play of country hired shepherds in gray cloaks, with curtailed dogs in strings, sometimes laughing together and sometimes killing one another; and missing Whitsunales, cream, wassail and morris dances, began to be angry." Defending the hybrid form of tragicomedy, Fletcher mixes traditional concepts of dramatic decorum: "so that a god is lawful in this as in tragedy, and mean people as in a comedy." Here we might consider how such definitions fit *A Midsummer Night's Dream,* and recalling the mocking remarks in *Hamlet* on the nicety of dramatic typology, we may forgive Fletcher his touchy recollection of his unreceptive firstnight audience.

Furthermore, with its original, *Il Pastor Fido,* his play, which seems to have been in Milton's mind as he wrote *Comus,* may resolve a conflict between the festive comedy of Shakespeare and the type of drama Shakespeare assimilated through the dramaturgy of romance—that is, the masque.[5] Fletcher's

[5] See Bernard Weinberg, *A History of Literary Criticism in the Italian Renaissance* (Chicago, 1961), II, ch. xxi, "The Quarrel over Guarini's *Il Pastor Fido.*" Weinberg notes that this quarrel compressed and raised the central issues of Renaissance critical theory more sharply than had any previous polemical debate, largely because tragicomedy seemed to undermine the notion of fixed generic categories which belonged to "a system of airtight and immutable genres" (1103). By substituting the end of pleasure for that of pure form and approved content, the tragicomic is almost "sufficient to wreck the systematized thinking of the Ancients. There are no longer any permanent Forms, but in their place an indefinite number of species, each of which invents its own subjects, characters, plots, styles. Invention of this kind is the poet's right. Rather than being bound by precept, he is free to improvise such artistic forms as seem to him likely to succeed with his audience. Against the old thesis that the precepts of art determine the poet's practice is set the new thesis that the poet's practice determines the precepts of art" (1104–1105). This suggests that John Fletcher was interested precisely in the audience's knowing that a new rule was being created by him, not that the old rules were simply abandoned; tragicomedy, in other words, was a new and self-consciously hybridized form. See Marvin T. Herrick, *Tragicomedy: Its Origin and Development in Italy, France, and England* (Urbana, Ill., 1962); and Eugene Waith, *The Pattern of Tragicomedy in Beaumont and Fletcher* (New Haven, 1952).

preface points to the difficulty of reconciling the primitive ritualism of festive theatre with the elegance of pastoral drama, which is surely the neatest form in which ideas of state, of culture, of religion may be brought into the comic drama. *A Midsummer Night's Dream* draws on deliberately primitive and popular myth, whereas the poetry of ideas requires, for its purest expression, to be given over to something like pastoral, if not to pastoral drama as a strictly stylized genre. *As You Like It*, which contains the masque of Hymen, is typically Shakespearean in that it does not allow the standard of courtly behavior to impose, as ultimate arbiter, a pastoralism of pure idea upon the benign simplicities of Audrey and Touchstone. The standard by which Shakespeare measures is the natural; the standard by which most Renaissance pastoral measures is the artificial, whether it be the artifice of refined courtly behavior, courtesy, or the extrapolated turns and bows of the pastoral "shepherd," that artificial creature to whom Dr. Johnson took such violent exception in his review of *Lycidas*.

To the extent that Renaissance English drama becomes more artificial and courtly as it develops, the natural standard will decline and will be replaced by more sophisticated criteria. Ian Fletcher's description of *The Faithful Shepherdess* shows just how far this movement could carry the drama toward abstraction, if not toward a new species of allegory: "Like its Italian predecessors, *The Faithful Shepherdess* presents a map of love, ranging from the frontiers of lust, true chaste love, both physical and spiritual, to a new extreme, positive virginity, Fletcher's version of Italian platonizing." "Map of love" does not describe what Barber would call a festive drama. Clorin, whose speech expounding the magical powers of chastity appears to be echoed in *Comus*, may rightly be termed "an emblem of that supernatural power which governs instinctive nature," [6] and we are ready to accept an allegorical reading of such a play. John Fletcher employs a highly symmetrical method of doubling and grouping his characters, so that pair after pair appears, to experience the abstract testing of principle.[7] This new kind of theatrical magic is less variable, less humane than that practiced and studied in the festive Shakespearean comedy.

To call the festive ritual "primitive" may mislead. But it reminds us that whatever magic Shakespeare employs is mythically structured to reinforce belief in the great recurrences of nature, thereby giving the artifice of dreams, as they ornament the play, a strength and popular soundness which otherwise would be missing. It might, however, be best to reintroduce the distinction between an Apollonian and a Dionysian vision. Clearly the latter informs these festive comedies in spite of the intellectual delicacy which, as always, Shakespeare exhibits in many playfully metaphysical passages. But his intellectual games with appearance, reality, imagination, fancy, will, desire, and knowledge—all these entwined themes of his revels—follow rules laid down by Dionysus, the ancient impostor-god of the theatre. When Shakespeare wants an Apollonian twist, he gets it formally by the direct use of the masque, for in this genre an Apollonian order prevails.

The magic of Dionysus is ritual dance magic; that of Apollo is prophetic and oracular magic, the magic of verse itself in its purest forms. The masque provides a theatrical forum for

---

[6] Ian Fletcher, *Beaumont and Fletcher* (London, 1967), 22.

[7] Ben Jonson uses the term "ingemination" in *Loves Triumph through Callipolis* (1631) to mean the doubling of a song-stanza. The twinning effect is a strongly ritualistic reinforcement of the stanzaic balance; see Herford and Simpson, VII, 741. Frequently masque figures are doubled, e.g., Eros and Anteros in the last of Jonson's entertainments, *Loves Wel-come at Bolsover* (1634).

both sorts of play and for both kinds of magic. The great virtue of Barber's analysis is that it allows the discrimination among various theatrical magics, which may combine in single plays or may appear separately as the informing styles of one dramatic genre or another. The masque, though danced, obeys an Apollonian law. It *bases* its action upon the idea of rule, as contrasted with the sportive basis of the earlier Shakespearean comedies. Both types of drama may accept "misrule" centrally, but the masque is more chary about its acceptance of Revel and tends to control him more rigidly than does the "festive comedy." In differentiating between masque and festive comedy, however, we have to tolerate only the crudest measurements of their difference. In both forms magic and reality interact in all sorts of ways. *A Midsummer Night's Dream*, for example, is the archetypal festive comedy, yet it remained a court favorite and left itself open to submergence under added shows and pageants, which actually happened when Dryden and Purcell converted it to *The Fairy Queen*.[8] Because they are formal and stately, the masques of *The Tempest, Cymbeline,* and *As You Like It* contaminate the festivity of the plays they climax. Shakespeare's genius, equal to his judgment, allowed the contamination. With the court masque likewise we shall also find a practice of mixing, of miscegenating the magic modes, and although by taking Apollonian order for its base the masque limits its power, it also can partake of other energies when it develops the devices of antimasque.

[8] In Henry Purcell and John Dryden's *The Fairy Queen* (1692) there were a dance of monkeys, a "Grand Dance of 24 Chineses," and numerous other interpolations. The ultimate in a certain kind of illusionism came with Beerbohm Tree's 1911 production of *A Midsummer Night's Dream*, in which real rabbits sported in the stage-woods.

The crisis of aristocracy

Burckhardt, having singled out the existence of both sacred
and secular triumphs in Renaissance Italy, observed that "the
secular *trionfi* were far more frequent than the religious."
This is remarkable and important, because the aim of secular
pageants was to insist on the timely political occasion. "They
were modelled on the procession of the Roman Imperator as
it was known from the old reliefs and from the writings of
ancient authors." [9] Recent studies of the *joyeuses entrées* of
various princes in northern Europe during the sixteenth century indicate that again, as with the Italian models, the fundamental form of the Renaissance triumph was a political
display. [10] The usual concoction was "a strange mixture of antique, allegorical, and purely comic elements," and these might
be varied to suit the particular victory or happy event that
was celebrated. Complex as their origins are, the pageants of
the Renaissance seem generally to derive from this need to
celebrate, publicly or privately, the triumph of a given power.
It might be a military victory; it might be a marriage; it
might be a coronation; and as Burckhardt observes:

When there were in reality no triumphs to celebrate the poets
found a compensation for themselves and their patrons. Petrarch
and Boccaccio had described the representation of every sort of
fame as attendants each of an allegorical figure; the celebrities of
past ages were now made attendants of the prince. The poetess

[9] *Civilization*, II, 416.

[10] In Jean Jacquot, *Fêtes*, see the discussion by Frances Yates of
the propagandist aims of pageantry; she points out that "everyone
gained from these occasions, because they were sumptuary expenditures that stimulated commerce and trade, so that finally every one
profited thereby. The art of dumping money out of windows is
fundamental in all societies, and during the Renaissance appears in
this form" (I, 458–462).

Cleofe Gabrielli of Gubbio paid this honour to Borso of Ferrara. She gave him seven queens—the seven liberal arts—as his handmaids, with whom he mounted a chariot; further, a crowd of heroes, distinguished by names written on their foreheads; then followed all the famous poets; and after them the gods driving in their chariots. There is, in fact, at this time simply no end to the mythological and allegorical charioteering, and the most important work of art of Borso's time—the frescoes in the Palazzo Schifanoia—shows us a whole frieze filled with these motifs.

In the main the artists tried to excel in magnificence of display: "At the Venetian festivals the processions—not on land, but on water—were marvellous in their fantastic splendour." [11] Burckhardt is an important commentator on these matters, not only because of the historical evidence he amassed, but also because it appeared to him that these splendid, awe-inspiring festive occasions provided a key to the inner life of the Italian Renaissance. They were, for him, its perfect insignia. They represented all its magnificent energies in aesthetic form. This fact makes their ephemeral nature all the more expressive and all the more problematic for the artists engaged in their creation.

Yet there is an odd marriage to be made between the ephemeral and the eternal, as late Shakespearean drama shows, with its tendency toward the fixed visionary endings provided by the masque and its insistent worrying of the problem of rebirth. Shakespeare's "festive comedy" refers its audience to an actual present world of things as they are, a world to be

[11] Burckhardt, *Civilization*, II, 417, 418, 420. See Jacquot, *Fêtes*, I, 93–98, for illustrations depicting aquatic festivities, by Antoine Caron. In the more elaborate festivals of the Medici, during the period 1539–1637, aquatic designs were often used; see A. M. Nagler, *Theatre Festivals of the Medici: 1539–1637* (New Haven, 1964), Plates 33, 36, 37, 40, 57, 65 (which shows a *naumachia* in the courtyard of the Pitti Palace, in 1589), and 75–88 (all showing barges for *The Triumph of the Argonauts*).

rejuvenated by the comic benediction of the Lord of Misrule. This revelry is comic in a style that cannot be found in the late romances.[12] Their anxiety over man's mortality and their devices of miraculous delivery from death both depend upon the developed practice of the masque and its particular magic. Without their masques, *Cymbeline* and *The Tempest* are inconceivable, and the use of statuary in *The Winter's Tale* (with its masque presenter, Time) and of the miraculous sea change and Temple of Diana in *Pericles* (with its mytho-mystical presenter, Gower) belongs to the same general dramatic style. In all these plays the idea of man's ephemeral nature is set against the seemingly permanent state of the masque vision. This amounts almost to a theatrical trick or oxymoron, whose paradox, of ephemeral permanence, was a major obsession with the greatest of masque masters, Ben Jonson. We find in his comments and in his practice a double awareness of the problem: he speaks of the glory of the scene itself, of the fact that its splendor is a vanishing burst of light —bright, then dark; he also suggests that the spectators of the masque and the festive dancers are themselves the most ephemeral creatures in God's universe. For they have risen on Fortune's wheel, and although in his official capacity he cannot openly say much about mutability, his remarks on the ephemeral nature of the masque as a genre can be read as an oblique commentary on the nature of royal and lordly ascendance.

In fact, as we try to locate the critical problem of the masque and its magic style in relation to Milton, we find that its comment upon princely power is central. This arises from the nature of the genre itself: the court masque, like the

[12] In *A Natural Perspective: The Development of Shakespearean Comedy and Romance* (New York, 1965), 91, Northrop Frye says that "the greater the emphasis on reconciliation in comedy, the more the defeated forces of the comedy tend to become states of mind rather than individuals."

Italian festival procession and the lesser English genres of pageant and interlude, belongs to a ceremonial type, and its form and purpose depend therefore on the objects of ceremonial attention. Common to all such works, we find, is an interpenetration of actors and audience, and since the audience is royal or at the least noble, the actions of such works are peculiarly inflated by the status of their audience. The masque, as Northrop Frye observes, "is usually a compliment to the audience, or an important member of it, and leads up to an idealization of the society represented by that audience. Its plots and characters are fairly stock, as they exist only in relation to the significance of the occasion. . . . It thus differs from comedy in its more intimate attitude to the audience: there is more insistence on the connection between the audience and the community on the stage. The members of the masque are ordinarily disguised members of the audience, and there is a final gesture of surrender when the actors unmask and join the audience in a dance." [13] This account can be elaborated to fit the intricacies of some of the more complicated Stuart masques, but it remains generally true that the unmasking gesture of the masquers will always betoken a "more intimate attitude to the audience," thereby implicating the masque in the general political fate of that audience.

Perhaps because he sensed the mutability of royal power, Ben Jonson was led to distinguish his own librettos from the scenic effects of Inigo Jones and to argue that although these were brilliant, they were ephemeral, whereas his own verses would outlast the momentary flash of light. He even recommended that the princely participants in the masque study his own text, after the occasion was over, in hopes that its lasting force would redeem the lost moments of glory. In the preface affixed to his *Hymenaei*, Jonson defended the primacy and permanence of his libretto. His remarks imply

[13] *Anatomy of Criticism* (Princeton, N.J., 1957), 287–288.

that the masque, when read as literature, is a triumph over time.

It is a noble and just advantage, that the things subjected to *understanding* have of those which are objected to *sense*, that the one sort are but momentarie, and meerely taking; the other impressing, and lasting: Else the glorie of all these *solemnities* had perish'd like a blaze, and gone out, in the *beholders* eyes. So short liv'd are the *bodies* of all things, in comparison of their *soules*. And, though *bodies* oft-times have the ill luck to be sensually preferr'd, they find afterwards, the good fortune (when *soules* live) to be utterly forgotten. This it is hath made the most royall *Princes*, and greatest *persons* (who are commonly the personaters of these *actions*) not onely studious of riches, and magnificence in the outward celebration, or shew; (which right becomes them) but curious after the most high, and heartie *inventions*, to furnish the inward parts: (and those grounded upon *antiquitie*, and solide *learnings*) which, though their *voyce* be taught to sound to present occasions, their *sense*, or doth, or should alwayes lay hold on more remov'd *mysteries*. And, howsoever some may squeamishly crie out, that all endevour of *learning*, and *sharpnesse* in these transitorie *devices* especially, where it steps beyond their little, or (let me not wrong 'hem) no braine at all, is superfluous; I am contented, these fastidious *stomachs* should leave my full tables, and enjoy at home, their cleane emptie trenchers, fittest for such ayrie tasts: where perhaps a few *Italian* herbs, pick'd up, and made into a *sallade*, May find sweeter acceptance, than all, the most nourishing, and sound meates of the world.

For these mens palates, let me answer, O *Muses*.[14]

[14] H. and S., VII, 209–210. The full title is *Hymenaei; or, The Solemnities of Masque, and Barriers, Magnificently performed on the eleventh, and twelfth Nights, from Christmas; At Court: To the auspicious celebrating of the Marriage-union, betweene Robert, Earle of Essex, and the Lady Frances, second Daughter to the most noble Earle of Suffolke.* By Ben: Jonson, *Iam veniet Virgo, iam dicetur Hymenaeus.* The masque was performed January 5, 1606. On Lady Frances' marital career, see Spencer and Wells, *Book of Masques*, 151.

Jonson here compresses the entire ethical and literary theory of the genre into a single prefatory note. The Italianate culinary allusions are significant, because Italy had been the original home of triumphal entertainment, and the "more remov'd mysteries" of Jonson's art were partly of Italian derivation. But Jonson's patriotic sentiments are hardly defensive; he may have suspected that he lived in the company of the greatest dramatists the world had seen in some two thousand years. Of Shakespeare he wrote: "He was not of an age but for all time."

The preface to *Hymenaei* also implies a theory of the occasional poem. By insisting on the *literary* triumph of the masque over the mutability of time, Jonson maintains, in part according to a Platonic tradition, that the logically connected themes of the work can withstand the transitory flux. The visual devices of masque are, by themselves, incapable of ideal stability; they fade from memory and fame alike, and only through the conditional immortality of print will they hold a place in time. Jonson perceives, it would seem, that the triumphal Renaissance occasion is, more than any other kind of aesthetic moment, a reminder that even aristocracy is subject to political mutability. And yet, recalling *The Triumphs* of Petrarch, Jonson claims that in the triumphal work of art the dance of death becomes an ambiguous dance of life.[15]

---

[15] Hugo von Hofmannsthal, in "Shakespeare's Kings and Noblemen," in *Selected Prose*, ed. Hermann Broch (New York, 1952), 255, says: "In the performance of *Twelfth Night* by Beerbohm Tree and his troupe, the play ends—and it is said that this was not the director's brilliant idea, but an old English tradition—with each gentleman offering a hand to his lady, and thus, in couples, the Duke and Viola, Olivia and Sebastian, and behind them their retinue dance across and off the stage. Hand in hand they dance, those who had inflamed and tortured one another, sought and deceived and enchanted one another. Thus these figures become figures of a dance, pursuing and not finding, chasing the Wrong and fleeing the Right. This is now

Sir John Davies' *Orchestra: A Poem of Dancing* shows the typical Elizabethan ambivalence toward the dance. Antinous sings in praise of dancing in order to woo the chaste Penelope, who at a climactic moment exclaims:

> And even this self-same Love hath dancing taught,
> An art that showeth th' idea of his mind
> With vainness, frenzy, and misorder fraught;
> Sometimes with blood and cruelties unkind,
> For in a dance Tereus' mad wife did find
> Fit time and place, by murdering her son,
> To avenge the wrong his traitorous sire had done.
> What mean the mermaids when they dance and sing
> But certain death unto the mariner?

Although Antinous can answer these objections by distinguishing between the effects of love and lust, a doubt remains, and the idea of dancing itself still carries a weight of paradox. As a whole, *Orchestra* makes motion so cosmologically complete that stability itself loses its fixed basis. If, as Ribner has said and Colie has shown, "the early seventeenth century is the age of paradox," and if "this is the dominant literary exercise of the time, developed in the best of Jacobean prose, and a cardinal element in its metaphysical

---

the final figure, and for an instant something wafts past it like a shadow, a fleeting memory of the Dance of Death which also makes everything equal, as everything here is equal and together, hands in hands, is creating a double chain, a 'figure' wherein the single destiny has as much value as a single spot of colour on an ornament, as a single theme in a symphony. Even if this idea were re-created out of an old tradition, it was nevertheless once, the first time, a stroke of genius on the part of one director who invented this perfect symbol of binding together the human bodies (in whose gestures he has expressed for five acts the experiences of each single character), of binding them together at the last moment by a rhythm and expressing in them the wholeness of the Whole. You will say that this director was also a poet."

poetry," [16] we may also ascribe a large measure of para-doxical intent to Davies' earlier iconography of the dance. Critics have tended to depict his vision in what we may call an optimistic light; but the work he subtitles *A Poem of Dancing*, like Ulysses' speech on degree in *Troilus and Cressida*, allows at least a strong countercurrent.

This multivalence of attitude toward the dance and there-fore toward masque dancing is reflected in the larger problem of the history of speculative music, music as cosmic image, during the Tudor and Stuart period.[17] The sky is not so much

[16] Irving Ribner, "Jacobean Tragedy: An Introduction," in D. L. Stevenson, ed., *The Elizabethan Age* (New York, 1966), 250. The major study of late-Renaissance paradox in English literature is Rosalie Colie, *Paradoxia Epidemica* (Princeton, N.J., 1966).

[17] See Manfred Bukofzer, "Speculative Thinking in Medieval Music," *Speculum*, XVII, No. 2 (1942), 165-180. In "Allegory in Baroque Music," *Journal of the Warburg and Courtauld Institute*, III, Nos. 1-2 (1939-1940), 1-21, Bukofzer says, "The Analogies in Music may refer only to one voice, or to all the voices, to the rhythm, to the harmony alone, to the setting and instrumentation alone, or simply to the intensity" (9). Bukofzer places these elements in a larger per-spective in *Music in the Baroque Era* (New York, 1947), 370-371, 390 ff. Much of Bukofzer's work has been amplified and brought into relation to literature in Gretchen Finney, *Musical Backgrounds for English Literature: 1580-1650* (New Brunswick, N.J., 1967). Of her own work Mrs. Finney says: "The 'music' implied in the title, *Musical Backgrounds*, might be called 'speculative music,' or better— to use baroque terminology—*musica theorica*. This kind of theory had nothing to do with composition of music, *musica poetica* (*poetica* referring to the creation of music). It had nothing to do with musical performance—methods of singing or playing—*musica prac-tica*. Speculative music dealt with the nature of sound, with the posi-tion and function of music in the entire system of human knowledge, and with music's usefulness to man. It included, finally, metaphysical speculations on the harmony of the universe, for it was widely taught in the Renaissance that the whole cosmos operates according to musical law" (ix). It will be seen that, with some hesitation, I tend to hold, in opposition to Mrs. Finney's strong statements here, that the poetical and practical aspects of music also should enter into a critique of *Comus*.

tuned and then untuned; it undergoes ambiguous changes throughout the period. On the other hand, Hollander has shown, the untuning of the sky, however paradoxical and complex the process may be, does shake the monumental principles of Renaissance poetics, until after the appearance of Dryden's great musical odes and *Secular Masque* the triumphal style gives way to what, following Pope, Rachel Trickett has dubbed "the honest muse," [18] or else to mere burlesque. Honest the earlier muses were not, for their powers depended on Machiavellian courtly conditions of belief. Neatly enough, at the close of *Orchestra* the text says that "here are wanting some stanzas describing Queen Elizabeth," which reminds us of the doubtful congruities between Penelope and the Virgin Queen.

There is little virtue in simplifying the curve of historical change between Skelton and Dryden, but we do observe that between the two poles absolute monarchy went through a steady rise under the Tudors and James I, a sunburst under Charles I ("There grew up a passionate sentiment of loyalty to the Crown"),[19] an eclipse with the Civil War, a metamorphosis during the Commonwealth and Protectorate, a delicate revival with the Restoration, and a final transmogrifying at the moment of the Glorious Revolution. The whole movement of Tudor rule, especially that of Henry

[18] *The Honest Muse: A Study in Augustan Verse* (Oxford, 1967).

[19] J. N. Figgis, *The Divine Right of Kings*, ed. G. R. Elton (New York, 1965), 141; see also G. R. Elton, *The Tudor Revolution in Government: Administrative Changes in the Reign of Henry VIII* (Cambridge, 1960); J. E. Neale, *Elizabeth I and Her Parliaments* (New York, 1958; repr. 1966), I, II; and A. F. Pollard, *Factors in Modern History* (London, 1907; repr. Boston, 1960), ch. iv. Of Michelet's epigram, "Le nouveau Messie est le roi," Pollard says, "Nowhere was the king more emphatically the saviour of society than in England" (67). Cf. Norman Cohn, *The Pursuit of the Millennium* (New York, 1961).

VIII, was toward focal concentration; the royal house sought increased bureaucratic centralization, and this had the effect of giving the prince a royal charisma which was to carry over into all forms of art which had anything to do with ideas of power. The prince gave power its *raison d'être* and its organizational system. Political nature was throughout a two-hundred-year span organized around the sun of the monarch's presence, a political fact which found its ideal imagery in plays like *Richard II*, poems like *The Faerie Queene*, and masques without number. Only when the nature of actual politics changed radically could this triumphal solar system of art give way to a duller plurality of centers, chief among them a large new parliamentary establishment. Curiously, as the poems of Marvell show, the princely ideal was not destroyed by the Civil War and the rule of Cromwell, who might have become a model Davidic king.[20] Around this ideal Marvell built the ambivalent imagery of his *Horatian Ode*. Something Whiggish had to enter the picture before the persons of royal and princely rank would cease to act as "personators of these actions."

The Caroline death throes of royal festivity call up the specter of Hobbes, whose political theory of princely absolutism perhaps marks a death of that system in the realm of political fact. Hobbes's notion that to achieve an adequate "common power" men have to "reduce all their wills by plurality of voices unto one will," besides resulting from the first of his six fundamental observations on humanity ("that men are continually in competition for honor and dignity"), provides a theory about the fictions in which this competi-

[20] As is argued by J. A. Mazzeo, "Cromwell as Davidic King," in *Renaissance and Seventeenth-Century Studies* (New York and London, 1964), 183–208. John M. Wallace, *Destiny His Choice: The Loyalism of Andrew Marvell* (Cambridge, 1967) is the most complete study of Marvell's political stance.

tion is mirrored, namely the entertainments at court. *Leviathan* is the perfect commentary on the highly political Caroline masques—*The Triumph of Peace, Salmacida Spolia*, and *Coelum Britannicum*—with their continual, rather desperate cry for absolute royal prerogative.

After 1688 kings, princes, and lords remained as rich and in some ways more powerful than ever, but as individuals they no longer held the center of the political stage; parliament now finally and firmly held it; aristocratic power had to be exercised through parliamentary means. Parliament, however, could not provide the one image essential to the ideal festal art: it could not, by its very nature, be a focus of power. Its whole purpose was to *disperse* the sources of power over a large and increasingly representative body within the commonwealth. By contrast the Tudor and Stuart kings had drawn all power into themselves, and through this concentration provided the ideal solar source of energy, whose analogue in art was the glamor of "our radiant queen," the glory of Gloriana and her noble compeers. This glory slowly faded from the scene, and although the political and economic historian, examining the "century of crisis," [21] will not be happy with a history determined by aesthetics, aestheticism played an overlarge role in the history of this golden age. Poetry provided imaginative models of statecraft and, reciprocally, political thought influenced the imagination.

The power of the prince may in fact have undergone all sorts of subtle and not so subtle erosions during the reign of Elizabeth, and her bank balance at the time of her death would suggest their gravity; yet Elizabethan and Stuart masque

[21] See H. R. Trevor-Roper, "The General Crisis of the Seventeenth Century," in *Crisis in Europe: 1560–1660*, ed. Trevor Ashton (New York, 1967); and Christopher Hill, *The Century of Revolution: 1603–1714* (New York, 1966).

makers, particularly the latter, never ceased to produce works of unparalleled cost and splendor, right up to the very end of the Caroline era. For their collaboration with scene designers, poets like Jonson were paid more than for a play in the public theatre. The masques served, among other purposes, to impress important foreign visitors, and their propagandist aim was shared by courtiers greedy for a part in the general splurge. Lawrence Stone has described this state of affairs in his *Crisis of the Aristocracy:*

All these various forms of excessive expenditure sprang from an attitude of mind which put generosity and display before thrift and economy, and which was encouraged by the growing popularity of attendance, often unrequited attendance, upon a deliberately and conspicuously extravagant court. This generalized ostentation in manner of life and death reached its peak in the late Elizabethan and Jacobean period, and can be attributed mainly to the fierce competition for social status which in a transitional period of uncertain values tended to find expression in both medieval and renaissance forms, in hospitality and servants in the country, and clothes and gambling at the Court. Superimposed upon this general tendency, however, was a personal recklessness of behaviour whose cause was more psychological than social.[22]

Although Stone cautions against relying on the notorious cases of noble malaise "to make generalizations about a class as a whole," it yet seems clear that men like Oxford, Rutland,

[22] *The Crisis of the Aristocracy: 1558–1641* (abridged ed.; New York, 1967), 264–265; see also Stone, "The Fruits of Office: The Case of Robert Cecil, First Earl of Salisbury, 1596–1612," in *Essays in the Economic and Social History of Tudor and Stuart England: In Honour of R. H. Tawney* (Cambridge, 1961), where Stone examines the astonishing scale of Cecil's tax-farming and other ventures, and his equally remarkable expenditures on land and houses—an average of £ 13,500 per annum between 1608 and 1612.

Southampton, Bedford, and Essex were indeed reacting against the stolid guidance of their guardians, chief among them Lord Burghley—the model for Spenser's "Stoicke censours," we might add. The tiresome counsel of worldly prudence robbed these young courtiers of their sense of autonomy. As Stone observes,

To listen to Polonius for a few moments in a theatre is one thing; to have to put up with him pontificating at every meal-time for years on end is another. No wonder these young men adopted a way of life of absurdly prodigal extravagance; it was the only revenge they could take on a guardian to whom waste and imprudence were deeply horrifying. The knowledge that so many of his charges had both disliked him and gone to the bad must have puzzled and saddened this well-meaning old gentleman.[23]

This picture clarifies the marvelous extravagance of the masque. The disaffected nobility could, paradoxically, show disdain for their own state, which Cecil more than any other courtier had helped to create, simply by taking part in the ostentatious adulation of the court which is represented in the masque.

Wonder in the masque: A philosophic bias

In the material we are about to examine one motif will be reiterated, the necessity for wonder and wondrous displays to the success of the masque. This aesthetic bent needs to be set in a historical context, which is, roughly speaking, that the reigning philosophical influence upon poetry, that of Neoplatonism, conceives of the "dignity of man" as precisely this, a wonder. This is the burden of Pico della Mirandola's famous *Oration.* Commenting on the ancient maxims "There is nothing more wonderful to be seen than man" and "A great mira-

---

[23] *Crisis of the Aristocracy,* 265.

cle, Asclepius, is man," Pico concluded that man in his ideal
state was free through his mind to "observe whatever is in
the world." Pico imagined God saying to man, "With freedom of choice and with honor, as though the maker and
molder of thyself, thou mayest fashion thyself in whatever
shape thou shalt prefer." The freedom of choice was complete, and man could remake himself in either a fine or a
degenerate form. "Thou shalt have the power to degenerate
into the lower forms of life, which are brutish. Thou shalt
have the power, out of thy soul's judgment, to be reborn into
the higher forms, which are divine." Pico is explicit on the
nature of this exceptional freedom: it is based on the power
of man to metamorphose himself as he cultivates the rational,
divine powers of his mind. "Who would not admire this our
chameleon?" Notably, for the history of the masque, "it is
man who Asclepius of Athens, arguing from his mutability
of character and from his self-transforming nature, on just
grounds says was symbolized by Proteus in the mysteries.
Hence those metamorphoses renowned among the Hebrews
and the Pythagoreans." [24]

Possession of this chameleon-like power requires the syn-
cretic discipline of the Hermetic, Pythagorean, Cabalistic,
Neoplatonic, Pagan, and Christian mysteries, and all decisions
of philosophy are subjected to a criterion of mystery, so that
nothing will pass as truth which does not in some way share
in "the divinity of a greater world," which can only be known
through the true, benign magic, the *mageia*, "a perfect and
most high wisdom." Like other Renaissance magians Pico
can speak of this knowledge only in the most enthusiastic
tones, calling it "the ineffable theology of the supersubstantial

[24] *Oration on the Dignity of Man*, tr. E. L. Forbes, in *The Renaissance Philosophy of Man*, ed. Ernst Cassirer, P. O. Kristeller, and
J. H. Randall (Chicago, 1948), 223, 225–226.

deity; the fountain of wisdom, that is, the exact metaphysic of the intellectual and angelic forms; and the stream of knowledge, that is, the most steadfast philosophy of natural things." [25] By nature Pico seems always drawn to the highest of the magic realms described by Cornelius Agrippa in *De Occulta Philosophia*, the "ceremonial or religious magic." Pico reaches this level mainly through his double praise of Mageia and Cabala. "These" says Frances Yates, "are the basic themes of his whole song." Pico's style of magic thinking is not unlike that of Ficino, which "worked through the imagination, by conditioning the imagination through various ways of life and rituals towards receiving inwardly the divine forms of the natural gods. It was the magic of a highly artistic nature, heightening the artistic perceptions with magical procedures." Miss Yates concludes that "it is also chiefly in this imaginative and artistic sense that we should understand the influence of the Renaissance magic of the type inaugurated by Ficino and Pico. The operative Magi of the Renaissance were the artists, and it was a Donatello or a Michelangelo who knew how to infuse the divine life into statues through their art." [26]

[25] *Ibid.*, 236, 252.

[26] *Giordano Bruno and the Hermetic Tradition* (Chicago, 1964), 102. See C. G. Nauert, *Agrippa and the Crisis of Renaissance Thought* (Urbana, Ill., 1965), chs. ix and x, "Agrippan Magic and Renaissance Culture" and "The Magical World." Nauert says, "Toward the end of Book Three of *De Occulta Philosophia*, Agrippa devoted several chapters to outlining methods for the elevation of the soul, to prepare it for receiving divine and angelic aid in magical works. The aim of such magical mysticism was not just to secure more power but also a precaution against the magician's being deceived by demons. Agrippa explicitly warned that true piety was necessary for these ceremonies, and that if it were lacking, the *magus* might find himself being misled by evil spirits" (258). The Agrippan demonology resembles that in *Comus:* "Good demons are of three

The main method by which this artistry worked was clearly through what has been called, in Edgar Wind's important study, the "pagan mysteries in the renaissance." [27] Frye has noted that characteristically the masques used mythological materials, "which the audience is not obliged to accept as 'true,' " while "the ideal masque is in fact a myth-play like the *auto*, to which it is related much as comedy is to tragedy. It is designed to emphasize, not the ideals to be achieved by discipline or faith, but ideals which are desired or considered to be already possessed. Its settings are seldom remote from magic and fairyland, from Arcadias and visions of earthly Paradise." [28] A major source for such visions was bound to be the pagan mysteries Wind has described, since they possessed, besides an element of religious cult or convention, an equally strong element of religious wonder. A magus like Pico would not be content to provide for artists a mere catalogue of ideals to be reaffirmed in ceremonial rites, pageants, or festal masques. What is provided in these works, when they display a magian influence, is the energy of the

---

main ranks: the supercelestial, which have no relation to any bodies but transmit divine light to the lower orders; the celestial intelligences, which rule the various planets; and ministering demons, which watch over men. There are corresponding orders of dark or rebellious demons. . . . Each man has three guardian spirits, a sacred one subject not to the planets but only to God; a spirit of his nativity; and a spirit of profession, which changes as one changes occupations. These spirits, he thinks, give a man certain capabilities and make him suited to prosper in certain places or occupations and not in others" (269–270). On the sources and problems of Milton's angelology, see C. A. Patrides, *Milton and the Christian Tradition* (Oxford, 1966), 46–51, 64–68. The angelology of *Comus*, like that of Milton generally, is profoundly influenced by pseudo-Dionysian tradition.

[27] *Pagan Mysteries in the Renaissance* (London, 1958).
[28] *Anatomy of Criticism*, 288.

Neoplatonic talisman or of the cabalistic or Pythagorean symbol. Such materials were, as we might expect, not exempt from orthodox religious scrutiny, nor were any of the great magian Italians exempt from clerical suspicion. "If even Ficino's mild cult of the natural gods as a kind of medical therapy involved him in difficulties with theologians, Pico's difficulties from the same quarter were bound to be much graver and deeper, for, by harnessing natural magic to Cabala, he took magic right up into the supercelestial world of divine and angelic powers." The ceremony of the divine magic did not, however, always involve an arcane poetic language. Pico would advise the student to sing the Psalms of David, which "are spoken of as incantations as powerful for the work of Cabala, as the hymns of Orpheus are of value for natural magic." [29] An early biographer said of Milton that in later life, "David's Psalms were in esteem with him above all poetry," [30] and perhaps from the perspective of Pico's *Oration* we can add a specifically extra-Puritan bias in favor of the Psalms. If so, it is a bias toward the incantatory, something hardly felt during the modern era, when the Psalms have disappeared from their former central place in the canon of poetry. Incantation itself becomes the chief appeal and power of these "hymns of David," and the likeliest approach to any magian poetry will be to remember that the Psalms were available examples of the sacred *furor poeticus* on which

[29] Yates, *Bruno*, 104.

[30] John Phillips, *The Life of Mr. John Milton*, in Helen Darbishire, ed., *The Early Lives of Milton* (New York, 1965), 33. On psalm-singing, see P. M. Scholes, *The Puritans and Music in England and New England* (New York, 1962), 253–269, *et passim*. "If some Puritan genius had been at hand to cast the emotions of the seventeenth century into original verse he could not have come closer to its intimate expression than did the age-old Psalms. They therefore enrolled David as a Puritan!" (254).

all other poetic efforts could be modeled. To the extent that masques and triumphs celebrate noble ceremonies, they are infused with speculative music, like that the Psalms and Orphic hymns possessed for the Renaissance.

Throughout this cult of magic theory, of course, there is a bias toward *celestial* magic. This, the subject of Cornelius Agrippa's second book, provides the gateway to the highest forms of religious arcanum, but its emphasis on the constellations and on the physical presence of the stars and planets and, in general, on the celestial universe gives such magic a peculiarly important influence on works of art. For the celestial bodies possess number, organization, order in the highest degree, and above all, brilliance, which presents to the eye of the beholder an inherently magical sight. The stars dazzle—hence Sidney names his personae Astrophel and Stella —while the planets wander in their special ways, to be watched and understood as magical mirrors reflecting the wanderings of men on earth. The science of the stars includes a range of occult lore, astrological in the main, which can be regarded as the source of divine *influence* over heroic action. Thus Ficino, according to Walker, revived in *De Vita Coelitus Comparanda* "a theory of astrological influence, ultimately stoic in origin, which postulates a cosmic spirit (*spiritus mundi*) flowing through the whole of the sensible universe, and thus providing a channel of influence between the heavenly bodies and the sublunar world." [31]

This theory informs the opening lines of *Comus*, and it is widely applicable, since the notion of an influential court of the stars, held in state by the will of the Almighty and shedding its benign influence on man, is basic to the structuring of a Platonized pantheon. A clear example is in the invocation

[31] Walker, *Spiritual and Demonic Magic*, 12.

to Sibylla spoken by Iris, the celestial messenger in Daniel's *Vision of the Twelve Goddesses.* Entering "from the mount where they were assembled (decked like a rainbow)," she speaks as follows:

I, the daughter of wonder (now made the messenger of Power) am here descended to signify the coming of a celestial presence of Goddesses determined to visit this fair Temple of Peace which holy hands and devout desires have dedicated to unity and concord. And leaving to show themselves any more in Samos, Ida, Paphos, their ancient delighting places of Greece and Asia, made now the seats of barbarism and spoil, vouchsafe to recreate themselves upon this western mount of mighty Brittany, the land of civil music and of rest, and are pleased to appear in the self-same figures wherein antiquity hath formerly clothed them and as they have been cast in the imagination of piety, who hath given mortal shapes to the gifts and effects of an eternal power for those beautiful characters of sense were easier to be read than their mystical *Ideas* dispersed in that wide and incomprehensible volume of nature. And well have mortal men apparelled all the graces, all the blessings, all virtues, with that shape wherein themselves are much delighted and which work the best motions and best present the beauty of heavenly powers.[32]

Sibylla then introduces the twelve goddesses in the order of their figural significance, their "shadows": "Thus have I read their shadows, but behold! / In glory where they come as Iris told."

The reverential tone recalls another familiar Renaissance kind of flattery, namely to do honor to a noble person. Honor, said Lord Bacon in his essay "Of Ambition," "hath three things in it; the vantage ground to do good; the approach to kings and principal persons and the raising of a man's fortunes. He that hath the best of these intentions, when he

[32] Spencer and Wells, *Book of Masques,* 32.

aspireth, is an honest man and the prince that can discern of these intentions in another that aspireth, is a wise prince." The masque as a genre attempts the dramatization of these three elements of honor and the "honest" aspiration toward them.[33]

Perhaps the resort to magic seeks to resolve a peculiarly tense condition of courtly thought and action during this period. It is a time of political uncertainty, of continual crisis, as Trevor-Roper and others have emphasized. It is also time when philosophers study temporal short-cuts achieved through method.[34] On the doorstep of a modern era of science, more than one thinker and poet stands with Sir Thomas Browne in "divided and distinguished worlds." Magical procedures are significant because they bond alchemy and philosophy, thaumaturgy and Christian faith. It seems significant that Jonson, author of masques, wrote *The Alchemist* and *The Magnetic Lady*.[35] Such work debunks thaumaturgic belief, as *Volpone* debunks the conspicuous spending powers of the rich (those "studious of riches") who helped create the masques. Such satires point to the fashion of the times; it was always possible, within the highly artificial courtly ambience, to pretend that the natural world was alive with occult meanings. Per-

[33] Cf. William Empson, in "Honest in Othello," *The Structure of Complex Words* (New York, n.d.); also, Rachel Trickett, *The Honest Muse.*

[34] As shown in Neal Gilbert, *Renaissance Concepts of Method* (New York, 1960); see also Eugene Rice, *The Renaissance Idea of Wisdom* (Cambridge, Mass., 1958), 60–61, on "conditional wisdom."

[35] This sort of satire is to be distinguished from the in-group satire of the 1616 masque, *Mercurie Vindicated from the Alchemists at Court*, where "Mercury, persecuted and perplexed in the antimasque, wins through when the radiant vision of the real makers of men floods through the gloomy recesses of the alchemists' workshop and drives away the workers and the botchers. Nature and natural forces triumph while 'Art' is humiliated" (H. and S., X, 546–547).

haps Jonson would have held that under the controlled conditions of the court, where he and Jones rivaled the king himself, natural philosophy was indeed "natural magic." [36]

Miracle: Probability in the masque

Endless contemporary testimony exists to show that spectators found the masking devices miraculous. Time after time the machines of Sebastiano Serlio or Inigo Jones struck the audience as somehow uncanny, because they moved or dissolved in thin air or otherwise metamorphosed in ways not visible to the inspecting eye. Even Jonson himself, reporting the effect of his own *Hymenaei*, tries to convey this impression of the inexpressible: "Such was the exquisit performance, as (beside the *pompe, splendor,* or what we may call *apparelling* of such *Presentments*), that alone (had all else beene absent) was of power to surprize with delight, and steale away the *spectators* from themselves." Jonson tried to achieve this transport of the spectators by making them *auditors,* as Orgel has shown, and his more literary masque rivaled the visual effects created by Inigo Jones. Jonson exploited all the forces of mythopoeic construction, for example in the person of his Wonder, in *The Vision of Delight.* Wonder wonders to himself how all the magic changes of nature can occur in the world of the masque, and concludes with a question, "Whose power is this? what God?"—to which Phantsie replies, pointing directly at King James:

> Behold a King
> Whose presence maketh this perpetuall *Spring,*
> The glories of which Spring grow in that Bower,
> And are the marks and beauties of his power.

[36] See Kitty Scoular, *Natural Magic* (Oxford, 1965), especially 29 ff., on varieties of this magic; e.g., Tesauro distinguished four types, derived from nature, art, opinion, and deception.

Here the magical coercion consists in the mythic union of two creative forces, that of the poet (who is really creating the piece) and that of the king (who creates it indirectly, by permitting its performance and providing its perfect ambience). Such effects can work on the literary level, "as if by magic," because a theatrical pun connects the prince and poet. The *double entendre* is a perspective device. It was against such poetic methods that, presumably, Inigo Jones had to compete, though he too would have felt *his* mythic coincidence with the king. For he too was a double of the king-creator. When we examine a work like *Salmacida Spolia*, where Jones took a direct hand in writing the scenario, we find him envisioning the destiny of the Queen and her ladies—but Jones shows less intimacy with his courtly players than does Jonson, who seems, on the surface at least, to have held toward James I something of the attitude Molière held toward Louis XIV: "Il y a deux rois de France—vous, Sire, et moi-meme."

The stage directions of the epiphany in *Salmacida Spolia* bear quoting, because they indicate what splendor Jonson's rival could in fact manage theatrically:

Whilst the Chorus sung this song, there came softly from the upper part of the heavens a huge cloud of various colours, but pleasant to the sight; which, descending to the midst of the scene, opened, and within it was a transparent brightness of thin exhalations, such as the Gods are feigned to descend in; in the most eminent place of which her Majesty sat, representing the chief heroine, environed with her martial ladies [they had been sent down from heaven by Pallas Athene to quell Discord, a "malicious fury"]; and from over her head were darted lightsome rays that illuminated her seat; and all the ladies about her participated more or less of that light, as they sat near or further off. This brightness with many streaks of thin vapours about it, such as are seen in a fair evening sky, softly descended; and as it came near to the earth the seat of Honour by little and little vanished, as if it gave way to these heavenly graces. The Queen's Majesty and her ladies were in Amazonian habits of carnation, embroidered with silver, with plumed helms, baldrics with antique sword hanging by their sides—all as rich as might be; but the strangeness of the habits was most admired.

After the King and his lords had "taken out" the Queen and her ladies and come down into the room and danced their entry, and after a fifth song had been performed and another dance ended,

their Majesties being seated under the state, the scene was changed into magnificent buildings composed of several pieces of architecture. In the furthest part was a bridge over a river, where many people, coaches, horses, and such like, were seen to pass to and fro. Beyond this on the shore were buildings in perspective, which shooting far from the eye showed as the suburbs of a great city. From the highest part of the heavens came forth a cloud far in the scene, in which were eight persons richly attired representing the spheres. This, joining with two other clouds which appeared at that instant full of music, covered all the upper part of the scene; and at that instant, beyond all these, a heaven opened full of deities; which celestial prospect, with the Chorus below, filled all the whole scene with apparitions and harmony.[37]

And no wonder, we may add, that as the printed account maintains, this masque "was generally approved of, especially by all strangers [i.e., foreigners] that were present, to be the noblest and most ingenuous [sic] that hath been done here in that kind." The account continues: "The invention, ornament, scenes, and apparitions, with their descriptions, were made by Inigo Jones, Surveyor General of his Majesty's Works," while William D'Avenant made only the verses and the

[37] Spencer and Wells, Book of Masques, 358.

prose dialogue. "The subject was set down by them both. The music was composed by Lewis Richard, Master of her Majesty's Music." [38] The postscript gives some idea of the production difficulties in matching the talents of the necessary artists, a managerial problem equaled, doubtless, only in the production of opera or, in later times, of films, where technical subdivisions are vastly more numerous than in artistic media previously invented. Like the film, the masque required multiple gifts and a coordinating hand. Unquestionably, if a conflict between the major partners occurred, it would damage the one effect the masque had to have, spectacular *éclat*. Reaching toward this aim by literary devices, Jonson was working against heavy competition. The set designer was the man of the hour. He could claim to be the dominant partner, since magical coercion of belief was the primary aim of the partnership.

The control of belief which the masque aims at requires the creation of theatrical astonishment. Masques moved toward, through, and beyond what we may call "miraculous moments," that is, moments in which the audience admires—as the term "miracle" and the name Miranda imply.[39] Nothing is more frequent, as Allardyce Nicoll observes, than the insistence, in both libretto and outside commentary on the festive occasion, that at its high points the masque seeks the "marvelous": "In the *impresa* and in the masque alike the

[38] *Ibid.*, 361.

[39] As in Plato's *Cratylus*, "name" here implies "essence." Miranda's name suggests that she can only wonder at nature, and in Shakespeare's *The Tempest* the word "wonder" is directly associated with her name by Ferdinand: "O you wonder!" . . . "No wonder, sir, But certainly a maid" (I, ii, 426–428). Then, in her company, Ferdinand speaks of himself as "a single thing, as I am now, that wonders / To hear thee speak of Naples." Meanwhile, she divinizes him, and says, with a pun on "tempest," "there's nothing ill can dwell in such a temple."

quality of *meraviglia*, or wonder, was called for—the exciting of that admiration aimed at the entire spectacle." Frequently the allegorical necessities of the masque would demand a use of surrealistic, grotesque, or daemonic emblems, and these could not fail to astonish. The acrobatic antimasque dance might itself be fearful; in Jones's set for *Britannia Triumphans*, "the whole scene was transformed into a horrid Hell, the further part terminating in a flaming precipice, and the neerer parts expressing the Suburbs." [40] Quite the opposite, but equally amazing, would be the aerial glister of a divine messenger, a standard feature in the masque.[41] Irene, the goddess of peace, appears in the *Arches of Triumph* of 1604, "richly attired," "her upper garment of carnation loose, a robe of white under it powdered with stars and girt to her." [42] This expresses the idea of external glory, whose inward lineaments had been given by *The Faerie Queene*.

The glorious vision is perhaps most perfectly rendered in the penultimate speech of Jonson's *Hymenaei*, where an "angel or messenger of glory" envelops the appearance of Truth in a panoply of glittering ornaments:

> Upon her head she wears a crowne of starres,
> Through which her orient hayre waves to her wast,
> By which beleeving *mortalls* hold her fast,
> And in those golden chordes are carried even,
> Till with her breath she blowes them up to heaven.
> She weares a robe encas'd with eagles eyes,
> To signifie her sight in *mysteries;*

[40] Allardyce Nicoll, *Stuart Masques and the Renaissance Stage* (London, 1938; New York, 1963), 155, 115.

[41] For the iconography of this tradition, see Thomas M. Greene, *The Descent from Heaven: A Study in Epic Continuity* (New Haven, 1963), especially 363–418, on Milton.

[42] Nicoll, *Stuart Masques*, 180. See, above, the description of Iris in Daniel's *Twelve Goddesses*.

Upon each shoulder sits a milke-white dove,
And at her feet doe witty serpents move:
Her spacious armes doe reach from *East* to *West*,
And you may see her heart shine through her breast.
Her right hand holds a *sunne* with burning rayes,
Her left a curious bunch of golden kayes,
With which *heaven* gates she locketh, and displayes.
A christall mirror hangeth at her breast,
By which mens consciences are search'd, and drest:
On her coach-wheeles *hypocrisie* lies rackt;
And squint-eyd *slander*, with *vaine-glory* backt,
Her bright eyes burne to dust: in which shines fate.
An *angell* ushers her triumphant gate,
Whilst with her fingers fans of starres shee twists,
And with them beates backe *Error*, clad in mists.
Eternall *Unitie* behind her shines,
That *fire*, and *water*, *earth*, and *ayre* combines;
Her voyce is like a trumpet lowd, and shrill,
Which bids all sounds in *earth*, and *heav'n* be still.
And see! descended from her chariot now,
In this related pompe shee visits you.   [ll. 885–912]

The devices of Truth's costume were woven in actual threads, and when she descended in response to the angelic announcement, she explained the mystical significance of each *impresa*. But at the moment of epiphany her appearance was intended to "steale away the spectators from themselves." (From this perspective we can perhaps better appreciate the technique Shakespeare exploited in the barge scene of *Antony and Cleopatra;* he simply imposed upon the messenger speech of Enobarbus the hieroglyphic of a masque, and in this way improved upon the splendid source in North's Plutarch; *Antony and Cleopatra* is full of such borrowings from masque practice.)

Often the audience would be ravished by a deliberate sensuality, wrought up to excess, as in Francis Beaumont's *Inner Temple Masque*, where four Cupids enter "attired in flame coloured Taffita close to their body like naked Boyes, with Bowes, Arrows and wings of gold: Chaplets of flowers on their heads, hoodwinckt with Tiffany scarfs."[43] Samuel Daniel's Diana appears in "a greene Mantle imbrodered with silver halfe-Moones and a croissant of pearle on her head."[44] Everywhere, when spring came in the masque, there were chaplets and garlands, and one character who wore a garland of roses about his head also wore a rainbow "circling his head about his shoulders." The lore of the masque is a catalogue of such effects. Their overall force, as vision, always suggested the magnificence of gold, and not infrequently the scene would appear to be "seeming all of Goldsmiths worke."[45] About the shrine in William D'Avenant's first masque, *The Temple of Love* (1635), we are told:

The Temple instead of Columnes had terms of young Satyrs bearing up the returns of Architrave, Freeze and Coronice, all enrich'd of Goldsmith's work. The farther part of the Temple running far from the eye was design'd of another kind of Architecture, with Pillasters, Neeches and Statues, and in the midst a stately gate adorn'd with Columns and their Ornaments, and a Frontispiece on the top, all which seemed to be of Burnish'd Gold.[46]

In another work, Jonson's *The Masque of Beauty*, the north wind, Boreas, wore another sort of jeweled decoration, the

---

[43] Nicoll, *Stuart Masques*, 175. The full text is in Spencer and Wells, *Book of Masques*, 132–142.

[44] *Vision of the Twelve Goddesses*, in Spencer and Wells, *Book of Masques*, 27.

[45] Nicoll, *Stuart Masques*, 115.   [46] *Ibid.*, 110.

icicle: "His haire and bearde rough, and horride; his wings gray and full of snow, and ycicles; his mantle borne from him with wyres, and in severall puffes; his feet ending in Serpents tayles; and in his hand a leave-lesse Branch, laden with ycicles." [47] These details from the iconographies of Cartari and Ripa became, in plastic execution, more weird and exotic and impressive than those in any wood-block print. In them the *impresa* put on a persona.

The description of Daniel's *Tethys Festival*, where the use of golden effects was more extreme than usual ("mask-heads of gold," "a rich Vayle adorned with flutings and inchased worke," "a round globe of gold full of holes," "Pillasters of gold, mingled with rustic stones," "hanging Labells of gold"), tells us that something had to be done to diminish an almost monochromatic golden sheen: "All this whole Scene was filled with the splendor of gold and silver; onely some beautifull colours behinde to distinguish them [all the disparate ornaments of mask heads, spouting "naturall seeming waters," swans, festoons of maritime weeds, great shells and the like] and to set off the rest." [48] Everywhere there is an emphasis on the "rich and curious" interweaving of ornamental designs, particularly in the scene and in the costuming of the gentlemen and lady masquers—we read that typically "every part was richly Embroydered with pure silver." [49] We have ample testimony that spectators valued this alchemy. Nagler has noted the spontaneous outcries of audiences at the long series of magnificent entertainments given to the Medici family; his list abounds with expressions like "con molta meraviglia," "cosa mirabile," "mirabilissimo," and "maraviglioso festino." [50]

---

[47] *Ibid.*, 163. The text is also in H. and S., VII, 181–194.
[48] Nicoll, *Stuart Masques*, 71.   [49] *Ibid.*, 211.
[50] *Theatre Festivals of the Medici.*

Much of the wonder came from the invention of movable scenery, such as was produced by the "cloud machines" of Serlio and imitated by Inigo Jones and his English colleagues. Using "turning machines," whether or not, strictly speaking, they were *periaktoi*, the masque maker could persuade his audience to accept illusions of dissolving appearances. Here the "mechanick" art of the scene designer reached its acme, and here the technology of magic-making was taken over by the visual media. Such assaults on the credulity of audiences were, if anything, made more powerful by the gradually increased use of proscenium frames. By surrounding the scene with an arch or frame, however richly that frame might be decorated to conform to the device of the masque, the set designer was able to highlight the visual detail he so lavishly expended. Furthermore, the art of stage-lighting developed rapidly in the same direction, adding éclat to the merely scenic. Filling the scene with "ample and glistering light," sometimes directing the light *against* the audience, the designer could prevent them from seeing how the scene was being changed before their very eyes. Once again, as with the overall effect of the proscenium arch, the theatric effect sought was that of complete deception. With careful lighting the mechanism of the cloud machines could be disguised, and since they were "of relievo, embossed," they might appear "tralucent as naturals," which means, as Nicoll observes, "that they were cut out so that one flat showed through an opening of that in front while the material of which they were made allowed the light behind to filter through." [51] Such effects were tied to the newly discovered arts of perspective, by means of which space was measured by a succession of planes all parallel to the picture plane. Sequences of gradually narrowing proscenium arches increased the sense of focus

[51] *Stuart Masques*, 136.

toward the back of the scene. This technique of scenic focus finally organized all the devices of the masque into a single magical illusion.

The masque absolutely requires focus, if only because that is the means of surprising and convincing the spectators. A diffused attention would destroy the effect of wonder, whereas a focused attention would greatly increase the shock and the hypnotic effect of all the set designer's marvels. We again have ample testimony that the precise effect of the wondrous spectacle, besides being illusionistic—so that the accounts of the masques are full of words like "seeming," "appearing"—is best defined as suddenness. As Nicoll notes, Ariosto himself had described the effect of the newly invented curtain as sudden; it was designed, says Nicoll, "not to form a means of concealing change of scene but to surprise the audience by a sudden revelation of the scenic glory." [52] " 'Suddenly' is a word we meet with frequently in the descriptive accounts, and there can be no doubt that the artist's main endeavour was to secure so swift a passing away of the existing set and so rapid an appearance of its successor that spectators should fail to observe the means whereby the one was made to transform itself into the other." [53] Even music, as we have seen, may be a "sudden music," and if this is the case with music, it is true *a fortiori* of vision. When the scene flies open "on a suddaine," the audience is startled and held transfixed.

The illusionist purpose appears in a comment of the great stage and machine designer, Nicolo Sabbatini:

When in *intermedii* [the English interludes were simpler] it is necessary for machines to ascend to the sky or descend thence to

[52] Allardyce Nicoll, *Development of the Theatre* (New York, 1937), 104.
[53] Nicoll, *Stuart Masques*, 22.

the stage, one must have a "cut" heaven, both for convenience and for the delight and wonder which audiences take in it, since they cannot see how the machines which rise from the earth disappear or how they descend from the heavens to the stage.[54] Sabbatini so elaborated these illusionistic devices that his manual for designers includes instructions

How to show the whole scene in flames; how to make a hell appear; how to make mountains and other objects rise from the stage; how to transform a man into a rock or a similar object; how to transform rocks or stones into men; how to make the sea rise, swell, get tempestuous or change color; how to make ships or galleys or other vessels seem to move over the sea; how to make dolphins and other marine monsters appear to spout water while they swim; how to make the Heavens in sections; how to make a cloud with people in it descend directly onto the stage from the Heavens.[55]

All these tricks of theatrical magic depended on a technique of bedazzlement—and the artists were not content with a willing suspension of disbelief. They wanted to force the spectators into this suspension, whether they liked it or not. Thus, from the rhetorical point of view, there is something fundamentally anti-imaginative in the visualizing procedures of the masque, a fact which Ben Jonson and Milton fully appreciated. (The same anti-imaginative force might deaden the modern movie.) In the meantime, however, the set designers had their day and enjoyed a complete triumph over both imagination and judgment.

[54] Nicoll, *Development*, 102.
[55] Nicolo Sabbatini, *Manual for Constructing Theatrical Scenes and Machines* (*Practica di fabricar scene e machine ne' teatri* [Ravenna, 1638]), in *The Renaissance Stage: Documents of Serlio, Sabbatini, and Furttenbach*, tr. A. Nicoll, J. H. McDowell, and G. R. Kernodle; ed. B. Hewitt (Coral Gables, Fla., 1958).

The politics of the vanishing point

One standard Elizabethan theatrical term for the space above the stage was "the heavens," [56] and therefore whenever an ascent or descent from the heavens occurred in the masque, there might be a double sense to the stage direction, symbolic as well as theatrical. This sort of double meaning occurs in the second line of *Comus*. The Attendant Spirit announces to the audience, "Before the starry threshold of *Joves* court / My mansion is." This mansion, home of all the angels, seems to be coextensive with heaven itself, for within it

> those immortal shapes
> Of bright aerial spirits live insphear'd
> In regions mild of calm and serene air,
> Above the smoak and stir of this dim spot,
> Which men call Earth.

Throughout such prologues the audience was encouraged to think on two levels: first on the level of theological symbolism, second on the level of theatrical fact. The appearance of the arranged scene would correspond to the words of the Spirit; in all such cases in the masque, the imaginary was as much as possible given life in material form.

"Mansion," like "the heavens," was a technical theatre term. Since the Middle Ages it had been the name for the major scenic device of the mystery cycles. The mansions were symbolic houses, castles, palaces, thrones, tents, hills, or

[56] On the "heavens," Nicoll says: "Somewhere below the roof or 'shadowe' but above the gallery, there were the 'heavens' from which chairs and similar objects could be let down. Already in 1584 Higgins had defined the 'heavens' in his *Nomenclator* as 'The skies or counterfeit heaven over the stage, from whence some god appeared or spoke'" (*Development*, 123).

simply places (loci) where major episodes of the mystery were conceived as having their locale. They were placed around the unlocalized central space known usually as the platea, and their number and variety depended entirely on the requirements of a particular story.

In an ordinary short episode of a mystery cycle commonly two or three were demanded, but sometimes as many as six or more appeared for one drama. *The Death of Judas* from the *Ludus Coventriae* requires Pilate's house, Herod's house, Hell, the bedroom of Pilate's wife, and the cross; the *Assumption of the Virgin* of the same cycle has the house of the Episcopus, three houses of the Princes, the Temple, Heaven, and Hell. When, however an entire cycle was presented (including scores of these small plays) obviously the number was considerably increased.[57]

Nicoll notes that three such mansions held particular interest for their audiences and for the designers: the terrestrial paradise, the celestial paradise or heaven, and hell. In the contemporary descriptions of the way such places could be constructed we see a dim anticipation of the later pageant and court masque; we have, for example, "Paradise made of paper in the midst of which shall be branches of trees, some with flowers, others laden with all kinds of fruit, such as cherries,

---

[57] Allardyce Nicoll, *Masks, Mimes and Miracles: Studies in the Popular Theatre* (New York, 1963), 195. See also Hardin Craig, *English Religious Drama of the Middle Ages* (Oxford, 1955), 115–127, especially 122, on "the naive convention of disregarding distances," and 125, defining the "pageant" as that device which was paid for by the guilds: "This pageant is obviously a platform on wheels covered with a detachable ornamental roof probably held up by posts. It is open on all sides, but when our first parents were naked and unashamed the three painted cloths were hung round about the pageant at an appropriate height as in the *Ordo Adae*. The truth of the matter is, pageants must have varied greatly from one to another according to the demands of the scenes that were to be represented."

pears, apples, figs, grapes and similar things made by artifice." [58] Yet it is not the construction of the mansion which
seems important in the traditional development of the theatre
of wonder, from mystery play to masque, but rather the way
the mansion is to be viewed.

The medieval mystery had grown from the simplicity and
unity of the *Quem Quaeritis* type, with its focus on an altar
or similar single point, toward the system of "multiple setting,"
which "places before the spectators a number of widely
separated 'scenes' at one and the same time. As the mysteries
develop and are taken out of the church this system is retained,
with the necessary modifications demanded by the vastness of
the subject-matter and the great numbers of localities required
for the performance of the plays." [59] It is not until the advent
of the Elizabethan theatre, with its gradually more and more
focused design, that mystery is taken from this multiple setting
and given the highly concentrated format in which the

[58] Nicoll, *Masks, Mimes and Miracles*, 204.
[59] *Ibid.*, 294–295. See L. B. Campbell, *Scenes and Machines on the
English Stage during the Renaissance* (Cambridge, 1923; repr. New
York, 1960); and G. R. Kernodle, *From Art to Theatre: Form and
Convention in the Renaissance* (Chicago, 1944). The creation of a
spatial reality, i.e., space as an experienced volume, is one main consequence of perspective. John White, in *The Birth and Rebirth of
Pictorial Space* (New York, 1958), 123, says: "Even the bare sum-
mary of a few aspects of Alberti's new construction [as in Book II
of *Della Pittura*] reveals the automomy achieved by the idea of space.
During the thirteenth and fourteenth centuries it was possible to see
space gradually extending outwards from the nucleus of the individual solid object, and moving, stage by stage, towards emancipa-
tion from its tyranny. Now the pictorial process is complete. Space is
created first, and then the solid objects of the pictured world are
arranged within it in accordance with the rules which it dictates.
Space now contains the objects by which formerly it was created.
. . . The result is an approximation to an infinite, mathematically
homogeneous space, and the creation of a new, and powerful means
of giving unity to the pictorial design."

intensely illusionistic masque becomes possible. For the masque goes well beyond the performance possible in a public theatre, toward a focused visual scene. This happens not merely because the masque uses artificial lighting. It occurs in its most intense form as a result of the influence of perspective on the practice of set designers.

In the theory of perspective the masque found its natural scenic theory, and its method coincided with a new means of localizing the mysterious mansion. Kernodle has summarized the new theatrical format according to three principles to which it, unlike the medieval or the Elizabethan public theatre, can be said to adhere.[60] "First, an exact relation, unknown before, was established between audience, actor and setting when the eyepoint from which the stage picture was viewed was fixed at one definite point (the duke's box). The vanishing-point for all lines of depth was fixed opposite that eyepoint, at the center of the picture." This principle gave rise to the extraordinarily symmetrical designs of Serlio for tragic, comic, and satirical scenes, designs which seemed determined to force the viewer down a tunnel of sight until his eyeglance struck exactly the bull's-eye of the vanishing point.

The second principle is that of "constancy," according to which "all the space of the stage picture was unified by the concept of one picture plane and one frame." This would immediately work against the older method of allegorical signification, which had depended upon the discontinuity in space of the elements being represented—exactly the effect that was most powerful in the presentation of the mystery-play mansions, with their abrupt incongruities of relationship

[60] *From Art to Theatre*, 178 ff. Masque theatre tended, along with other proscenium usages, to lead into a *picturesque* art, with obvious consequences for the allegorical representations made possible in this medium.

(and their simultaneous coexistence before the spectators). "Yet there were," as Kernodle observes, "many difficulties to be overcome before all the space of the stage was pushed back of that plane and a single proscenium established." Kernodle inclines to the view that although Jonson may be credited with the introduction of the proscenium in 1607, in *The Masque of Blackness*, its adoption was slow and fitful in England, where, instead, many compromises were evolved allowing the retention of native stage procedures, some of which violated the singleness of perspective space. But once the singleness found its way into the canons of the masque, it could only enhance the effect of magic, since the very events which were most extravagant could thereby be forced to occur within, to be compressed into, a single unified space. This compression would itself be a dramatically wondrous effect. The mansions were now subjected to neoclassic economy.

Similarly with the third principle of perspective theory. Since space was to be "measured by a succession of planes all parallel to the picture plane," the stage designer could realize this measurement on the set by "the duplication of similar or identical forms, one visible behind the other." Here too the new method allowed a much more highly structured and more homogeneous space than had ever been used to organize the mansions of the mystery plays. Since proscenium arches and frames were employed to create this perspective of receding planes, once again we get a method of theatrical focus.

It is the first principle, however, which governs the evolution of the masque. The immediate result of the establishment of an eyepoint and a vanishing point is to replace the multiple setting with a single setting. At one blow the gothic variety of the mystery had to give place to a more classic mode, whose singleness of focus was to be its greatest strength. During the earlier period there could hardly be a focusing of the eye upon a single object, with its single vanishing point. This was not so with the Renaissance stage.

Only when a new aristocratic society brought in a courtly audience in which only a few people counted was perspective possible. The Renaissance architect had to reverse completely the older relationship of scenery to audience. In early medieval drama the scenic element was merely a nucleus. The actors, in a small arc, were placed around this center. The large democratic audience formed a circle outside—a circle that almost surrounded both scenery and actors. When there was more than one unit, the audience moved along to surround the next nucleus, just as the public might view the frieze in art. The form was a time art, the audience democratic.[61]

How different are these social conditions from those of the masque and private theatre, with their royal boxes and long, narrow auditoriums.

The space art of perspective, which depended on a single fixed eyepoint, was possible only when duke and cardinal in the Renaissance were rich enough and important enough to create an aristocratic theatre just to please themselves. For the first time, the architect could build a scene for a small ducal party and forget completely such other people as were permitted to look on at the princely entertainments. In the medieval theatre there were many viewpoints on the arc of a circle, with each scenic element as a center. The rich Italian princes, at the beginning of an age of absolutism, made themselves the center of the circle: the scenic elements were on the arc of the circumference. Scenery was no longer a nucleus but began to inclose the actor, as it has continued to do to the present day.[62]

The technique had political consequences. By giving all attention to the prince and his party, in their spectator roles (not their roles as participant dancers, which depend upon and are doubtless influenced by the magical show), masque makers like Inigo Jones were bound to increase their own powers of illusionism. For the first time it became possible, through this aristocratic mode, to concentrate the gaze of some spectators on the one central epiphany which the masque was attempting. In the house of the lord there were no longer many mansions, but only one at a time. In its most extreme form this principle meant that only a very small number of spectators could see the "vision" in its pure state, that is, as viewed from the eyepoint, exactly opposite which the designer placed the stage artifice, precisely at the vanishing point.[63] All others who crowded into the hall to see the show might get a good idea of the spectacle and certainly could enjoy dancing, which moved the vision across a wider space. But they could not experience the sudden, thrilling epiphany of a crowd of divinities or heroes when the scene "broke open" in a flash of brilliant light. Nor could they savor equally wondrous disappearances through the vanishing point. Their sense of the occasion would inevitably be spoiled by democratic dullness and lack of focus, whereas the prince and his favorites would know an uncanny *participation mystique* as they took in the sudden appearance or languid dissolution. The politics of the masque would, in these perfect theoretical terms at least, appear to be built right into its optical system.

The net effect of such a powerful system is that the rhetoric of the visual media appears to possess the greatest magic of

[63] The "vanishing point" may be defined as the point at which receding parallel lines appear to converge. On the precision with which Inigo Jones could measure such geometric and optic relations, see Rudolf Wittkower, "Inigo Jones, Architect and Man of Letters," *Royal Institute of British Architects Journal*, LX (1953), 83–85; also János Scholz, ed., *Baroque and Romantic Stage Design* (New York, 1962), Introduction.

the various competing charms disposed throughout the masque. In the internecine strife between the mixed media there appears to be one winner, vision. The next question to raise is whether sight or sound could have the last word. We have yet to explore the implications of the rivalry between sense modalities, but first we should recall the climate of this rivalry.

3 An Expostulation with Inigo Jones

The famed quarrel between Inigo Jones and Ben Jonson has been shown by D. J. Gordon to have issued, in considerable measure, from a professional disagreement about the hierarchy of the liberal arts, from which, before the Renaissance, architecture had been excluded and into which, as a consequence of Albertian and Palladian arguments, architecture was now forcing its way.[1] Granting that all high art had similar ends, Jonson disputed the claim that architecture could stand beside poetry as a high and liberal art, and he particularly resented the role played by Jones in establishing this claim. Resentment was all the more bitter because Jones appeared to be gaining the sacred precincts at Jonson's expense; the immediate basis of the quarrel was the collaborative

[1] See D. J. Gordon, "Poet and Architect: The Intellectual Setting of the Quarrel between Ben Jonson and Inigo Jones," *Journal of the Warburg and Courtauld Institute*, XII (1949), 152–178; and Jones-Davies, *Inigo Jones, Ben Jonson et le masque*, ch. iii. On the medieval system of the arts, see Ernst Curtius, *European Literature in the Latin Middle Ages* (New York, 1953), chs. iii and iv, also Excursus, No. xxiii, "Calderón's Theory of Art and the *Artes Liberales*," largely a discussion of the relation between poetry and painting.

part each artist played in creating masques for the first Stuart kings of England.

At the outset we have to grant the technical virtuosity of Jones's achievement, as displayed in the magnificent collection of designs preserved at Chatsworth.[2] Contemporaries applauded "the only Renaissance architect in England,"[3] for to an extent unparalleled among architects, Jones seemed to be what Chapman had precisely accused Ben Jonson of *not* being, "one Compleat man."[4] Summerson observes that "behind Jones the architect there is always Jones the philosopher, a shining intelligence in the lay intellectual circles which became a power in English society under James I."[5] In 1570,

[2] Catalogued and described by Percy Simpson and C. F. Bell, *Designs by Inigo Jones for Masques and Plays at Court* (Oxford, 1924). Stephen Orgel is preparing a comprehensive new edition of Jones's designs, which will strengthen the artist's claim to imaginative vision.

[3] John Summerson, *Inigo Jones* (Harmondsworth, Eng., 1966), 31.

[4] *An Invective Wrighten by Mr. George Chapman against Mr. Ben: Johnson*, l. 191. This curious poem appears in P. B. Bartlett, ed., *The Poems of George Chapman* (New York, 1962), 374–378. Bartlett says: "The poem reads like a fulmination written soon after reading Jonson's *Execration* [*upon Vulcan*], hence probably in 1623 or 1624." H. and S. (X, 693) argue (from evidence in the manuscript note of Burghe) that the poem was written in 1634, shortly before Chapman's death.

[5] *Inigo Jones*, 73. See also Rudolf Wittkower, "Inigo Jones, Architect and Man of Letters," 83–90. Aligning the studies of Jones with the "Renaissance ideal of universality which through Baldassare Castiglione's *Cortegiano* and later Peacham's *Compleat Gentleman* (1622) had been given the widest currency at the English court," Wittkower shows that "more than once Inigo expressed in an oblique way that theory and practice were two facets of the same thing" (86). As an instance Wittkower cites the allegorical proscenium arch of *Albion's Triumph*, which Jones produced with Aurelian Townshend. Furthermore, Jones's annotations of Plato and Plutarch show that he made an Albertian analogy between musical harmony and architectural "number." In this he reflects the view held by Sir

Dr. John Dee had claimed philosophic range for architecture:

Thus much, and in the same wordes (in sense) in one onely Chapter of this Incomparable *Architect Vitruvius,* shall you finde. And if you should, but take his boke in your hand, and slightly loke through it, you would say straight way: This is Geometrie, Arithmeticke, Astronomie, Musike, Anthropographie, Hydragogie, Horometrie, &c. and (to conclude) the Storehouse of all workmanship.[6]

These fulsome praises grant wide speculative range to architecture, but it remains to be seen whether we should stress the word "workmanship" or not. If we should, then Dee's assessment would lead us to place architecture on the periphery of the liberal arts, not at their center.

That a decision favoring architecture was difficult may be gathered from the mixed allegiance of Edmund Bolton, author of *Hypercritica: or A Rule of Judgment, for writing or reading our History's* (1621). Bolton was actively concerned with the earliest attempts at establishing a scientific "royal society," and he admired Jonson. In *Hypercritica* he says, "If I should declare mine own Rudeness rudely, I should then confess that I never tasted *English* more to my liking, nor more smart, and put to the height of Use in Poetry, than in that vital, judicious, and most practical Language of *Benjamin Jonson's* Poems." [7] But against these terms we may set the words of Bolton's dedication in a book he gave Inigo Jones, in late 1606, expressing his belief that through Jones "there is hope that

---

Henry Wotton, in his *Elements of Architecture* (1624), "that the Images of all Things are latent in Numbers." Wittkower holds that "this metaphysical belief . . . accounts for the seriousness and vitality of [Jones's] classicism."

[6] Campbell, *Scenes and Machines,* 81.

[7] J. E. Spingarn, *Critical Essays of the Seventeenth Century* (Oxford, 1908–1909), I, 111.

sculpture, modelling, architecture, painting, acting and all that is praise-worthy in the elegant arts of the antients, may one day find their way across the Alps into our England." Italy spelled new arts of vision and new theatrical styles. The year 1606 was an important one for Jones, for in that year construction began on "a new Banqueting House, of brick and timber, built on the site of its decrepit Elizabethan predecessor and built, we may surmise, to accomodate the new style of masque which Ben Jonson and Jones had lately introduced. This building, finished in 1609, had a life of only eleven years, being burnt down in 1619; but we know enough about it to be sure that the interior, at least, was classical. . . . [Jones] was, in fact, almost certainly the architect." [8] Nor can it surprise us that when Jones created the now famous replacement for the burned-out hall, his designs were in a similar classical vein, but on a more elaborate scale. His new Banqueting Hall, the "tragick scene" of the late Jacobean and Caroline masques and of Charles I's execution, eclipsed all prior monuments of its kind in England, taking its place among the great architectural façades. The Banqueting Hall sought comparison with the Escurial, which, however, was far grander than the Hall.[9] Perhaps this magnificent structure

[8] Summerson, *Inigo Jones*, 28–29.

[9] See Jonson's epigram "To Inigo Marquess would be: a Corollary"; also *The Escuriall*, in N. W. Bawcutt, ed., *Shorter Poems and Translations of Sir Richard Fanshawe* (Liverpool, 1964). The Escurial fascinated Fanshawe, who had seen it some time between 1633 and 1638, when he was in Spain; his poem on the ship "Sovereign of the Seas" begins, "Escuriall of the Sea . . . ." On the numerological design of the building, see René Taylor, "Architecture and Magic: Considerations on the *Idea* of the Escorial," in D. Fraser, H. Hibbard and M. J. Lewine, eds., *Essays in the History of Architecture Presented to Rudolf Wittkower* (London, 1967), 81–109. The Escurial appears to have been built according to an astrological system of circles, squares, triangles, and stars.

haunted Ben Jonson's jealous soul because it "contained" the performances of masques. Jonson could see in Jones a genuine rival, a virtuoso of scenery, architecture, and costume so consummate in his art that his fame really hurt. Ben thus counterattacked with the full armory of his satirical skill. Shortly after the performance of *Chloridia* in 1631, he expostulated.

An Expostulation with Inigo Jones

MR Surveyor, you that first begann
From thirty pound, in pipkins, to the man
You are; from them leapt forth an Architect,
Able to talk of Euclide! and correct
Both him & Archimede! damne Architas,
The noblest Inginere that ever was!
Controll Ctesibius! overbearing us
With mistooke names, out of Vitruvius!
Drawne Aristotle on us! & thence showne
How much *Architectonice* is your owne!
Whether the buylding of the Stage, or Scene!
Or making of the properties, it meane!
Vizors, or Anticks! or it comprehend
Some-thing your Surship doth not yet intend!
By all your Titles, & whole style at ones,
Of Tyre-man, Mounte-banck & Justice Jones,
I doe salute you! Are you fitted, yet?
Will any of these express your place? or witt?
Or are you soe ambitious, 'bove your Peeres,
You would be'an Asinigo, by your ears?
Why, much good doo't you! Be what beast you will,
You'will be as *Langley* sayd, an Inigo still.
    What makes your Wretchednes to bray soe loud,
In Towne, & Court? Are you growne rich? & proud?
Your Trappings will not change you. Change your mynd.

Noe velvet sheath, you weare, will alter kynde.
A wooden Dagger, is a Dagger of Wood
Though gold or Ivory haftes would make it good.
What is the cause you pompe it soe? I aske;
And all men eccho, you have made a masque!
I chyme that too: And I have mett with those,
That doe cry up the Machine! & the Showes!
The majesty of Juno, in the Clouds!
And peering forth of Iris, in the Shrowdes!
The ascent of Lady Fame! which none could spy,
Not they that sided her, Dame Poëtry,
Dame History, Dame Architecture too,
And Goody Sculpture, brought with much adoo,
To hold her up. O Showes! Showes! Mighty Showes!
The Eloquence of Masques! What need of prose,
Or Verse, or sense, t'express Immortall you?
You are the Spectacles of State! T'is true
Court Hiero-gly-phicks! & all Artes afford,
In the mere perspective of an Inch board!
You aske noe more then certeyne politique Eyes!
Eyes, that can pierce into Misteryes
Of many Colours! read them! & reveale
Mythology, there, painted on split-deale!
O, to make Boardes to speake! There is a taske.
Painting, & Carpentry, are the Soule of Masque!
Pack with your pedling Poëtry to the Stage,
This is the money-gett, Mechanick Age!
To plant the Musique where noe eare can reach!
Attyre the persons as noe thought can teach
Sense, what they are! which by a specious, fyne
Terme of the Architects, is called *Designe!*
But, in the practisd truth, *Destruction* is
Of any Art, besyde what he calls his!
Whither? o whither will this Tire-man growe?
His name is Σκενοποίος, wee all knowe,

The maker of the Propertyes! In summe,
The Scene! the ingine! but he now is come
To be the Musique-Master! Fabler too!
He is or would-bee the mayne Dominus doo
All, i' the Worke! And soe shall still, for Ben:
Be Inigo, the Whistler, & his men!
Hee's warme on his feete, now, he saies! & can
Swim without Corke! Why, thank the good Queen Anne.
    I am too fatt, t' envy him. He too leane,
To be worth Envy. Hence-forth I doe meane
To pitty him, as smiling at his Feat
Of Lanterne-lerry: with fuliginous heate,
Whirling his Whymseys, by a subtilty
Suckt from the Veynes of shop-phylosophy!
What would he doo now, giving his mynde that way,
In praesentation of some puppet-play?
Should but the kind his Justice-hood employ
In setting forth of such a serious Toye!
How would he firke, lyke Adam over-doo
Up, & about! Dyve into Cellars too,
Disguisd! and thence drag forth Enormity!
Discover Vice! Commit Absurdity!
Under the moral! shewe he had a pate
Moulded, or stroakt up to survey a State!
    Oh wise Surveyor! wyser Architect!
But wisest Inigo! who can reflect
On the new priming of thy old signe-Postes;
Reviveing with fresh colours the pale Ghosts
Of thy dead Standards: or (with miracle) see
Thy twice conceyvd, thrice payd-for Imag'rye,
And not fall downe before it? and confess
Allmighty Architecture? who noe less
A Goddess is, then paynted Cloth, Deal-boards,
Vermilion, Lake, or Cinnopar affords
Expression for! with that unbounded line,

Aymd at, in thy omnipotent *Designe!*
What Poësy ere, was painted on a Wall,
That may compare with thee? what story shall
Of all the Worthyes hope t'outlast thy one,
Soe the Materialls bee, of Purbeck stone!
Lyve long the Feasting Roome. And e're thou burne
Againe, thy Architect to ashes turne!
Whom not ten fyres, nor a Parlyament can,
With all Remonstrance, make an honest man! [10]

"*A wooden dagger*"

What a blast of satirical wind! Ben at his greatest and most informative. Beneath the envy of the rising court favorite, between the lines of purely social animus, we can read a detailed, sober, analytic account of the aesthetic principles and theatrical practice by which Inigo Jones was seeking to outdo the art of poetry.[11] For poetic vision Jones had substituted

---

[10] I have used the text of W. B. Hunter, *The Complete Poetry of Ben Jonson* (New York, 1963), 391–395.

[11] Gordon, in "Poet and Architect," discusses the extended burlesque of architectural pretension in the antimasque of *Neptune's Triumph* (1624), as expressed by the Cook (H. and S., VII, 684–685). According to Gordon, "In his own copy of Vitruvius' *De Architectura* he [Jones] had read and studied thoroughly at least the first chapter, *Quid sit Architectura, et de Architectis instituendis*" ("Poet and Architect," 162). Gordon's analysis of *Love's Welcome at Bolsover* (H. and S., VII, 807–814) shows that in it, and especially in the portrait of Coronell Vitruvius (another satire on Jones), Jonson sums up the full complexity of Neoplatonic image-making, and in particular the relation of music to number. The Coronell says, "*Time*, and *Measure*, are the Father, and Mother of Musique, you know," and later compliments the dancers on being "Musical, Arithmeticall, Geometricall Gamesters! or rather my true Mathematicall Boyes! It is carried, in number, weight and measure, as if the Aires were all Harmonie, and the Figures a well-tim'd Proportion" (H. and S., VII, 810). The dance figures the music, and the latter underlies the former, gives it its meaning.

mechanical engineering, for verbal grace the props of the tedious "tyre-man," for the genuine titles of poetic fame the "surship" of His Majesty's Surveyor of Works (Jones was also a J.P. at Westminster); by all these travesties Jones had usurped the poet's rightful place of honor. Ben Jonson took immense delight in the fact that Inigo is almost the Latin name for the Vice of the morality plays, and he gives Jones the Vice's weapon, a wooden dagger. The Devil is "an Asinigo," and no gentleman.[12] William Drummond recorded, with what measure of accuracy we can only guess, that Jonson "said to Prince Charles of Inigo Jones, that when he wanted words to express the greatest Villaine in ye world he would call him an Inigo." [13] And Jonson averred to his Scottish host, "I said he was ane arrant knave & I avouch it," while one of the *Epigrams* depicts Jones as an "An ingener, in slanders, of all fashions. . . . The townes honest Man's her arrant'st knave." [14] If Jones is the Devil, his "Allmighty Architecture" is a golden calf, and his "unbounded line" and "omnipotent *Designe*" express a false, deceiving wit. By an assault on the innocent eye, he has killed the true *ingenium*.

The satirical argument against Jones assumes the validity of the Great Chain of Being: degree has suffered a wound through the advancement of this "upstart crow." Jones himself took a high moral and intellectual tone when he argued

[12] It seems difficult to disentangle all Jonson's allusions to Jones. The most obvious ones are, besides the poems in which Jones's name appears, the characters In-and-In Medlay in *A Tale of a Tub* (1633); Vitruvius Hoop, in the original 1596–1597 version of that work; Lanthorn Leatherhead in *Bartholomew Fair;* and Iniquo Vitruvius in *Love's Welcome at Bolsover.* Herford and Simpson discuss the satires against Jones—no less than eight clear cases in all—in X, 689–691.

[13] H. and S., X, 692; quoted from *Conversations of Ben Jonson with William Drummond of Hawthornden* (1619).

[14] No. cxv, ll. 29–34.

for the relocation of architecture as a liberal art, as well he might. We therefore debase the quarrel if we fail to perceive that for Jonson, at least, the elevation of Jones, which the *Expostulation* (along with several other satiric portraits of Jones) caricatures in detail, and specifically the elevation of the architect over the poet, was an attack on the logic and system of the arts. All creativity, Jonson would argue, must depend, as a civilizing process, on the hierarchic mysteries of degree, and since poets had been mythic kings from the earliest times, it followed that any change in status was a rebellious attack upon authority itself, and by extension (he might even add) upon the principles of monarchy. Jonson would have to hold that in the beginning the word was the primary creative power, and he would have to hang on tenaciously to this doctrine, because while it had heavy religious reinforcement, it could be challenged in the light of new and growing archaeological discoveries. The vogue of "Egyptian" mythology might give the palm to geometers, draftsmen, designers, and pyramid builders. Exactly because the primacy of each art was at stake, and because financial support from the court was the prize to be won, Jonson's invective had to maintain that Inigo Jones was subverting the good order of all the arts—a subversion which amounted to a diabolic Italianate plot, with the machines of the masque becoming the machinations of the Devil.

"Musique where noe eare can reach"

The central issue in Renaissance poetic theorizing, as it neared the end of the sixteenth century, may be described as the pressure from composite forms: that is, critics, whether dealing with Tasso's *Gerusalemme* or Guarini's *Il Pastor Fido*, felt obliged to defend or attack the rich combinatory largesse of such poets, whose works embody multiple aesthetic modes (magic symbolism in Tasso, tragicomedy in Guarini) and whose brilliance, in its tendency toward synesthetic bravura, heralds the coming of the baroque era. During the late sixteenth century, in England as in France and Italy, a new sense of the compounding of aesthetic modes was beginning to transform the grounds of critical theory. In England music was a dominant art during Elizabeth's reign, her composers among the leading musicians of Europe. Their pre-eminence did not survive the competition with the public plays during her reign and that of James; but their ethos did survive, and in the masques, even more than in public drama, music brought ideas of cosmic harmony into the theatre. Simultaneously, the scenic department was expanding its activities. In the Blackfriars Theatre drama drew attention to elaborate staging.[15] What was true of the elaboration of music and scene in England was true *a fortiori* of their Italian and French counterparts, where, as usual, modal developments in the arts (though not actual achievements) advanced ahead of similar changes in England.

The problem of mixed modes appears, in fact, to be the critical thorn in the side of Renaissance aesthetics. Artists of every calling were playing about with combinations of modes (music + words, music + pictures, dance + words, music + scene + words) as if the basic fact of synesthetic combination itself guaranteed the new artistic goal, which was no longer the search for truth, divine or secular, but a more ecstatic, more expressive aim: magical ease.

So anxiously did this late Renaissance period seek the authoritarian brilliance of prince, nobility, royal house and all its appendages, that as we have seen, even the optics of

---

[15] See A. M. Nagler, *Shakespeare's Stage*, tr. Ralph Manheim (New Haven, 1958); and G. E. Bentley, "Shakespeare and the Blackfriars Theatre," *Shakespeare Survey*, I (1948), 38–50.

court drama aimed at creating the marvelous. Weinberg has observed that this pursuit was so general that critics of the period found it almost impossible to distinguish between the different species of poetry:

New difficulties arise, for we still have found no means of determining the species of poetry. The general form of the "mirabile," achieved by the proper combination of the credible and the incredible, is common to all species. Besides, it appears in every part of every poem: Patrizi goes back to his original array of poetic properties and discerns the presence of the marvelous (sometimes in quite equivocal ways) in every one of them. The effect of the marvelous, which becomes identified with the end, is also universal to all genres.[16]

Noting, as Weinberg does, that Francesco Patrizi tries here and elsewhere to define poetry by its *ends*, by its effects, that is, according to a roughly "expressive" theory, we begin to see the origins of the new cult of Longinus. For it is basically the aim of Longinus' *On the Sublime* to speak about the marvelous, magical, sublime, enthusiastic effects of poetry, which Longinus can do because he concentrates (unlike Aristotle) on the textual *medium* of poetry, rather than on its structures. Precisely this concentration on the psychology of the medium distinguishes much late Renaissance poetry theory, and it results, I believe, from a genuine response to contemporary poetry, where synesthesia was the great new discovery. Synesthesia worked in different ways: the *ballate* of the Italian *madrigalisti* created songs, which could be danced to;[17]

[16] *A History of Literary Criticism in the Italian Renaissance*, II, 776.

[17] On the *canzone a ballo* and the *ballata* ("itself an ancient, indigenous, and popular form in the Mediterranean lands"), see Sir Maurice Bowra, "Songs of Dance and Carnival," in *Italian Renaissance Studies* (London, 1960), 328–353. The songs of dance and

at the end of *The Winter's Tale* a statue comes to life. Tragicomedy is a generic instance, mixing symbolic modes rather than theatrical sensations.[18] In many cases the mixing suggests mannerism.

Under these conditions Ben Jonson might have attacked Inigo Jones because the latter had imported the artificial Italianate vices of a new synesthesia without any corresponding intellectual virtues. If so, the attack is parlous, since Jonson himself also participated in the Italianate movement. True, his Roman tragedies explore neoclassic possibilities, while his humor comedies and his critical espousal of classical unities need not be aligned with any interest in synesthetic *meraviglia*. *The Alchemist* is full of mingled sights, sounds, and smells— superaesthetic, we might say—but not in order to establish the principle of mixture. If anything, Jonson the public

---

carnival reflect a double origin, in a courtly pursuit of noble love and in a popular pursuit of seasonal festivity. Bowra observes that "in developing the courtly and romantic possibilities of the *canzone a ballo* Lorenzo [de' Medici] and Poliziano followed an aristocratic tradition which believed in restraint and decorum and impeccable sentiments. Parallel to this was another tradition with a very different temper. Since *ballate* were sung at seasonal festivals, they had a strong popular element of satire, gibes, and lubricious jocosity" (341– 342). This distinction corresponds to the one I have drawn between "festive comedy" and reveling in the masque; the latter seems inevitably governed by the calm setting of the courtly vision, however rowdy it might appear. Some masques, e.g., *Christmas his Masque*, stay closer to the popular style throughout.

[18] Jonson, in his conversations with Drummond, showed some interest in tragicomedy: "That Guarini, in his Pastor Fido kept not decorum in making Shepherds speek as well as himself could"; "Flesher and Beaumont ten yeers since hath written the Faithfull Shipheardesse a Tragicomedie well done." Dryden, in his late essay the *Parallel of Poetry and Painting* (1695) admitted, ruefully, that "our English tragicomedy must be confessed to be wholly Gothic, notwithstanding the success which it has found upon our theatre, and in the *Pastor Fido* of Guarini."

dramatist innovates by a neoclassic return to rules. Shake-speare's late romances are more radically experimental than anything of Jonson, save perhaps the unfinished *Sad Shepherd*, if we insist on the new synesthetic standard. *Bartholomew Fair* perhaps involves a satire on the new mode, which is treated as festive extravaganza. *Bartholomew Fair* is a gigantic antimasque. An anonymous contemporary says of the play that in it you "behold and heare the strange sights, and confus'd noise in the Fair. Here a Knave in a Fooles coate, with a trumpet sounding, or a drumme beating, invites you and would faine perswade you to see his puppets; There a Rogue alike a wilde woodman, or in an Antick shap(e) like an Incubus, desires your company, to view his motion." [19] Jonson prefaced the 1612 quarto of *The Alchemist* with a complaint against contemporary plays: "Now, the Concup-iscence of Daunces, and Antickes so raigneth, as to runne away from Nature, and be afraid of her, is the onely point of art that tickles the Spectators." And as Herford and Simpson observe, the same terms are employed in *Bartholomew Fair* itself, while Jonson condemns the interpolated masques of late Shakespeare for "mixing his head with other mens heeles." Jonson, they say, "was indignant that an eminent and popular playwright should countenance, and so help to perpetuate, what he himself felt to be a degradation of dramatic art." [20]

And yet the annual court masques remain, testimony to Jonson's own involvement in this degradation. Clearly he thought that up to a certain point the masque was the natural, classic form in which to embody the mixture of spectacle, dance, song, and verse. The *Expostulation* then defines a scenic excess, and it suggests that even the masque with its extrava-gant arts of magic, had to undergo the scrutiny of classical moderation.

[19] H. and S., X, 176.   [20] *Ibid.*, X, 177.

If the assumptions of the *Expostulation* suggest an ambiguous basis for Jonson's criticism, once inside the poem we soon forget that he may be compromised by his own dramatic standards and practices. The poem assumes the powerful Renaissance notion that all the arts are controlled by the idea of "number," whether Platonic, or Pythagorean. Jones's particular aesthetic excesses are not bad because they are synesthetic—synesthesia is one defining property of the masque. They are bad because they invert the mysterious hierarchy of synesthetic effects and resources. Jonson believes that poetry, verse-writing even, as practiced in the neoclassic pursuit of measure, best embodies the theoretical music of the masque, and that all other media are derivatives of the primal melody of the poet. He objects to the "skenopoet's" practice because it embodies an unbalanced harmony.

The *Expostulation*, from line 30 on, has been taken to imply that Jones had appropriated the poet's role in fabricating the ending of *Chloridia*, by his own arrangement introducing Juno, Iris, Lady Fame, Dame Poetry, Dame History, Dame Architecture, and Goody Sculpture to round out a particularly brilliant display at the close. Not only was Jones now a *skenopoetes*, but a music master and a fabler as well, and he would soon be the Dominus-Do-All of masque-making. Jonson objects that his rival will "make Boards to speak," by planting the music where no ear can reach. Mythology, the essence and "soul of the drama," will now be at the disposal of a man who can paint his myths on wooden boards. This "eloquence of masques" is a perverse rhetoric, contrasted with the *eloquentia* that is conducive, in humanist theory, to the wisdom and justice of the true prince or hero.

When Jonson satirizes Jones in his *Tale of a Tub*, his character In-and-In Medlay uses two words obsessively, "feasible" and "conduce." These may be explained as the two keys to Jones's hieroglyphical art. On the one hand, despite his vast expense account, he always needed to save money and thus had to find "feasible" means of making his machines; the technical achievement was always a costly engineering problem.

On the other hand, these machines had finally to influence the audience, the spectators; by magic they had to "conduce" to the right sort of marvelous dazzle of the spectators' critical faculties. But in the very process of this mad magical mechanism lay the sources of a decadence in the *poetic* arts that traditionally gave the masque its original "device." Jonson could only hold that his emblem, which he occasionally took pains to define by using classical sources, analogues, explanations, and other marginalian glosses, was always a primarily mythological and literary device. Only a poet could control such a machine, since only a poet would know the truly central role of myth in poetry. The poet had to be the absolute monarch of this mythic art, and the genre would die if "painting, and Carpentry, are the soule of masque." [21] In aligning the allegorical "hinge" with the poetic arts of mythmaking, Jonson was being commonsensical. The devices of the "Choice of Hercules," the liberation of Andromeda, or the Circean metamorphoses of Ulysses' men were mythological and thus very conveniently catalogued and their stories recounted in the handbooks of myth and emblem, and these myths were originally stories of a poetical sort.

[21] *Expostulation,* l. 50. The attack on physically painted scenery follows logically from the Horatian theory that "*Poetry,* and *Picture,* are Arts of a like Nature. . . . Poetry was a speaking Picture, and *Picture* a mute Poesie. . . . Yet of the two, the Pen is more noble, then the Pencill. For that can speake to the Understanding; the other, but to the Sense" (Ben Jonson, *Timber: or, Discoveries,* in Edward Tayler, *Literary Criticism of Seventeenth-Century England* [New York, 1967], 111).

A yet more profound connection between the allegorical device and the necessities of myth may have governed Jonson's ideas. The device was in one sense just the starting point of each such work, an originating motif from which it was spun out in verses and designs.[22] This suggests that the device was inherently a fixed *visual* start for the whole. But the form of the masque changed this initial fixity of the allegory into an unforeseen mobility. Thus, although the masque found its origin in the device which "set" the scene, typically a blustering, seriocomic sequence would start the stage business, often descending to burlesque (as in the actions of the tavern group in *The Masque of Augures* or of the Cook and the Poet in *Neptune's Triumph*). These opening scenes produce a sensation of dramatic flux, of misrule and antimasque prelude. Then follow the antimasque dances, and then the formalizing dances of the main masque, with varieties of dramatic action interspersed, and all this tends toward a slowing of the flux into a more stately grandeur. The main masque itself is slow motion, and in it movement is gradually stilled. Then follow the revels, with a return to flux, and finally the "going off" of the masquers closes the evening's entertainment with a return to stability and silence—at some hour before dawn. Now, although it is scarcely possible to systematize the incredible variety of masque forms, even of Jonson alone, it is perhaps possible to hold that the overall form of the masque is a transition, through varied interludes of song, dance, and dialogue, from an early state of strong visual fixation to a later state of harmonious musical motion. Or, using our conceptions from film-making, from a still shot

---

[22] "Device" in Elizabethan literary parlance was synonymous with "poetic conceit," or "controlling idea," though it very often referred precisely to a given *impresa*, or emblem. Often, in masques, it is called a "hinge."

to slow motion, through sequences run at a regular speed. Jonson would have regarded such a transition as a ritual by means of which the images of the princely presence were forced through a sequence of initiatory motions. He would have stressed the motions and would have aligned the formative techniques of his own literary art with the larger idea of musical form.

Various tendencies of Renaissance aesthetics will authorize this view. Much the most important, for our purposes, is the argument put forward by the poets that number symbolism was a legitimate philosophic basis for true poetry. For it was clear that besides music itself, which was restricted in referential power (though explorations of musical mimesis were a mark of the Renaissance and baroque periods), poetry which employed its own kind of "numbers" could exercise an Orphic control over the passions and the mind in general.

The problem for Jonson in attacking Jones was therefore to identify the exact method by which Jones was perverting the general belief that numbers were divine music. He found this in the way in which Jones was abusing his own art, by overextending it. Architecture had gained immeasurably in dignity and status with the writings of Alberti and Palladio, who had evolved their theories from the classic writings of Vitruvius. These Renaissance theories of architecture transformed the principles of architecture, as a modular science, from a set of mechanical techniques into a set of mystical, Pythagorean, musical harmonies. Jones himself "founded his theoretical deliberations [on architecture] on the metaphysical belief in the universal efficacy and beauty of numbers." Thus he proved that Stonehenge was a Roman temple, since it was built according to "harmonical proportions." Sir Henry Wotton similarly organized his *Elements of Architecture* (1624) around the Pythagorean number cult. Not stone, but "a secret harmony in the Proportions" was what seduced the viewer of a fine building. Wittkower has remarked that Wotton followed Alberti's interpretation of Pythagoras when he explained how to reduce "Symmetry to *Symphony*, and the *Harmony of Sound*, to a kind of *Harmony in Sight*." [23] Partly because such "mystification" is bathed in skepticism, it was easy for Elizabethans, Jacobeans, and Carolines to grasp the "curious learning" of universal harmony as it conditioned literary art. For they were, if nothing else, addicted to Neoplatonist styles of imagination,[24] and thereby were attuned to the transcendental interpretation of myth. Mythology was the governing system of the verbal universe which Renaissance poets inhabited. Possessing this universe, daily expanding it, the poets of this time stood between twin temptations of an earlier allegorism and a later realism, and acceded to neither.

If then we are to assimilate the full extravagance of the mystagogical Renaissance, with its hermetic magic, its mem-

[23] Quoted in Rudolf Wittkower, *Architectural Principles in the Age of Humanism* (New York, 1965), 144.

[24] Cf. Ellrodt, *Neoplatonism in the Poetry of Spenser;* C. S. Lewis' review thereof, in his *Studies in Medieval and Renaissance Literature* (Cambridge, 1966), 149–163; Douglas Bush, *Mythology and the Renaissance Tradition in English Poetry* (New York, 1963); Erwin Panofsky, *Studies in Iconology: Humanistic Themes in the Art of the Renaissance* (New York, 1939; repr. 1962); P. O. Kristeller, *Renaissance Thought: The Classic, Scholastic and Humanistic Strains* (New York, 1961), and *Renaissance Thought, II: Papers on Humanism and the Arts* (New York, 1965); Wind, *Pagan Mysteries;* Sears Jayne, "The Subject of Milton's Ludlow *Mask*," in A. E. Barker, ed., *Milton: Modern Essays in Criticism* (New York, 1965), and rev., in Diekhoff, ed., *A Maske at Ludlow;* D. J. Gordon, "*Hymenaei:* Ben Jonson's Masque of Union," *Journal of the Warburg and Courtauld Institute,* VIII (1945), 107–145, and "Ben Jonson's Haddington Masque: The Story and the Fable," *Modern Language Review,* XLII (1947).

ory theatres, its Egyptian theomancy, its Cabala, its wild fascination with inconceivable devices of order-in-chaos, we must taste the complex flavors of a seemingly compulsive syncretism. Although this was the period of Montaigne, it was also the era of Sir Thomas Browne. Ghosts came into their own during the Renaissance, dramaturgically. Spirits could inform theatrical scenes. Philosophy meant mysterious laws, and the word "mystery" itself took on an ironic sense of "arcane technical craft." [25] Method masqueraded as madness, and madness as method. One socially relevant index to the founding of the Royal Society, later in the seventeenth century, is the emergence of the "mad scientist" as a modish literary subject. The Renaissance period marks the rise of such fanciful subjects—in Jonson's *The Alchemist*, for example—and if I stress the aesthetic importance of mixed media during this period, it is because methods of controlling the new cosmology had to include some desperate measures. Among these were the games of artists using mixed media. Palladio and Alberti were architects. It was natural for them to appeal to the mysterious authority of Pythagorean numbers. They were not alone, and their disciple Jones simply continued the line of speculative wisdom. It was because the line had real force during this time that Ben Jonson made it a point of principle to oppose it.

First of all, he could not, like the rationalist Lord Kames

[25] Shakespeare's uses of "mystery" seem peculiarly rich, if not numerous: e.g., *Measure for Measure*, IV, ii, 33 ff., where the hangman's art is a "mystery"; *Hamlet*, III, ii, 382: "You would pluck the heart out of my mystery" (referring to the art of the musical recorder); *King Lear*, I, i, 112: "The Mysteries of Hecate . . ." and V, 3, 16: "Take upon's the mystery of things, / As if we were God's spies"; *Troilus and Cressida*, III, iii, 201: "There is a mystery—with whom relation / Durst never meddle—in the soul of state; / Which hath an operation more divine." There are eighteen occurrences in all.

two centuries later, deny the architecture-numbers analogy as an empirical matter. Kames could say: "To refute the notion of a resemblance between musical proportions and those of architecture, it might be sufficient to observe in general, that the one is addressed to the ear, the other to the eye; and that objects of different senses have no resemblance, nor indeed any relation to each other." [26] Kames's wisdom in regard to the separation of aesthetic modes would yet be reversed in I. A. Richards' first critical work, where, with C. K. Ogden, he spoke of "synesthesia." [27] But from his own perspective Kames was entirely sensible, and he adduced his evidence of the separations between media with the full authority of British empirical psychology. Before him and before Lockean, Hobbesian developments had taken place, however, there was every reason to think along more mystical lines, which is precisely what Jonson was doing. Thus it is important that he objects to Jones's inept use of Vitruvius, whom he accuses Jones of misinterpreting (ll. 7–8), and later mocks Jones under the name Vitruvius Hoop. The first part of the sobriquet speaks for itself. But "Hoop" is more interesting. It seems to have at least two meanings; the first an implication of rotund emptiness, mockingly suggests that Jones was a slender man. But secondly, the Vitruvian ideal was transformed during the Renaissance into the idea of the round, of the circle as achetype for all true temples. Whenever a church or other important building had to partake of the divine form, it had, in the spirit of Nicholas of Cusa, to fit other shapes (hexagons, squares, even triangles) inside the

[26] Wittkower, *Architectural Principles*, 152.

[27] C. K. Ogden and I. A. Richards, *The Foundations of Aesthetics* (2d ed., New York, 1925). Strictly, synesthesia requires a merging of senses, so as to approach the metaphoric effect of Donne's "loud perfume" or Crashaw's "sparkling noyse." See Frank Warnke, ed., *Dictionary of Poetry and Poetics* (Princeton, N.J., 1965), 839–840.

governing form of the circle. The hoop was the perfect Vitruvian form, and Jones should have known that in exalting Vitruvius he was appealing to an ancient emblem of God, the circle, and therefore to a principle which poetry commanded, through *its* perfection of the eternal return of verses.

With the cooling of time we can see that Jonson had no particular right to assume that poetry alone should command the heights of this sublime conception. Why not the magic of Renaissance architecture also? Any spectator of the wonders of Italian architecture, not to mention the lesser magnificence of Jones's Banqueting Hall, can testify that the magic of number belonged also to the arts of stone. But so Jonson saw the battle, and it is the lines on which the battle is drawn that are important to us now.

Perhaps we can back away from the quarrelsome confusion of Jonson versus Jones if we grant that they were both right, and that, in the containment of their own careers, they could not see that their quarrel implied a larger unresolved question: How can variant modes of aesthetic response be brilliantly coordinated? It was their quite human assumption that the outcome depended upon their own genius—as if Ben could outdo his rival by sheer virtuosity, or Inigo could outdo his by absolute architectural invention. Practically and ephemerally, Ben Jonson lost the fight. His idea of perfect numbers did not sufficiently excite King Charles and his court. Jones's splendors did. And of the two, which could survive? More likely the poetry, as Jonson knew, echoing Shakespeare's sonnet: "Not marble nor the gilded monuments / Of princes shall outlive this pow'rful rime."

This enormous presumption, based partly on the power of the relatively new print culture which, unprecedently, induced him to publish his *Works*, shows among other things a strong belief in the ear. "Music where no ear can reach"—

music is what the ear reaches. Spectacular sights are not music, because they are not reached by the ear. Ergo, spectacle is not true in the Pythagorean sense of truth. Musical harmony cannot inform the sights and the eloquence of the mere show. Only the ear can know the musically rendered passing of time. Music moves with time and is thus relatively at rest; architecture sits, and therefore "falls behind." Architecture for Jonson is not, as Goethe thought it, "frozen music."

Here we move yet closer to the source of rupture between the two men: only poetry (or a natural music, not architecture certainly) can confer the ultimate perfection on the audience—the perfection of a conditional immortality. Almost as if he were a Puritan exegete, or Milton writing *Paradise Lost*, Jonson ascribes the role of ultimate vision, not to sight, but to sound. When the Archangel in *Paradise Lost* wants man to know human history in all its ephemeral show, he shows it to him from the mountaintop. When he wants him to know the typological truth of history, he lets him hear about it. He preaches a sermon. He lets sound echo through the soul like the spirit of number itself. Through the ear one can redeem the ephemeral, but not through sight, which loses it in the passing flux.

Jonson's love of occasional poetry and his expertise in writing it lend particular credence to this view of his hierarchy of values. Jonson could from his own experience identify "Ben Jonson his best piece of poetry": he knew, from the death of his own child and the birth of the poem in which he commemorated the child's life and death and his own part in both, that whatever poetry is, it is not a grandiose mechanical plaster cast of eternity, not a myth painted on a canvas, not a scene visually magnificent as long as its "mechanic art" remains undetected by the spectator. He perhaps believed that the real consumer of art has to be an audience; it cannot be spectators. Jonson, because he commanded words, could *say* to Jones what they both were doing. Verbal signs could define visual language. True, he was angry or pretended anger, and he may have misrepresented his ingenious colleague. But, as the annals of the masque will show, there is no clearer, more exact, more honest appraisal of what a Jones could do than the judgment against him in the *Expostulation*.

"*Things sacred from prophane to separate*"

The wonder of Renaissance poetics was its general self-awareness. Poets experimented in the most daring way with the problems of belief that arose when spiritual and material worlds, body and soul, human and angelic, daemonic and god-like, or human and daemonic would collide with each other. Shakespeare explored every boundary between fact and fancy, history and fiction, error and truth. Spenser established the mythic principles of a protean romantic vision. This was a time, in short, when artists knew "things sacred from profane to separate," as the *Ars Poetica*, in Jonson's translation, said poets had been taught to do by Orpheus.

Modern studies of the mythography of the period have shown that for the Renaissance generally *mythology is a language*, and a language has "deep structures" and all sorts of dialects. Before pretending to get rid of the intricacies of mythology, the modern critic must try to work out its grammar and only then can he go into the nicer, more precise analysis of style or diction, at least if his interpretations are to fit the main facts.

The grammar of masque depends on a magical mode of causation. Furthermore, since the Renaissance is a period when boundaries between sacred and profane are under scrutiny, under pressure, the discussion of mythographic grammar has to begin with this distinction. Not accidentally, we notice,

Panofsky started his forays into Renaissance iconology by considering such painters as Piero di Cosimo, whose cosmogonic images invite the sacred-profane contrast, and Titian, whose famed *Sacred and Profane Love* is almost, throughout its history, an index to the illusions that grip the fantasy of Western man as it oscillates between ideas of the sacred as ideal and puritan, of the profane as sensual and libertine.[28] Such a painting does not dispose of the dichotomy, but entertains it, and this entertainment of the balance should be our touchstone for the period. For the ambiguity of the distinction, which seems to have been resolved by Orpheus and the prophetic poets, is not finally disposed of. Mystery is still, with the coming of Renaissance science, very much akin to philosophy. Any attempt to fasten religion on an idolatrous set of painted images will be a design to destroy the Orphic arts. For these must essentially remain secret within the mind.

Such is the aesthetic background of the *Expostulation* when it decries the "hieroglyphics" of the masque scene. These would hypostatize sacred truths and thus prevent us from knowing the true relation of sacred and profane, which is deeply ambiguous. Ambiguity is one condition of mystery. This is not always a matter of ambivalent, tabooed attitudes, though they may pull the believer this way or that, violently.

[28] See Panofsky, *Studies in Iconology*, chs. ii, v. To the degree that *Comus* suspends the dichotomy of two loves, the sacred agape (of the Lady) and the profane eros (of Comus), it also shares in the fiction of mediation which Titian represented through the image of Cupid, and Milton through the Attendant Spirit. "That Cupid is placed between the two Venuses, though somewhat closer to the 'terrestrial' or 'natural' one, and that he stirs the water in the fountain may express the Neoplatonic belief that love, a principle of cosmic 'mixture,' acts as an intermediary between heaven and earth" (152). The Attendant Spirit plays something of this mediating, "stirring" role by—as it were—directing, or stage-managing, the events of the masque.

Rather, as the Renaissance poet perceives, we simply cannot be sure about the mysterious. We certainly should not be taken in by wooden emblems of such complex truths. Jones, by violating complexity, violates simple truth. Simple truth here lies in the perception of multiple truths, and the unity of this multifarious universe lies in its "pied beauty."

Jonesean oversimplification was, despite its courtly uses, a debased form of mystery—that was the substance of Jonson's first diatribe. Having once failed to admit or allow into the masque at least the metaphysics of his own vanishing forms, Jones had denied all possibility of a synthesis of sight and sound. For the synthesis had to occur, as the poet knew, and he was never vitally opposed to scene and imagery ("picture") in poetry—he had mentioned the *Ars Poetica* of Horace several times, to argue the opposite view. But what he did oppose was a misconstruction of the sacred. Nothing sacred, he would claim, could be achieved if the scene designer showed a glistening transmogrification of the prince at the top of a pyramid. Sacred ecstasis was not gasping at the transformation of a mechanical cloud. A painting on a property wall was not sacred. The sacred was at least spiritual and could only reside, quintessentially, in the realms of idea, number, and mind. The imagery of the scene was a legitimate prod to the numinous experience, but not, as Jones wanted everyone to believe, its essence. That lay elsewhere.

If we seek a single criterion to denote the sacred in its proper ambiguous relationship with the profane, we can do no better than to employ that dichotomy which Jonson and other Christians of his time customarily used. From every pulpit in the land they learned that there was "sacred space"— churches were "sacred places"—and they knew that around such centers, timeless and perfect in their isolation from human depravity, there lay the endless wasteland of human error. This dialectic of temples and error was nothing new. But during this epoch it came more readily to hand than ever before, as mythographic languages became richer. The *moving* musical image of the temple—round dance or song—could be counterpointed against the mazy wanderings of the wasteland, where motion was the uncontrolled, undisciplined wilderness of the antimasque.

The Vision of the Twelve Goddesses, archetypal in this respect as in others, gives a picture of the degree to which the formal dancing could flow harmoniously:

Which as soon as she had ended, the three Graces in silver robes with white torches appeared on the top of the mountain, descending hand in hand before the Goddesses; who likewise followed three and three, as in a number dedicated unto sanctity and an incorporeal nature, whereas the dual, *Hierogliphice pro immundis accipitur* ["means, hieroglyphically, the impure"]. And between every rank of Goddesses marched three torch-bearers in the like several colours, their heads and robes all decked with stars and in their descending the cornets sitting in the concaves of the mountain and seen but to their breasts in the habit of satyrs sounded a stately march which continued until the Goddesses were approached just before the temple and then ceased, when the consort music (placed in the cupola thereof, out of sight) began: whereunto the three Graces, retiring themselves aside, sang whiles the Goddesses one after another with solemn pace ascended up into the temple and delivering their presents to the Sibylla (as it were but in passing by) returned down into the midst of the hall, preparing themselves to their dance, which, as soon as the Graces had ended their song, they began to the music of the viols and lutes placed on one side of the hall. Which dance being performed with great majesty and art, consisting of divers strains framed unto motions circular, square, triangular, with other proportions exceeding rare and full of variety, the Goddesses made a pause, casting themselves into a circle, whilst the Graces again sang to the music of the temple and prepared to take out the Lords to dance. With whom after they had performed certain measures, galliards, and corantos, Iris again comes and gives notice of their pleasure to depart.[29]

Jonson, like Daniel, recognized that the circling, geometric dance gave flow to the visual scene, but since the scene maker had invented a variety of movable visual machines, he had to make a distinction between a legitimate choreographic set of motions and mechanically produced scenic illusion. One of his masque-making triumphs was the development of the antimasque, which permitted this distinction; in the two main antithetical elements of Jonsonian form it is possible for the temple to be represented in round dances and their derivations, while error is represented by the jagged antimasque.

The destiny of the masque, as it develops with Jonson, is the liberation of the genre from its own visual materials. This is the chief significance of the tendency toward a more and more literary purpose which Orgel has demonstrated. The visual in which Jones finally triumphed over Jonson is fixation of thought. Yet the masque as myth liberates the imprisoned hero or heroine from the fixations of one tyranny or another. The genre is valid partly because it questions the power structure it appears to be supporting blindly. In common with other serious forms, the genre is somewhat equivocal and works by showing that there is always an evil as well as a benign monarchy. There is the true prince and the demonic parody of the prince, and both are subject to the vanishing point. Most of the masques of the period suggest Spenser, particularly the liberation of Amoret from the enchanter Busirane, and even the descent of the gentleman and lady masquers from their clouds, mountains, towers, and bowers

[29] Spencer and Wells, *Book of Masques,* 29–30.

takes the form of a liberation from prison. After the revels, or sometimes just before them, they go back up to their prison, though it has, by their revels, been redeemed. Their Olympus or Palace of Wisdom or Mount Atlas is redeemed because *they* have been redeemed, by going through the motions of the masque.

Milton, following Jonson and the other literary masters of the form, set out in *Comus* to write the transcendental version of this archetypal liberation. He wrote a final work in the genre, close to the end of its classic English phase, after Jonson and Jones had fully explored the possibilities of the form. But what was still for Jonson an uncertain battle between song and spectacle, movement and fixation, was a freer medium in Milton's hands. He went beyond his predecessors, it would seem, not only because he had such remarkable lyric gifts, but even more because he resolved the stylistic quarrel between sight and sound. He related both sight and sound to the literary dynamism of the form, which was thaumaturgic. Appreciating the "mythomystical" nature of the masque, he saw therein an unrivaled chance to mix all the modes already brought together in the disparate genres of tragicomedy, *ballet de cour*, opera, pageant, and masque itself, and in a thoroughly original way he forced imagery from all the available media of masque into the verbal confines of his text. Through words alone, *Comus* achieves transcendental form, the shape required by a work of art if it is to federate, or unify, the rivals among its mixed media. Separation of sacred and profane is the prelude to their "mysterious" reunion.

4 Transcendental Form

In *The Lives of the Poets,* where he is describing *Paradise Lost,* Dr. Johnson writes that "Milton's delight was to sport in the wide regions of possibility; reality was a scene too narrow for his mind. He sent his faculties out upon discovery, into worlds where only imagination can travel, and delighted to form new modes of existence, and furnish sentiment and action to superior beings; to trace the counsels of hell, or accompany the choirs of heaven." Milton, he continues, would characteristically choose "a subject on which too much could not be said, on which he might tire his fancy without the censure of extravagance." Such choices, and the aesthetic they imply, may be ascribed to a preference for "transcendental forms." Such forms seem to arise in literary history when authors have apparently exhausted all the natural resources of their art and seem also to arise, with less reason, when a cultural group believes it has entered a period of definitive decadence or even final apocalypse.

Initially we may define a transcendental form as any poetic structure that by design includes more than its traditionally accepted generic limits—the classical limits of its genre— would allow it to include. As containing form this structure will apparently be held together by an immanent order. As symbolic matrix, however, this closed and immanent order will display a countering activity of all its details, exploding out from the containing frame, transcending limits formally accepted. Such a form is, in Edmund Husserl's language, a world, since for him "a world itself, is an infinite idea, related to infinities of harmoniously combinable experiences— an idea that is the correlate of the idea of a perfect experiental evidence, a complete synthesis of possible experiences." Again, in Husserl's terms, each detail within such a world is an "immanent transcendency." [1] Now, whereas one could apply the method of Husserl's *Cartesian Mediations*, in the manner of Georges Poulet and others, to show that the masque in general, and *Comus* in particular, constitutes a perfect genre for "transcendental experience," it will be more useful to our analysis at this point to ask what general aesthetic problems arise in connection with transcendental forms. A return to philosophical speculation may later become desirable, since it may clarify Milton's "egotistical sublime." It may also elucidate the paradoxical manner of so much Miltonic myth-making.

While the critical theory of Kenneth Burke has often been devoted to the problem of the transcendental symbol, his definition of the transcendentalism of Emerson will serve to remind the reader that all such symbolism is a kind of "pontification," "the building of a *terministic bridge* whereby one realm is *transcended* by being viewed *in terms of* a realm 'beyond' it." Burke argues for Emerson's *Nature* and more widely for other similar works that insofar as things of this world, "things here and now," are treated in the terms of a realm *beyond*, "they thereby become infused or inspirited by

---

[1] *Cartesian Meditations: An Introduction to Phenomenology*, tr. Dorion Cairns (The Hague, 1960), 28, 50.

the addition of a *new or further* dimension." [2] This kind of thinking in turn may be grasped as a powerful system of revelation; nature can be treated "in terms of" a supernature, or, as Emerson phrased it, "The universe becomes transparent, and the light of higher laws than its own shines through it." Or again, "Sensible objects conform to the premonitions of Reason and reflect the conscience." From such statements the historian of philosophy can trace a long line of thought back to the Platonic theory of ideas, the source for all such theories of mediation. To the extent that poetic fictions attempt such crossing from one realm to another or attempt a vision of the material in terms of the ideal, they too have a root in the Platonic tradition, and during the Renaissance this inheritance is strong. Neoplatonic thought is radically transcendental, and the major literary forms in a period of influential Neoplatonism will show transcendence. Yet it is one thing to speak of "transcendence" within a work, and another of the "transcendental form" of a work. The former is textual—the parts are set forth to yield an image of one world "in terms of" another world beyond it. Yet the modular nature of all symbolic textures provides that certain overall forms will follow from those textures. Thus, to give a homely analogy, it is possible to make much better curvilinear architectural forms with poured concrete than with wood or cinder blocks. The modular unit influences the containing shape. Infinitely delicate details articulate the whole universe. There lies our main problem with the masque, for even though the texture can be shown to be predominantly magical, as we have seen, there remains the question of containing form.

Proleptically, but not unfairly, we could leap forward in

[2] "I, Eye, Ay—Concerning Emerson's Early Essay on 'Nature,' and the Machinery of Transcendence," in *Language as Symbolic Action* (Berkeley, 1966), 187, 190.

time to Hegel's "sublation," his *Aufhebung*, to reach the definitive instance of the transcendentalist yearning, which holds that "the work of art is not only for the sensuous apprehension as sensuous object, but its position is of such a kind that as sensuous it is at the same time essentially addressed to the mind." [3] In English literary history Coleridge most strongly expresses the nostalgia for the whole that will contain the infinitely outbursting natural world. Writing to his friend Thelwall in 1797, Coleridge admits the anguish of such a relation to nature:

I can *at times* feel strongly the beauties, you describe, in themselves, and for themselves—but more frequently *all things* appear little—all the knowledge, that can be acquired, child's play—the universe itself—what but an immense heap of *little* things?—I can contemplate nothing but parts, and parts are all *little*—!—My mind feels as if it ached to behold and know something great—something *one and indivisible*—and it is only in the faith of this that rocks or waterfalls, mountains or caverns give me the sense of sublimity or majesty!—But in this faith *all things* counterfeit infinity! [4]

How this natural environment can be like a "a living Thing/ Which acts upon the mind," or a transcendental ground of

[3] Quoted by W. K. Wimsatt, "The Concrete Universal," in *The Verbal Icon* (New York, 1954; repr., 1960), 72. Harry Berger, Jr., in "Archaism, Vision, and Revision: Studies in Virgil, Plato, and Milton," *Centennial Review*, XI (1967), 24–52, glosses (and uses) the Hegelian term *aufheben* as follows: "As I understand Hegel's notion, when you sublate something, you 1) transcend it or negate it, pass it by, render it obsolete, 2) recognize *that* you have transcended it, therefore 3) you sustain it, hold it up so it does not vanish, for you give it a new life and direction in your life, you assign it historical significance and bestow on it a career going beyond itself which it could not have had without you."

[4] *The Collected Letters of Samuel Taylor Coleridge* ed. E. L. Griggs (Oxford, 1956–1959), I, 349–350.

higher knowledge, is the puzzle that certain poets set out to resolve, not by theorizing, but in the creative act of making transcendental forms. To solve this puzzle three critical categories may serve: size, medium, and virtuosity.

Size

Although the problem is classical, having been raised by Aristotle in the *Poetics*, literary size is by no means easy to define or to understand. There is no ready definition of psychological magnitude. Yet by tradition the epic forms, besides their "rhythm of recurrence," [5] have been noted for their grandeur, their amplitude. It seems therefore revealing that Johnson should have called *Comus* a "drama in the epic style," since largeness of scope is almost sufficient to define the epical mode. Size also involves psychic relations between form and function—most lyrics are short because their themes and feelings are intense, though not necessarily brief or succinct. A nostalgic lyric nicely represents the difficulty of our problem. Feelings of longing seem to spread out in waves, enlarging and dilating the soul. Romantic poetry generally concerns itself with the *size* of our feelings.

Larger scope of action and image normally results from the cosmic ambitions of the epic author. He usually wants to develop a cosmos proper to the heroic myth. This cosmo-logical striving may be overt, as in *Paradise Lost* or the *Divine Comedy* or the *Ring* cycle, where scope is limited only by the boundaries of a divine science fiction. It may be veiled, as in the Homeric poems, where the gods hover in a strange accessory daemonic role, half in and half out of the human world. This is not the place to attempt a catalogue of the literary varieties of cosmic image and action; it suffices to say that in works of transcendental scope we are most im-

[5] Frye, *Anatomy of Criticism*, 251–262.

pressed by their sheer size, and this in turn is an impression of cosmic grandeur.

In principle, on the other hand, the definition of "cosmic scope" does not itself have to include a criterion of absolute size. Unity of diverse parts is rather the central concept, which indeed is recognized in the term "microcosm," which shares cosmic order, but not large size, with "macrocosm." If anything, cosmicity implies here that size is less important than coherence under conditions in which fragmentation would readily occur. Politically the unity of the Soviet Union or the United States is transcendental, and such federations are remarkable, as Kenneth Burke has reminded us, exactly because of their transcendence of inner differences. On such a political model the ultimate transcendental form would be a federation of the largest size capable of a coherence directly proportional to the stresses being contained and served by that large form. The "mystifications" which we observed in describing the masque as a type of political representation sustain the dynamic of the transcendental model. The political leader, the president of a vast federated republic, must necessarily "mystify" his governmental powers in order that they may persuade, or seem to persuade, the varied constituency he controls as head of state. Power thus "mystified" and mediated by symbols will acquire authority and will avoid the stigma of pure force. By analogy, the masque and its mixed media and their powerfully focused magical controls reflect the desire to invent a transcendental political rhetoric. Elizabethan and Stuart history suggests further that the growing sense of a British *imperium*—the term "British Empire" had been advocated by the alchemist Dr. Dee [6]—and the increased pressure of internal

---

[6] Richard Koebner, *Empire* (Cambridge, 1961), 62; W. J. Trattner, "God and Expansion in Elizabethan England: John Dee, 1527–1583," in *The Elizabethan Age* (New York, 1966), ed. D. L. Stevenson.

political forces, besides leading to the explosion of the Civil War, were the natural climate for a development of this transcendental dramatic mode. Courtship and its mysteries were undergoing their greatest trial, and their mythic languages were enlarged by masque makers to permit the containment of violence (antimasque) by order (main masque). Court masques normally are limited in the length of text they follow. Perhaps 300 lines would mark the average lower limit; *The Vision of Delight* has 247 lines; a more complex Jonsonian masque, *Oberon*, has 381; Carew's *Coelum Britannicum*, one of the longest, has approximately 1150; *The Gypsies Metamorphosed* has 1492; in its final published form *Comus* has 1023. We can obviously not claim literal vastness for the genre. We can more easily claim the opposite. But the actuality of masque is that the entertainment, if we include the revels, took several hours, and the overall effect of masque is quite missed when we simply count lines. The line count gives the lower limit of the masque as microcosm; the masque's dramatic actuality gives a totally different upper limit, where its range of reference to the macrocosm is such that it always suggests a larger world of political and social beliefs. One's sense of the occasion would be orgiastic. A feast of symbols, a dazzle of the senses, a revel of body and mind—these are transcendental to the degree that their medium is an intricate economy where nothing symbolic is wasted, and where the effects of astonishment and wonder are maximized.

So far, if masque is transcendental in such ways, it would appear hard to differentiate it from any standard allegorical process. The norm for allegory is an extended analogy drawn between microcosm and macrocosm. On the other hand, there seems to be a difference when we consider the style or the purely aesthetic aspect of allegory. It can be shown that the inherent tendency of allegory is toward endless, obsessive rumination and extension, so that, typically, the allegorical quest never ends. Nor is there any inherent reason for the allegorical battle ever to be won, for compulsive rumination finally escapes closure and in fact lives off the denial of closure. The "unfinished" masterpieces in this mode, works like *The Faerie Queene*, palpably demonstrate what psychoanalysts would call "the effect onto infinity." But works of the transcendental order seem rather different, however much one discerns family resemblances. They ought to go on forever but somehow insist upon closure. Their closure is often almost violent—more obviously perhaps in music, where, for example, the transcendental aspirations of Beethoven produce his manifest reluctance to end the final codas of his Fifth and Ninth symphonies. In fact, violent as the coda may be, its closure is all the more powerful for undergoing the pressure not to end. We could doubtless accumulate examples from baroque architecture, beginning with the Bernini arrangement of the piazza of St. Peter's or in poetry with Marino or with Crashaw—the one clear case of English baroque sensibility— and his *Hymn to St. Teresa*, whose flaming, iterative conclusion would provide another parallel. Such cases do not prove a point; they do, however, suggest the problem of containment as it occurs where there is the most direct evidence of a desire to write fictions, make buildings, compose musical concords, according to a system of transcendent expansion.

Were the term "baroque" not quite so variously discussed in the historical criticism of the arts, it would serve as an appropriate label for much of the transcendental form-making that concerns us here. In the baroque we can see the essential paradox: that the themes or materials tend to explode, while the artist does his best to contain this explosion.[7] What he does

[7] Consider the spiral form of steeple created by Borromini or the spiral columns of Bernini, in St. Peter's.

not do is rearrange the explosive materials so that their inner war is dissipated. He does not select. He does not reduce to classic simplicity. If he wants a simplification of choices, he gets it by compressing the materials, and his transcendentalism is defined by a sort of "compression ratio." By the same token he does not seek to reduce inner pressures by expanding the scope of his work; as the work gets bigger, the pressures are increased even more. *Paradise Lost,* for example, does not become less pressured, less intense because Milton added the final two books of world history; instead, the poem attains an even more dynamic inner life, an even more explosive form.

The increase of intensity accompanying an increase in scope, which appears paradoxical at best, recalls the metaphysical theories of Nicholas of Cusa, where God is simultaneously both the center and the circumference of the universe. This *concidentia oppositorum* is cosmological; it originates the shifts of thought outlined by Cassirer in *The Individual and the Cosmos in Renaissance Philosophy;* we see an emerging Renaissance belief in the freedom of the human spirit as a force indwelling in that same universe through which God manifests himself as both center and boundary. Cassirer traces the complex lines between Cusan cosmology and the arguments of Carolus Bovillus, showing that man (and especially the poet) can reach perfect self-consciousness through a fourfold rise of *esse, vivere, sentire, intelligere,* until he arrives at the almost Hegelian formula "according to which the meaning and aim of the mental process of development consists in the 'substance' becoming 'subject.' " [8] Further along this track of the liberation of his Promethean mental authority, Renaissance man learns that nature is not just an *ob-ject,* a thing thrown down against the ego, but is

[8] *Individual and the Cosmos,* 89. On Bovillus, see Rice, *Renaissance Idea of Wisdom,* 106–123.

rather a scene or setting or *Stimmung* in which the creative mind comes to life: "Nature is not sought and represented for its own sake; rather, its value lies in its service to modern man as a new *means of expression* for himself, for the liveliness and the infinite polymorphism of his inner life." Even magic shares in this trend; it is justified largely because it is *inside* rather than outside nature. Finally, Cassirer's account shows that for the modern mind a new conception of space opens new ideas of freedom. Space ceases to be the boundary containing things, the pod containing the seeds, the skin, the wall, the encasing armor.

The unbounded universe of Giordano Bruno displays the new philosophy of transcendental forms.

For Bruno, the space in which the universe exists is not the farthest boundary in which, so to speak, the universe is embedded and wrapped; rather, space is the free medium of movement, extending unhindered beyond every finite border and in all directions. This movement cannot and may not find any obstacle in the "nature" of any individual thing, or in the general constitution of the cosmos. For movement itself, in its universality and in its limitlessness, constitutes nature as such. Infinite *space* is required as the vehicle of infinite *power;* and this, in turn, is nothing but an expression of the infinite *life* of the universe. In Bruno's thought, these three movements are never sharply distinguished. As in the Stoic and the Neo-Platonic physics, upon which he leans, the concept of space merges with that of the aether, and this, in turn, with the concept of a world soul. Here again, a dynamic motif breaks through, and overcomes, the rigidity of the Aristotelian-Scholastic cosmos.

Bruno thus formulates the myth of "heroic frenzies," the *eroici furori* of his dialogue, in which, as Cassirer puts it, "the new view of the world represents itself in the form of a new, urgent, and swelling impulse." More precisely, "Man, the

Ego, appears to the universe, the world, at once as the enclosing and the enclosed." [9] This is the transcendental form-maker's destiny, to seek shapes at once enclosed and enclosing. He cultivates his mind as, in Ficino's words, "the faculty of containing."

Medium

To turn to our second category: what most needed containment was the masque's baroque mixture of media. Exploiting various media which extended different senses, the masque was bound to raise special problems of containment, which are painfully clear in the quarrel of Jones and Jonson, and which were pleasantly resolved in the degree of co-operation they did achieve. Even in the case of close and seemingly sympathetic collaborators like Henry Lawes and Milton, the wealth of media is potentially so great that it threatens to oppress the will to achieve any final unity. Some counterforce is necessary to channel the multiple means of utterance. However we describe this channeling, it reduces them to a singleness of voice, the kind of oneness that we found in the fact that masque is always an implicit dramatic monologue. By speaking in the "second voice," the poet creates an overriding persona that may govern the subordinate personae of the action. Most often, as we have seen, the governing persona is close to the poet himself and assumes a Daedalian stance—with Campion Orpheus and with Jonson Daedalus himself. This Daedalian "presenter" may unwind the tangle of the masque debate in any number of ways, but over all his particular devices there hangs one main destiny, to unify the voices of the many, to make the mixed media cohere so that a transcendent unity may be achieved.

The critical approach that will reveal this unity in its true

[9] Cassirer, *Individual and the Cosmos*, 144, 187, 189.

dimensions will be modern, if not employing a German Romantic or Coleridgean theory of imagination, then preferring Walter Pater's "perfect identification of matter and form." In defining the aspirations of the School of Giorgione, Pater discovered the virtue or active principle of this school in its double use of music, first of musical *genre* scenes and second of an elusive musical coherence. Perhaps only a modern sensibility (and this began to grow in the Renaissance) could maintain the balance between the claims of each specific medium—the "untranslatable order of impressions" created by sight, sound, touch, smell, and taste—and the claims of "the law or principle of music." That an exceedingly sensitive critic like Pater could maintain this balance in his essays on the Renaissance suggests a necessary historical bias in the criticism required by *Comus:* The self-consciousness of the modern era is a prerequisite of any sure estimate of the method of a transcendent unification of form and matter.

Such a method is hard to describe exactly, and we are forced to use impressionistic terms. Again, although there is testimony in early criticism that the wondrous appeal of the masque and such genres is in a transcendence of materiality—and this is the main point of Prospero's famed speech about his own masque—we can get closer to the problem if we think in more modern terms. The modern poet most deeply engaged in recapturing the art of transcendental forms is Hugo von Hofmannsthal, the reincarnation of the spirit of Calderón, who in turn had written the *autos sacramentales* which border so closely upon the territory of masque.[10] Hofmannsthal attempted a wide variety of transcendental

[10] Hofmannsthal's *Jedermann* (1911) and the other two festival dramas are discussed in Brian Coghlan, *Hofmannsthal's Festival Dramas* (Cambridge, 1964), which includes comment on the poet's critical essays of the period.

forms, and not merely in his festival dramas, *Das grosse Salzburger Welttheater* and *Der Turm*, both of which recreate earlier themes of Calderón. Even more striking is the collaboration between Hofmannsthal and Strauss, since the visionary language of an opera like *Die Frau ohne Schatten* is reinforced by the post-Wagnerian complexity of Strauss's music. For our purposes, however, a critical lecture, "Shakespeare's Kings and Noblemen," delivered in Weimar in 1905, will suggest the true nature of the unitary voice in masque.

Hofmannsthal began with the assumption that the reader of Shakespeare must possess "the gift of imaginary performance." He attempted to describe the effect of artistic wholeness that results from the employment of this "very specific creativeness" which is the proper response to Shakespearean vision. The ideal reader is driven by passion to see each of the plays "as a Whole." He takes in not only the play's tragic reflections of life as it is lived, but also "a thousand more delicate, more hidden, more sensual, more symbolic things—which, with their intertwining diversity, form the mysterious unit whose passionate servants they are." [11]

When asked to define the forces of this mysterious unity, Hofmannsthal had to reply (as we might expect of a good Viennese) that the varied strands "merge into a melodious Whole, which in its heroic elements and the recurrent theme, is reminiscent of a Beethoven sonata." And again, "The Whole is interwoven by this music." This, from such a different part of the world, is strikingly reminiscent of the analytic categories of G. Wilson Knight, who might himself have spoken the Austrian's words:

Or rather everything joins into it, everything surrenders to this

[11] *Selected Prose*, 249.

music, everything which is placed side by side, everything breathing at the other, mingling love and hatred in their breath, everything that glides past the other, that delights or terrifies, all that is sublime and all that is ridiculous—yes, all that is there and not there, is so far as in each work of art those things which do not appear in them also play a part by spreading their shadows around the Whole. Only the combination of all this can produce the unutterably sweet music of the Whole.

Almost obsessively, Hofmannsthal reiterated this theory of the power of the whole and with it the vision of a Shakespearean music, "the whole music of these poems." What is important for us is not so much the precision or imprecision of the modern poet's view, as that, starting from an initial sympathy with the making of transcendental forms, Hofmannsthal specified the direction criticism should take: toward the analysis of the mystery of this "musical" totality. His statement that "a play begins to live only after we have heard its whole music" drew attention rightly to the problem of the "gigantic *ensemble*," a phrase Hofmannsthal preferred in spite of difficulties ("I could speak of the music of the Whole, of a harmony, of a spiritualization, but all these words strike me as somewhat wilted, slightly soiled by the touch of human hands"). Having hit upon the idea of ensemble, the rest is easy. The transcendental form is "an *ensemble* wherein the difference between great and small has been cancelled in so far as one lives for the sake of the other, the great for the small, the dark for the light, where one seeks the other, emphasizes and restrains the other, colours and discolours, and where finally for the soul there exists nothing but the Whole—the indivisible, intangible, imponderable Whole." What follows in the lecture might well be a fanciful evocation of *Comus*: "As in a phantasmagoria, everything has changed. The naked landscape, hitherto so sad and deserted, is full of voluptuousness. The darkness doesn't oppress, it exalts. The near is as mysterious as the far." [12] Reduced to the difficulty of further defining this quite mystical vision of Shakespeare, Hofmannsthal rightly referred to the "atmosphere" of the plays, which is predominantly one of nobility. Again, we might reject Hofmannsthal's views as the projections of an alienated member of the Viennese aristocracy, but that is rather like basing arguments against Freud on his having lived in Vienna at the turn of the century. Instead we should take comfort from the position of Curtius, who found in Hofmannsthal a perhaps decadent, but quite genuine, visionary poet whose grasp of the nature of transcendental forms was consummate, as we should expect from an admirer of Calderón. [13] Finally, although Hofmannsthal's language appears "impressionistic," this is only an appearance. One can try to convey atmospheres and musical wholeness as clusters of private impressions, as, one might say, mere analogies. But Hofmannsthal, like Pater, was pleading for the critical use of "atmosphere," "music," and "wholeness."

Virtuosity

In a long tradition going back to the Greeks, this rhetoric finds a place in the practices of the rhapsodes, who (if we exclude various prophets) were the original rhetorical virtuosi. A major historical link is Longinus' treatise *On the Sublime*, since it describes the methods of creating an ecstatic literary effect in which diction and phrasing are so passionately informed with expressive power that they reach an inspired "height" of utterance. In its root, "virtuosity" implies "power," and there is always a hint that the virtuoso enjoys the exercise of power for its own sake.

[12] *Ibid.*, 251.   [13] See Curtius, *European Literature*, 143–144.

Virtuosity is most familiar in the history of musical performance, and particularly in the rise of the star performer during the nineteenth century. Liszt is the greatest of the great among virtuosi, and he typically composed and performed "transcendental études." His compositions include the pianistic form of operatic transcription, for not only is opera an immense theatrical mode, but its transcription for solo instrument exaggerates this scope yet further. By reducing the vastness of an operatic score to a size capable of management by ten fingers and then, through technical devices of "the sustaining pedal," creating the illusion that the pianist has *three* hands, the transcriber achieves a magical effect.[14] He is enclosed by the grandeur of the "grand opera," but he also encloses that grandeur. His sublimities are paradoxically bounded by his dazzling technique, which makes it all look or sound easy. Karl Tausig affected, in contrast to Liszt's more popular flamboyance, the pose of detached ease in his virtuosity. This absolute command, which is enhanced by obstacles, might be called "Paganini's G-string principle," after Paganini's triumph over the breaking of his violin strings

[14] On the rise of the virtuosi, see Arthur Loesser, *Men, Women and Pianos* (New York, 1954); and Harold Schonberg, *The Great Pianists* (New York, 1963). A vivid picture of the virtuoso ambience may be found in Amy Fay, *Music-Study in Germany in the Nineteenth Century* (Chicago, 1880; repr. New York, 1965). Miss Fay, a pianist herself, not only studied with Tausig and Liszt, but also closely observed the styles of Clara Schumann, Anton Rubinstein, Hans von Bülow, and the violinist Joseph Joachim—to name only the stars. *Music-Study* is the more valuable because it consists of somewhat "naïve" letters home and does not censor its enthusiasm: e.g., "I perfectly adore Joachim, and consider him the wonder of the age. It is simple ecstacy to listen to him." Elsewhere she praises Joachim for his powers of articulation and phrasing. For the Renaissance our records of virtuosity, even of well-known virtuosi like John Dowland, are less full.

at a concert. The principle asserts one way of going beyond simple flamboyance.

Renaissance poetry had its virtuosi, as had Renaissance music—that is the point of Richard Barnfield's sonnet "If music and sweet poetry agree," where two of the chief technicians of the time, Spenser and Dowland, are joined in aesthetic union. Among English poets Milton equally may strike the reader as a virtuoso; he is the kind of poet who can be saying nothing at all and can still sound impressive. But with him and with the forms he cultivated in his orderly plan of self-education, we enter a realm of higher virtuosity. For one thing, he is intensely aware of the "heav'n born" nature of his powers and wants to redeem them in a high service to God and fellow man. He wants a liveliness of spirit to permeate the matter of his verses and his tracts; in truth, for him each good book is "the precious life-blood of a master spirit," and that inner *vitality*, that force, that energy, that *genius*, is the mark of the poet whose destiny is the creation of one transcendental form after another. Nothing is more striking in Milton's career than his exhaustion of each literary type he essays; nothing would be more unfair to him than, let us say, our possessing only the *Arcades* (magnanimous though it is), if somehow we had lost its fulfillment, *Comus*. In each literary genre, including the small form of the sonnet as well as the largest dramatic and epic forms, Milton appears to have sought an ultimate performance.

Within every such event he crams as much symbolic and human interest as he can. The cramming itself is a virtuoso performance, and in his masques it is normal to the traditions of the genre. The quarrel between Jones and Jonson has illustrated at least the scenic and literary dimensions of masque performances. If we add to these the choreographic, the musical, and the diplomatic aspects, we get some idea of the challenge open to the virtuoso. Masque, as a genre, is the circus of Renaissance theatrical life. It demands the services of daemonically possessed artists if it is to fulfill its own formal implications. Without the artists' utmost enthusiasm, nothing good can come of masque. But with their enthusiasm or the illusion of it, almost any lack of taste will go undiscovered in the spectacle. Contemporary records of these events suggest that the creators of masques tried so to dazzle the spectators that their memory of all other masques would be erased. Again, this is paradoxical, for the method of bedazzlement included the allegorical teaching of political and social self-awareness. The paradox resembles that of the operatic transcription: the more one remembered the opera score, the more one was bewitched by the means of attaining that memory, and that bewitching magic itself rested on the need for the audience to appreciate the art of the soloist. Similarly, the masque may have been magical, charming, and thus narcotic; but it was narcosis with a difference, since the technique of thought control was to induce the audience to attend with an excess of enthusiasm to the thaumaturgic methods themselves. The masque makes its participants totally aware of art, of persona, of dramatic technique. The virtuoso self-consciously projects his awareness that he is a virtuoso, that he is playing the role of the godlike creator, that he is mediating the imaginative process and in fact is "performing" his creation. On this ground a number of Jonson's masques make the defense of artistic genius their "device."

Virtuosity, of course, is only persuasive when it goes beyond the bounds of normal caution, when it engages in what Ephim Fogel has called "generic competition." Its excitement, which recent musicians have claimed is no longer possible in the new electronic age, belongs to the arena of infinite risk-taking. The masque, like the transcendental performance of a romantic display piece, builds its magic on the audience's awareness that the whole work is so complicated and intense that things can go wrong at any moment. (Much of the "high-wire" feeling of masque can be ascribed to its generic relationship with the acrobatic arts, where "daring" is an aesthetic element of the whole.) Besides indicating what is often called "natural talent," but which is felt frequently to be supernatural talent, the virtuoso act is also an external sign of inner spirit, and here again we have the notion that transcendental forms are spirited and that spirit is an integral element of their aesthetic. There is no such thing as an unspirited or dispirited virtuoso performance, and by the same token the poetic form that aspires to a similar élan will always project artistic spirit as its primary meaning. It will, as often in the case of Milton, project the experience of immediate and overwhelming passion, as if the act of poetic utterance were almost too much for the poet to bear. Thus he will be able, quite convincingly, to speak to and of his muse; through his integral use of transcendental forms Milton escapes the *pro forma* address to the inspired power of verse and transforms his invocations into the moving utterance that we know ("superfluities so beautiful, who would take away?"). This familiarity with one's muse is Spenserian, it will be said. True, on a less exalted scale, and, I would argue, true in much the same way; both Spenser and Milton in their major works move toward the ultimate perfection of transcendental form; that is, they utter a prophetic poetry. But in their lesser genres they are more modest. Milton outdoes his master in these enthusiasms, and he signals his ambition in his numerous allusions and addresses to the art of music, in which he finds enshrined all the most exalted powers of aesthetic triumph.

Virtuosity achieves the effect of total enthusiasm largely because the virtuoso artist projects his own "giant personality." He must radiate the forces of his inspiration as an immediate effluence of this godlike personality. In formal terms this means that he will organize his expanding vision in ways that permit, not just virtuoso display, but special empowering effects, which may be termed "intensifiers." A good case of intensification is the musician's exaggerated "arching" of a *phrase*. Transcendental scope assumes an equipoise of "special effects," as they are called in movie-making. For the masque these would include all the more dramatic species of theatrical magic we have observed, with the striking use of grotesquerie, surrealism, the bizarre, the wide dynamic ranges of sudden crescendo and decrescendo—and in musical forms, the violence of chromatic art and the unexpectedness of sudden modulation.[15] Take *Paradise Lost* again, our cardinal instance of the Miltonic transcendental form. Its masks of Sin and Death, besides serving an allegorical function, intensify the scenic presence of the action, jarring and arousing the reader's sensitivity to a nightmarish superclarity in the poet's moral vision. Such figures were, to the dismay of neoclassic critics, extravagant; yet the art of transcendental form required their gothic extravagance, as a

---

[15] See Edward Lowinsky, *Secret Chromatic Art in the Netherlands Motet*, tr. Carl Buchman (New York, 1946); also Joseph Kerman, *The Elizabethan Madrigal: A Comparative Study* (New York, 1962), 212–220. Kerman concludes that the English composers of madrigals "see chromaticism as a disruptive force and tend to reject it accordingly. The essentially conservative nature of the English development is nowhere clearer than in its cautious treatment of Italian chromaticism." This earlier madrigalist caution makes the experiments of men like Lanier, Matthew Locke, and William and Henry Lawes all the more impressive, and makes Milton's interest in recitative composition all the more instructive. See Friedrich Blume, *Renaissance and Baroque Music* (New York, 1967), 121–125, on the new "style-consciousness" and the late baroque *Gesamtkunstwerke*.

means of virtuosic intensification. Again there is an underlying affinity between such extravagance and the extravagance of baroque.

Montage and perspectivism

We began with a problem of unifying the ununifiable, and
have suggested that scope and the mixture of media make this
a genuine challenge in the masque. The method of containment seems to demand something like Hofmannsthal's "music
of the Whole," and we can see two reasons why this is so.
For music has at least two necessary virtues. It traditionally
constitutes a method of achieving harmony, of "sym-phony,"
of "con-cert," of ensemble—and that method ministers to
the need for totality, for cosmic order. On the other hand,
music is an art which, since the Renaissance at least and most
notably in opera, permits a further scope for the virtuoso
use of dominant, overpowering single instruments, vocal or
other. Until the invention of the modern moving picture
there was much less expressive unity available to the theatre
unless it stuck close to purely verbal declamation. Scenery was
bound to disrupt, although every account of successful
masques indicates that scene makers like Jones sought to approach the technique of film montage. Even so, it was not yet
the era of Eisenstein's five levels of advancing musicality in
movie montage, by which sights began to flow, first in metric
montage, then rhythmic, then tonal, then overtonal, and
finally in pure synthesis through "intellectual" montage.[16]
Until the development of such means (and attempts persisted
in the nineteenth-century "magic theatre")[17] the poet had to

[16] Sergei Eisenstein, *Film Form and the Film Sense*, ed. and tr.
Jay Leyda (Cleveland and New York, 1964), 60–62, 72–83.

[17] During the nineteenth century the chief change to affect theatrical, as well as other scenic aesthetics, was the invention of the
camera. Daguerre's diorama was magic theatre, and it accompanied
research into the "magic" recording of images on plates and films.

seek transcendental *flow* in the analogy and in the logic of musical form. Music is the natural recourse for the poet who would create the atmosphere of transcendence. For this reason, it is natural that Milton should be wholly devoted to the myth of the blessings of music, which he renders in poem after poem.

The question remains, Is it possible that the need for transcendental closure arose only in the late Renaissance and baroque period? One answer would be that such a need had existed from the moment that Christianity achieved an accommodation with Platonic and Plotinian thought, and we see this reflected in the transcendental grandeur of the whole *Divine Comedy* and in lesser works of the medieval period.[18] But the need appears to have been more pressing during the later periods, whose sense of "the beyond" differed in context in one profound way from that of earlier times. For during this early stage of modern thinking there occurred the discovery of perspective, a discovery that directly influenced not only masques, but also all the arts of construction and vision, whether architectural or "architectonic" (Sir Philip Sidney's word).[19] The three terms "size" (scope),

[18] On the medieval synthesis, see M. D. Chenu, "The Symbolist Mentality," *Nature, Man and Society in the Twelfth Century,* ed. and tr. Jerome Taylor and L. K. Little (Chicago, 1968), 99–145.

[19] *An Apology for Poetry,* ed. G. G. Smith, in *Elizabethan Critical Essays* (Oxford, 1964), I, 161. The term occurs in a lofty excursus on the levels of excellence of the types of knowledge: astronomy, geometry, and so forth. Sidney observes that *all* types of knowledge, "all, one and other, having this scope—to knowe, and by knowledge to lift up the mind from the dungeon of the body to the enjoying his owne divine essence," belong to God's providence. "But when by the ballance of experience it was found that the Astronomer looking to the starres might fall into a ditch, that the enquiring Philosopher might be blinde in himselfe, and the Mathematician might draw foorth a straight line with a crooked hart; then loe, did proofe, the over ruler of opinions, make manifest that all these are but serving Sciences, which as they have each a private end in them-

"medium," and "virtuosity" reflect this new perspectivism. Visually the masque projected clear physical space which earlier theories had clouded and earlier practices had diminished. In medium a new ethos of measurement gave clearness to all the arts (music, for example, becoming increasingly conscious of its harmonic structure). In virtuosity the search for images of the creator's own power of phrasing led to an art of simultaneous precision and panache—the more technically "correct," the more inspired by the daemon of art. It seems proper that *Don Quixote* should have elicited Leo Spitzer's theory of "linguistic perspectivism," which expresses itself in a new, godlike artistry:

The artist Cervantes has extended, by the mere art of his narrative, the Demiurge-like, almost cosmic independence of the artist. His humor, which admits of many strata, perspectives, masks— of relativization and dialects—bears testimony to his high position above the world. His humor is the freedom of the heights, no fate-bound dionysiac dissolution of the individual into nothingness and night, as with Schopenhauer and Wagner, but a freedom beneath the dome of that religion which affirms the freedom of the will. There is, in the world of his creation, the bracing air with which we may fill our lungs and by which our individual senses and judgment are sharpened; and the crystalline lucidity of an artistic Maker in its manifold reflections and refractions.[20]

Perspective is the basis of René Girard's theory of "triangular" desire in the novel, where we discern the structure

selves, so yet are they all directed to the highest end of the mistress Knowledge, by the Greekes called *Arkitecktonike*, which stands, (as I thinke) in the knowledge of a mans selfe, in the Ethicke and politick consideration, with the end of well dooing and not of well knowing onely." The skills bringing forth "vertuous action" have the right to be called "Princes over all the rest," and the poets share in this nobility.

[20] "Linguistic Perspectivism in the *Don Quijote*," *Linguistics and Literary History* (Princeton, N.J., 1948), 73.

of Cervantean vision as a system of the "mediations" of love.[21] But the chorus of critical interest in perspectivism is general. It applies not merely to Renaissance literary forms. Panofsky observed that through techniques of perspective foreshortening, a fresh subjectivity was introduced into the visual arts, and Lowinsky adds, "It is uncanny how precisely these changes are echoed in the music of the Renaissance." [22] The subjectivity of foreshortening is the consequence of a new objectivity of optical theory; the new science makes possible the new vision, in every sense. The natural instrument of this Renaissance merging of science and imag-

[21] *Deceit, Desire and the Novel*, tr. Yvonne Freccero (Baltimore, 1965), ch. i. The novelists most interesting from the transcendental point of view seem to me to be Stendhal and Thomas Mann. (See R. M. Adams, "The Novel as Opera," in *New Views of Italian Opera*, ed. William W. Austin [Ithaca, N.Y., 1968].) Another reader might, however, prefer to instance Joyce and the ineluctible modality of the audible. Music has quite private values for Joyce.

[22] Edward Lowinsky, "Music of the Renaissance as Viewed by Renaissance Musicians," in *The Renaissance Image of Man and the World*, ed. Bernard O'Kelly (Columbus, Ohio, 1966). Lowinsky had quoted Panofsky. Lowinsky shows that mastery of perspective corresponds to the command of tonality, which emerges from the less structured sense of musical stability which characterized the period preceding the late Renaissance. By asserting a tonal center, the musician acquired a technique for moving to a tonal periphery; he thus achieved harmonic, as opposed to melodic, motion, and this enabled him to build the equivalent of the painter's perspective space, by using sheerly musical materials. Having first commanded such skills, the musician further extended them. He became free to *distort*, to exercise his "subjective" awareness—familiar to us, for example, in all modern painting—that even though they were physically and optically accurate, the perspectives of space and sound were not in line with our perceptions of things, in which sensorimotor skewings may occur. Thus "dissonance" arises in every medium. On perspective in the visual arts see chs. x–xiv, in Robert Klein, *La Forme et l'intelligible* (Paris, 1970), where there is also a complete bibliography of Klein's important studies in Renaissance aesthetics and poetics.

ination is Galileo's telescope in Milton's simile for the
vast shield of Satan:

> . . . the broad circumference
> Hung on his shoulders like the moon, whose orb
> Through optic glass the Tuscan artist views
> At ev'ning from the top of Fesole,
> Or in Valdarno, to descry new lands,
> Rivers or mountains in her spotty globe.

Freedom

If the discovery of perspective simultaneously complicates
both the objective and the impressionistic powers of art, its
fertilizing effect is not entirely a safe thing. On the one hand,
the linguistic perspectivism of Cervantes permits him to for-
mulate, at once, both the subtle and large images of human
experience. Through expert poetic management literature in
this period enters a golden age. Every genre displays an
eloquence proportional to the poet's love of language as a
variable and powerful instrument. On the other hand, as later
neoclassic theorists were fond of noting, there can be an
excess of inventive freedom. In England, Shakespeare plays
the role of Cervantes, and the Shakespearean canon would
be the creative limit beyond which Milton's genius would
seek to reach.

Erich Auerbach has described the dangerously rich art of
Shakespearean mimesis; it has "historical perspective," permits
an endless variety of decorum, and enjoys a "multiplicity of
subject matter, the freedom of invention and presentation
which distinguishes the Elizabethan and modern drama generally." It is a "mixed style," which demands the "mixture of
characters and the consequent mixture of tragic and comic
elements." Theatre audiences from that day to this have taken
vast delight in this miscegenating art. The mixed style is a

continuous source of refreshment in the theatrical experience; it is entertaining, if nothing else. But it is also potentially dangerous, since its freedom threatens to make freedom itself obsolete. As such it was soon to be attacked by all the forces of repression. In the plays, as Auerbach says, "the liberated forces show themselves as fully developed yet still permeated with the entire ethical wealth of the past. Not much later the restrictive countermovements gained the upper hand. Protestantism and the Counter Reformation, absolutist ordering of society and intellectual life, academic and puristic imitation of antiquity, rationalism and scientific empiricism, all operated together to prevent Shakespeare's freedom in the tragic from continuing to develop after him." [23] The artist, surrounded by a repressive climate, may simply give up. Or he may, with poets like Milton, Dryden, and Cowley, attempt the creation of transcendental forms.

Apparently the fear of decadence, if not the fact, marks the appearance of transcendental forms. In the twentieth century Thomas Mann exemplifies the search for a form that will both share in and retard the decay of his art. Gide's *Counterfeiters* may contain the "death of the novel," a possibility that both fascinates and repels the novelist. In this

---

[23] *Mimesis: The Representation of Reality in Western Literature*, tr. Willard Trask (New York, 1957), 281. On Prospero's epilogue to his masque, Auerbach observes: "This says two things: that Shakespeare includes earthly reality, and even its most trivial forms, in a thousand refractions and mixtures, but that his purpose goes far beyond the representation of reality in its merely earthly coherence; he embraces reality but he transcends it. This is already apparent in the presence of ghosts and witches in his plays, and in the often unrealistic style. . . . It is still more significantly revealed in the inner structure of the action, which is often—and especially in the most important plays—only erratically and sporadically realistic and often shows a tendency to break into the realm of the fairy tale, of playful fancy, or of the supernatural and demonic" (288).

sense, as T. S. Eliot said, "*Comus* is the death of the masque; it is the transition of a form of art—even of a form which existed but a short generation—into 'literature,' literature cast into a form which has lost its application." [24] Literature cast adrift from life becomes what Valéry might call "pure poetry," although even here the critic believes that the music of the pure is only the most intensely delicate apprehension of life.[25] Shakespeare, it is true, never indulges himself for long in the pleasures of high aestheticism. Rather, through numerous characterizations of men trying to express their needs, he affirms the poet's right to be heard. Utterance is the poet's freedom; the freedom of his created personae may follow, but his own freedom to speak out, to prophesy even, is the prior necessity.

Although much has been made in literary histories of the link between Milton and Spenser, we need to insist on the

[24] "Ben Jonson," in *Essays on Elizabethan Drama* (New York, 1960), 82.

[25] In various essays Paul Valéry spoke of the power of music, or even of sound, to evoke a universe. Thus, in "Pure Poetry," he says: "If a pure sound, that is, a relatively exceptional sound, is heard, a particular atmosphere is immediately created, a particular state of expectation is produced in our senses, and this expectation tends, in some way, to provoke sensations of the same order, and of the same purity as the first" (*The Art of Poetry*, tr. Denise Folliot [New York, 1961], 190). In "Poetry and Abstract Thought," the same sort of sound is said to produce "the feeling of a beginning, the beginning of a world; a quite different atmosphere would be created, a new order would arise, and you yourselves would unconsciously *organize* yourselves to receive it. The musical universe, therefore, was within you, with all its associations and proportions—as in a saturated salt solution a crystalline universe awaits the molecular shock of a minute crystal in order *to declare itself*" (67). In "Remarks on Poetry," Valéry distinguishes noise from sound: "The world of musical art, a world of sounds, is quite separate from the world of noises. Whereas a noise merely evokes in us some isolated event, *a produced sound in itself evokes the whole musical universe*" (203).

relative unimportance of this link. Milton was not unduly perturbed, surely, by the example of *The Faerie Queene*. Milton perceived the problem of being Milton: it was that he came after Shakespeare. As the most self-conscious sort of genius, he found himself, willy-nilly, post-Shakespearean. It was an impossible prospect, which he met by the sinister method of burying his meanings, interring them in his signs and syntax. He could not afford the Shakespearean openness, even if he had been able to imagine it. His epoch prohibited such "freedom of invention and presentation." With Sir Thomas Browne he might have said, " 'Tis too late to be ambitious. The great mutations of the world are acted, or time may be too short for our designes." [26] This was the challenge specified in Milton's first published poem; a sonnet on the monumental legacy of Shakespeare's works.

The relation between Milton and his two great predecessors may be archetypal for the poetry of transcendental forms, and the need to outdo them both, if regarded as a single complex need, may reveal the heart of the transcendental process. To simplify: if Spenser embodies the allegorical mode and Shakespeare the mimetic, the merging of these two modalities in a single large work like *Paradise Lost* will have both the transcendentalism of texture that we expect in allegory and the containment of this-worldly things that we expect in mimesis. Like a baroque façade, which has both classic design and romantic ornament, the transcendental form will combine opposed symbolic modes and will hold them, under pressure, in a state of high, even ecstatic tension.

Baroque Rome will readily illustrate this tension at numerous points throughout the city, as will the various works of Gian Lorenzo Bernini. In November 1644, John Evelyn noted

[26] Sir Thomas Browne, *Hydriotaphia: Urne-Buriall*, in *Religio Medici and Other Works*, ed. L. C. Martin (Oxford, 1964), 120.

in his *diary:* "Cavalieri Bernini a Florentine Sculptor, Architect, Painter & Poet: who a little before my Comming to the Citty, gave a Publique Opera (for so they call those Shews of that kind) where in he painted the Sceanes, cut the Statues, invented the Engines, composed the Musique, writ the Comedy & built the Theater all himselfe." [27] What matters here is not so much the actual fact: Could Bernini have done all that? What matters is the transcendental virtuosity of the pretense. Even Milton's own father, much earlier, had succumbed to the craving for sheer display, if we may believe the often credulous, genial John Aubrey. In the *Brief Lives* he reports that while Milton's father accumulated a "plentifull estate," he delighted in music and composed many songs. One of these was "a Song of fourscore parts for the Lantgrave of Hess, for which his Highnesse sent a meddall of gold, or a noble present." [28] One cannot help wondering what sort of chorus the Landgrave's *Kapellmeister* had trained. It is perhaps historically helpful to notice that no hard and fast dates isolate

[27] Presumably Gian Lorenzo Bernini (1598–1680); quoted in M. F. Robinson, *Opera before Mozart* (New York, 1966), 14n. On November 19, 1644, Evelyn notes: "I visited St. Peter's, that most stupendous and incomparable Basilica, far surpassing any now extant in the world, and perhaps, Solomon's Temple excepted, any that was ever built. The largeness of the piazza before the portico is worth observing, because it affords a noble prospect of the church, not crowded up, as for the most part is the case with such other places where great churches are erected." Throughout his account Evelyn appears to be impressed by the spaciousness of *prospect*, of vista, which the overall plan of this complex has achieved. For the work of massive scope it is not enough to erect structures of great size; their size must be dramatically presented to the eye, that is, given scope, by the development of viewing-space and an unfolding experience of texture. (*Diary of John Evelyn*, ed. William Bray [London, 1945], I, 118–124).

[28] Ed. O. L. Dick (London, 1949; repr. Ann Arbor, Mich., 1962), 199. Or was this piece in four voices, reading the text as: "a Song of four scoreparts"?

the period of such extravagance. Baroque tendencies began early and stayed late, even in England. Baroque may at any period emerge as the projection of man's childish delight in the gigantic. A chorale in eighty voices attempts to *surround* the listener, to swallow him up.

One hesitates to gloss over the technical difficulties of such enveloping arts. Shakespeare's example of continuous development throughout an extended theatrical career may have emboldened the young Milton, who at least had the model of a poet who was in his later plays attempting fusions of allegorical romance and mimetic drama. More important, perhaps, may have been the development of Shakespearean blank verse, which sought always more syntactic freedom. If the essence of virtuoso performance is the fluency of its medium, the poet must completely command the syntax of his verse, so that for him freedom will be implicit in his rhythms and thus not need to be explicit in his message. He must be free, rather than talk freely. His poem must have the quality of improvisation, which affirms the strictest compositional order even as it pretends continuous spontaneity.

The transcendentalist impulse of the allegorical author comes out in rigid multileveled fictions. The movement toward transcendental form, properly speaking, transfers this diffusive allegorical drive back into the texture of the poem. Such works then feel allegorical, though one cannot point to their allegory. The allegory is ploughed back into the soil. It is a happy accident, if not indeed a logical necessity, that one common ground upon which Spenser, Shakespeare, and Milton meet is their joint interest in the masque, for in this genre the poet, relying on fixed and conventional iconographies, can indulge in a free play of syntax. He can experiment with pure syntactic structure, not as a thing in itself, but as an expression of the poetic powers in their full range of freedom.

For if signs and semantics constitute the material stuff of literature, syntax puts them in order and gives them their mode of life.

5 *The Transcendental Masque*

That *Comus* is no ordinary masque has long been felt. In dedicating the published work to John, Lord Viscount Brackley, Lawes said that although *Comus* was "not openly acknowledged by the author, yet it is a legitimate offspring, so lovely, and so much desired, that the often copying of it hath tired my pen to give my several friends satisfaction, and brought me to a necessity of producing it to the public view." [1] These friends found an excellence posterity has confirmed. Yet beyond the eloquence of the "series of lines," to use Johnson's phrase, *Comus* has presented a problematic aspect in both theme and form.

The extraordinary bulk of critical commentary on the Miltonic treatment of chastity, a critique as subtle as it is learned—much if not all of it leading into the mysteries of Christian or Neoplatonic theology—will bear witness to the ambiguity of themes in *Comus*. We may perhaps be impatient with the questions, proofs, and counterproofs of thematic criticism. But we cannot dismiss the crisis implied in this lore.

[1] As in the 1645 edition, in Douglas Bush, *The Complete Poetical Works of John Milton* (Boston, 1965), 113. This work is hereafter referred to as *PW*.

No simple way out of tangled Miltonic image and theme will be forthcoming, and if a formal approach to *Comus* is proposed, it should be constantly attuned to the complications of theme which have made the work so tantalizing to its readers.[2] What needs to be done, following Robert M. Adams' lead,[3] is to explain the doubts of critics about *Comus*, yet without explaining them away. Generations of critics are never, taken as a whole, wrong. They are responding to something, and the historical critic in his turn should respond to this continuity of critical awareness. In dealing with *Comus* there is no need to deny its dramatic force. *Comus*, naïvely viewed, is a markedly dramatic piece. But how so? Perhaps it would be useful to take Dr. Johnson seriously and ask if, as he called it, *Comus* is not "a drama in the epic style."

Woodhouse wisely referred criticism of *Comus* to the remarkable passage of *An Apology for Smectymnuus* where Milton recounts the progress of his almost obsessive concern with idea of chastity.[4] Among several striking personal

[2] A wealth of allusion to learned articles, and so forth, in John Demaray, *Milton and the Masque Tradition*, should not obscure the limits of Demaray's argument, which seems to depend upon the notion that dance defines the masque as Milton evolves its genre in *Comus*, an assumption that would force one to equate *Arcades* with *Comus*, or even to argue that *Arcades* is the more perfect masque. Yet the most obvious thing about *Comus* is that it has almost no dances; they have none of the formal iconographic import and intricacy usually given to court-masque choreography. They sufficed on the occasion of the original performance, but since a printed libretto can also, if its author chooses, yield a dance-drama, we should begin with the fact that this libretto fails to do so.

[3] *Milton and the Modern Critics* (Ithaca, N.Y., 1966), repr. from *Ikon: John Milton and the Modern Critics* (Ithaca, 1955).

[4] A. S. P. Woodhouse, "The Argument in Milton's *Comus*," *University of Toronto Quarterly*, II (1941), 46; the passage will be found in John Milton, *Prose Selections*, ed. Merritt Hughes (New York, 1947), 156–159. Bush (*PW*, 110) says, "That all-important passage . . . needs to be read and reread," and quotes George Sandys'

reminiscences there runs a key motif: Milton set the problem of chastity in the context of a largely literary experience. He began his education in purity in the poetic world of "the two famous renowners of Beatrice and Laura," and proceeded in due time ("whither my younger feet had wandered") to "those lofty fables and romances which recount in solemn cantos the deeds of knighthood founded by our victorious kings," and thence "from the laureate fraternity of poets, riper years and the ceaseless round of study and reading led me to the shady spaces of philosophy, but chiefly to the divine volumes of Plato and his equal, Xenophon." Throughout the account we sense not only the pursuit of the "abstracted sublimities" of knowledge and virtue, but in the course of this pursuit, the sublimation of thought into character, so that we can well believe the poet when he announces his early won creed: "that he who would not be frustrate of his hope to write well hereafter in laudable things, ought himself to be a true poem, that is, a composition and pattern of the best and honorablest things; not presuming to sing high praises of heroic men or famous cities unless he have in himself the experience and pratice of all that which is praiseworthy." This is not hermetic pretension, though there is a smell of the magus about the poet as sublime poem; Milton here betrays that characteristically total involvement of his whole self with his thought, an involvement mediated by his poetic vocation. For through the poetic second voice, he would discover the self defined by all the prior patterns and compositions of the best and most honorable things.

The Johnsonian epithet comes into focus. A drama written

commentary on Ovid's Circe: "Men whose appetites 'revolt from the sovereignty of reason (by which we are only like unto God, and armed against depraved affections)' can never 'return into their country (from whence the soul deriveth her celestial original) unless disenchanted and cleansed from their former impurity.'"

in epic style would first of all flow like a narrative poem, and
secondly it would be a drama raised above the requirements of
realistic decorum to a level of inspired, prophetic, or epic
voice, that is, raised to the vehement level of style described
in Longinus' famed treatise. Johnson did not clarify the
distinction between the usual dramatic genres and the epic
drama, but Thomas Warton did, when in his edition of Milton (1791) he said that *"Comus* is a suite of Speeches, not
interesting by discrimination of character; not conveying a
variety of incidents; not gradually exciting curiosity; but
perpetually attracting attention by sublime sentiment, by
fanciful imagery of the richest vein, by an exuberance of
picturesque description, poetical allusion, and ornamental
expression." The prime mover of the drama in epic style
would seem to be the "sublime sentiment," with its usual
picturesque accompaniments.

In *Comus*, therefore, Milton is "unfolding those chaste and
high mysteries" which, in conjunction with the Holy Scrip-
tures, veil and reveal the secrets of divine wisdom. In the
terms of Pico della Mirandola the poet is at once both magus
and *interpres*. Chastity must be envisioned in the most sacred
languages, and, by conversion, the language of the poet,
arising in the devotion to the ideal of the chaste, must
achieve sublimity if it is to equal the transcendental challenge. Milton writes about chastity continuously, in tracts on
marriage, love, and divorce—even on freedom of speech and
thought—and in his major poems, all of which deal with
virtue as an effluence of chastity. The *Apology* suggests something even more radical about the Miltonic career: that it
was the literary enactment of one vast, many-sided *personal*
struggle for the comprehension of the idea of the chaste
mystery, and therefore that as a career the life of Milton
indeed has the prime requisite of a poem: namely, it has a

hero. Milton becomes a poet-poem in this heroic manner. The idea of chastity is for him a burning, luminous, radiant core of energy, and the recurrent theme of temptation, on which Frye has commented so eloquently, is but the dramatic trial of the chaste vision.[5] For chastity, like grace (if that is in any ordinary sense a "virtue"), metaphorically permits only perfect motion: that is, motion which redeems the wandering, mazy, labyrinthine error of ordinary life. Chastity finds its model of movement in the circular form of the Ptolemaic universe; it is perfect, like a sphere, with no beginning and no end. How then express its forms and implications? This is the mystery that Milton wished to suggest, and went so far as to describe, in the *Apology*.

Milton imagines himself living and acting on heroic lines. Frye has pointed out the difference between his "radical, revolutionary temperament" and the conservative temperament of Spenser.

The radical or revolutionary artist impresses us, first of all as a tremendous personal force, a great man who happened to be an artist in one particular field but who would still have been a remarkable man whatever he had gone into. His art has in consequence a kind of oratorical relation to him: his creative *persona* reveals his personality instead of concealing it. He does not enter into the forms of his art like an indwelling spirit, but approaches them analytically and externally, tearing them to pieces and putting them together again in a way which expresses his genius and not theirs. In listening to the Kyrie of the Bach B Minor Mass we feel what amazing things the fugue can do; in listening to the finale of Beethoven's Opus 106, we feel what amazing things can be done with the fugue. This latter is the feeling we have about *Comus* as a masque, when we come to it from Jonson

[5] Northrop Frye, *The Return of Eden: Five Essays on Milton's Epics* (Toronto, 1965), 9, 126 ff. Most problematic is the Miltonic idea of "temptation to premature action."

or Campion. Because the art of the revolutionary artist follows a rhythm of personal development external to itself, it goes through a series of metamorphoses: the revolutionary artist plunges into one "period" after another, marking his career off into separate divisions.[6]

The continuous revelation of a giant personality behind the mask is crucial to the work of an artist like Milton. But in assessing the work itself, we need a notion like "the transscendental." The formal peculiarity of this style of work is again finely suggested in Frye's distinction between the conservative and revolutionary aspects of poetry.

The revolutionary aspect of Milton also comes out in that curious mania for doing everything himself which led him to produce his own treatise on theology, his own national history, his own dictionary and grammar, his own art of logic. . . . Both kinds of genius may seek for an art that transcends art, a poetry or music that goes beyond poetry or music. But the conservative artists finds—if this metaphor conveys anything intelligible to the reader —his greatest profundities at the centre of his art; the radical artist finds them on the frontier. . . . Milton, like Beethoven, is continually exploring the boundaries of his art, getting more experimental and radical as he goes on.[7]

Comus fits into this radical experimentation; it transcends by formal pressures on the normal boundaries of the masque. It "transcends art" in this sense precisely, and I would hold that the other transcendence, of which Frye rightly speaks, is only the fulfillment of the more limited possibilities of classical selectivity and repose. There is, perhaps, a further distinction to be made, though it does not really contradict

---

[6] *Ibid.*, 90–91. Speaking of *The Tenure of Kings and Magistrates,* Frye observes that, as a revolutionary thinker, "Milton will appeal to precedent only with the greatest reluctance."

[7] *Ibid.*, 91–92.

Frye's notion, between the transcendence of the radical style and the perfectionism of the conservative style. The former issues, as Frye suggests, in a revolutionary attitude toward tradition, the latter in a neoclassic piety toward rules—at least if the energy of creation is not coequal with the energies of self-expression.

Comus, should it fit this broad view of Miltonic creativity, can be only partially illuminated by historical "sources" which are supposed to explain its power and its complexity. To argue that Milton had various models is to repeat the obvious, unless one further asks, What was his experimental attitude toward those models? For the transcendental re-creation of an inherited form is always so new and revolutionary in feeling and form that it will yield none of its secrets to the critic who is, at bottom, unconcerned with the radical mentality bringing such a work into being. In the case of *Comus,* as we shall see, the obvious use of a whole range of magic devices, persons, and scenes provides the setting for the radical encounter with masque as genre. Milton picks exactly the theme and variations which will permit him to exercise a virtuoso control over his masque.

The "handy but illogical" title Comus

Douglas Bush once characterized as "handy but illogical" the traditional name *Comus* for Milton's "A MASKE PRE-SENTED At Ludlow Castle, 1634: *On Michaelmasse night, before the* RIGHT HONORABLE, JOHN *Earle of Bridgewater, Vicount* BRACKLY, *Lord Praesident of* WALES, And one of His MAJESTIES most honorable Privie Counsell"—or as it is called in the *Poems* of 1645, "A MASK Of the same AUTHOR Presented at LUDLOW-Castle, 1634. Before the Earl of Bridgewater Then President of Wales."[8] We may gratefully concur that indeed *Comus*

---

[8] *PW,* introduction to *Comus,* 109.

is much handier than the wounded snakes of the published titles. Yet the convenient misnomer has teased the critics inordinately, and the trouble is revealing. Commenting on the evolution of the masque, Orgel says:

It was not until 1634 that a poet (who had certainly read *Pleasure Reconciled to Virtue*) was to conceive of a masque not as a court ballet, but as a drama about the will. That "Maske presented at Ludlow Castle" has been so consistently misinterpreted that, since the eighteenth century, it has masqueraded under the name of its villain, the leader of its antimasque. The modern title, *Comus*, is grossly unjust to the work: we would not think of referring to *Paradise Lost* as *Satan*.[9]

Perhaps everyone has misinterpreted the work. Yet there may be a certain wisdom in the title as it stands in popular usage, as there would be if a popular tradition had given *Paradise Lost* the title *Satan*. Perhaps Comus counts for more than his role as leader of the antimasque, and it may even have eluded most of Milton's readers and the audience at Thomas Arne's musical play, *Comus* (1738), that the villain was, technically and formally, the leader of the antimasque. Possibly a more obvious fact is the relevant one, that Comus is an enchanter whose presence gives pre-eminence to magic in a masque attempting to climax the masque tradition.

But no major critical issue should depend upon tags and titles. They are hints only. Accepting this caveat, we notice that the practice of publishing unhelpful titles was a common one. Typically we have *The Lords Masque* by Campion (1613) and *The Masque of the Inner Temple and Gray's Inn* by an anonymous author (1613), while from Ben Jonson's output we can select the following title-page entries: "B. Jon: HIS PART OF / king James his Royall and Mag-

9 *Jonsonian Masque*, 151–152.

nific*ent Entertainment through* / his Honorable Cittie of London, Thurseday the 15. of / March. 1603"; "THE / DESCRIPTION / of the Masque. / With the *NUPTIALL SONGS.* / Celebrating the happy Marriage of John, *Lord* / RAMSEY, *Vicount Hadington*, with the / Lady ELIZABETH RATCLIFFE, / Daughter to the right Honor: / ROBERT Earle of *SUSSEX.* / At Court / *On the shrove-Tuesday at night.* 1608;" and "THE SPEECHES / AT PRINCE HENRIES / BARRIERS."

These titles indicate one major facet of the genre: the primary importance of the occasion, the secondary importance of the particular emblem or theme used to realize the occasion. Yet such thematically nondescript titles gave way during the period after 1611, when Jonson consistently named the subject or theme of his masques. The convention thus appears to be that a lesser, less formal "entertainment" might get its title from its occasion only, while a true masque being more elaborate, called for an inconographic title. The printing of the scenario led in opposite directions: first, toward the commemoration of a past event—whose dramatis personae were, in principle, the nobles who took part—and second, toward the present experience of a literary drama through its script, where the dramatis personae were the mythical and allegorical persons being impersonated by the noble participants. Of thirty-six entertainments and masques, Jonson gave twenty-four some sort of iconographic title, and the bulk of the unhelpful occasional titles are given to entertainments. By this strategy in the publication of his works, Jonson seems to have wished to distinguish his own productions from the typical masques, "enterprises noble in aspiration but all too often ignoble in their accomplishments." [10] He wished to ennoble his poetical career.

[10] Spencer and Wells, *Book of Masques*, general introduction by G. E. Bentley, 1.

We may well ask what part the title of a work plays in its relation to fame; certainly poets who insist on giving the iconography of the "device" in their title pages would seem to be interested in starting the reader down the right road. This is the reason for the continuing interest of critics in the title of *Comus;* they are struck, as if Milton himself had affixed the enchanter's name, to think that here the normal expectations about the masque are violated or subverted. Critical comment on the title often reveals fundamental attitudes toward this and other masques. Sears Jayne, for example, has this to say:

> Even if Milton had named his subject in the title of the work, I imagine that very few in the Ludlow audience, or even in the cast (perhaps, as I have suggested, only Lawes himself, who had been given the "simples" by his "shepherd" friend Milton) would have recognized the esoteric concept which Milton had in mind in combining the familiar Circe myth with the unfamiliar Sabrina myth. By entitling it simply *A mask Performed at Ludlow Castle,* he kept the focus where, for that audience, it belonged, not on chastity, but on the glorification of the Earl and his family.[11]

This final statement assumes that occasion is the dominant factor, whereby Henry Lawes and later Milton himself were forced to give a nonthematic title. Yet Jayne has shown how little "that audience" could restrict the poet's fancy.

Modern critics have tended to ask, What would the iconographic title of *Comus* be if it were corrected, that is, properly extracted from the text of the work? Referring to the true title, *A Maske . . . ,* D. C. Allen admits:

> This may come as a surprise to some readers because the earliest critics refer to it as *Comus* and few modern Miltonists think of

[11] "The Subject of Milton's Ludlow *Mask,*" in Barker, *Milton;* 104.

it under any other title. The reason for this is clear; the character of Comus dominates the masque whether Milton intended it or not. One cannot imagine *Macbeth* if it were untitled getting the popular title of *Macduff*, or *Hamlet* becoming *Claudius*. Likewise if Milton's theme of chastity had been firmly brought home, this masque might be known as *The Mask of Chastity* or *The Mask of the Virgin*.[12]

Despite his own qualification, "whether Milton intended it or not," Allen's argument about the title depends on a certain view of Miltonic intention, and a considered belief that Milton failed to do what he intended—or at least complicated his intention so that a resolution of antithetical pulls failed to occur in *Comus*. One critical point holds firm, however: the title of the *Maske* is properly assigned, as tradition assigns it, to *Comus*; the common title, Allen claims, is right for the work we have. This response to the problem of nomenclature shows a refreshing dramatistic urgency, for it takes the action of masque seriously; it takes Dr. Johnson's querulous remarks equally seriously. We may agree or disagree with Allen that *Comus* fails as a masque of chastity, but in either case it would seem logical to conclude, with Allen, that "in *Comus* we are spectators at a pagan temptation" which gives the major role to the tempter. In terms of the present argument, temptation and thaumaturgy have obvious connections, which similarly point to the thematic centrality of Comus: if the heroine is to break through the spells of evil delight, she must possess her own countercharms. A temptation is not, strictly speaking, beyond resistance; but to resist temptation, as Oscar Wilde jokingly implied, is to perform a miracle. Dramatically, temptation scenes often end by the entrance of a *deus ex*

[12] *The Harmonious Vision: Studies in Milton's Poetry* (Baltimore, 1954), 39.

machina, because to the extent that temptation approaches a dilemma it leaves the optional world of trial and error.

The typical retitling, however, seeks to replace the name *Comus* entirely. Sears Jayne, for example, observed that it might have been called *A Masque of Parentage*, an interesting choice, but Jayne finally picked the Platonized *Masque of Chastity*. Such choices stem in part from the classic articles of A. S. P. Woodhouse, "The Argument in Milton's *Comus*" and "*Comus* Once More," in which he switched on the powerful machine of his favorite dichotomy, nature and grace, to analyze the prime Miltonic descendant of Spenser's *Faerie Queene*.[13] Leaving aside the details of the controversy arising out of Woodhouse's articles, we may say that he must have been roughly right about *Comus*, because he showed the Christian conventions of the period underlying the work. Even if there are metaphysical problems in arguing that on the last and dramatically climactic level the Lady's virginity (as opposed to mere continence or temperance, i.e., "chastity") is the exemplum of divine grace, the blessing of grace does hover over her; and her story surely in some general way justifies her as a divinely favored creature, the recipient of grace, deserving it through her faith, hope, and chastity.[14]

[13] "The Argument in Milton's *Comus*," *University of Toronto Quarterly*, XI (1941), 47–71; "*Comus* Once More," XIX, (1950), 218–223, also in Diekhoff, ed., *A Maske at Ludlow*. See also "Nature and Grace in *The Faerie Queene*," *Journal of English Literary History*, XVI (1949), 194–228 (repr. in Paul Alpers, ed., *Elizabethan Poetry: Modern Essays in Criticism* [New York, 1967], 345–379).

[14] As at l. 938: "Come, lady, while Heaven lends us grace, / Let us fly this cursed place." Bush observes, about l. 638, that haemony cannot represent divine grace because "if it were religious faith or divine grace, its efficacy would surely be less limited than it proves to be." This raises a question about the difference between an emblem, or an exemplum, and a magic force. Gale Carrithers, in "Milton's Ludlow Mask: From Chaos to Community," *Journal of English Literary History*, XXXIII (1966), 38, agrees with John Steadman ("Milton's

To argue that an Italianate philosophizing counts as heavily as Christian theology seems, from the perspective of critical method, not to shift emphasis greatly, but to strengthen it. To argue that the poem presents a *Platonized* Christianity is doubtless just to the poem, and this claim does not overthrow the main proposition according to which Woodhouse structured his original essay.

This proposition may be simply stated: the drama of the masque has thematic force, and we must discover the themes through a reading of that drama. Like other masques, *Comus* is radically thematic in argument, as it is radically magical in texture. A further reason for the "argument" school of criticism should be mentioned. Possibly because modern ideas of chastity seem relatively impoverished, as compared with those of Milton's day, the best critics have explored the grounds of the conflict and temptation—meanings of "chastity" and "temperance,"—which Milton's audience knew without thinking. The modern reader has needed to be reminded of the autobiographical passage in the *Apology for Smectymnuus*, which, better than any other work, gives the background of the argument. One virtue of returning to the *Apology* which is not often noticed is that, besides defining the "abstracted sublimities" of chastity, besides relating the quest for purity to the quest for a vocation, this passage reminds us that Milton thinks dramatistically of his thematic concerns. He associates his ideas with the fictions from which he first learned them and which, in relaying his ideas to other readers, he himself uses for mythic purposes.

Since then *Comus* takes its popular name from one of its

Haemony: Etymology and Allegory," *PMLA*, *LXXVII* [1962], 200–207) that haemony signifies knowledge. But surely the main point throughout *Comus* is that there are degrees of approach to the presence of grace and that for the mortal there is no absolute "state of grace"—even the Lady has to be saved by a set of counterspells.

dramatis personae, its title may be said to remove the work from the normal allegorical frame, shifting the masque toward mimetic drama. It was, I believe, one implication, though not an obvious one in D. C. Allen's *The Harmonious Vision*, that Milton was moving in such a direction when he wrote *Comus*. Allen saw Milton gradually acquiring the powers of the "prophetic strain" announced in the coda of *Il Penseroso*.[15] Milton knew that for his high purposes he would practice mythic syncretism, and this syncretism would indeed be what Allen calls a "higher compromise." Such a vision is based on methods of poetic accommodation not unlike that which leads to religious allegory. Milton's first major attempt was the *Nativity Ode*, which fails or succeeds depending on one's view of its transcendental aspect. The higher compromise makes Milton baroque or mannerist. Not only does it finally contort syntax; it also subjects time and space to all sorts of typological bendings and twistings. Allen argued in *The Harmonious Vision* that *Comus* failed to achieve the baroque unity, although as an experiment in a more realistic dramaturgy than was possible in the confines of *Arcades*, it enabled Milton to explore the possibilities (finally rejected) for a drama of "Adam Unparadised."

The theory of higher compromise is a theory of poetic and dramatic texture. Allen made the general point that *Comus* shows a "patchwork of styles," and in various ways argued that the "exterior structure" of the work is unsatisfactory to the extent that "the poem is not a masque at all." Too long, not fantastic enough, too tense in plot, too serious

[15] "The Search for the Prophetic Strain," in *The Harmonious Vision*, 3–23. See also Michael Fixler, *Milton and the Kingdoms of God* (London, 1964); Barbara Lewalski, *Milton's Brief Epic: The Genre, Meaning and Art of Paradise Regained* (Providence, 1966); and F. M. Krouse, *Milton's Samson and the Christian Tradition* Princeton, N.J., 1949).

in theme, too humorless, too emphatic in dramatic crisis, not emphatic enough in spectacle, dance, costume, and song —the list of *Comus'* faults can be prolonged, and it would merely be unfair to Allen's complicated argument to do more than suggest its main drift. This drift, it seems to me, is that from three points of view—structure, source material (which Allen calls the "pretext"), and orchestration—*Comus* suffers from internal conflicts which it cannot "pacify by a higher compromise." [16] The theory requires an examination of the tempter as dramatic agent.

Drama, transformation, and temptation

One way of describing the dramatic texture of *Comus* would be to say that it has two plots, a philosophic plot which is allegorical and a magical plot which is mimetic. If then Milton achieves success with the latter plot, he is managing to become more mimetic than he has been in earlier works.[17] Within the framework of his plan of a major poetic career he may have wanted to become more mimetic, since he was already planning his great epic. But this view begs the question, and it is better to show that a connection

[16] *The Harmonious Vision*, 30. Bush, in his introduction to *Comus* (*PW*, 111) observes: "In point of style, the masque may almost be called a mosaic of different styles, which range from Elizabethan pastoralism to Augustan classicism, though every line bears the stamp of its author." Rosemond Tuve, in *Images and Themes in Five Poems by Milton* (Cambridge, Mass., 1957), says, "We expect debate, not drama" (121). At the end of *Comus* "All is serene, tranquil, and slow" (155). Yet the critical history of *Comus* tells a different story: the work has appeared to many readers more dramatic, in some ordinary sense, than Miss Tuve thought it.

[17] See John M. Wallace, "Milton's Arcades," in Barker, *Milton*, 77–87. Wallace holds that *Arcades* "epitomizes the growing dissatisfaction with the Arcadian ideal. . . . For Milton, however, the conversion of the pagan world, not a compromise with it, was the only legitimate aim of a Christian."

exists between the plot whatever its mode) in *Comus* and the generally dramatic style which a major epic or dramatic poet has to command.

In all the many attempts to explain what the mimetic is, whether psychologically, theologically, or formally, insufficient use has been made of the fact that to imitate is to become converted into the object of imitation. This was perceived by Plato and before him had anciently been grasped by the Greek dramatists, who made Dionysus the god of the drama. Dionysus is the shapeshifter of the Greek religious system, a rather late divinity in the pantheon, whose cult is a cult of personal salvation and transformation, finally localized in the Mysteries. At the height of his worship, as at the height of the dramatic experience presented, archetypally, in Euripides' *The Bacchae*, the believer "became the god," became entheos.[18] The same sort of identity between mimesis and conversion exists in the parallel Christian sphere, where the "imitation of Christ" demands the entrance of the divinity into man, and man into divinity—a mystery embodied in the Communion service. Every genuine Christian drama is referable to the *imitatio Christi*, which yields the ultimate model of conversion to the good life. Thus Thomas à Kempis struc-

[18] Aristotle says that poetry itself is entheos. Entheus is a major figure in Campion's *The Lords Masque* (1613). Meric Casaubon, son of the famous Isaac, wrote in his *Treatise Concerning Enthusiasme* (London, 1655), on the probably beneficial effects of wine on poetic enthusiasm, concluding that it was "not impossible" that a man who drank water might also be a good poet—"But he had need to have good store of good bloud, or a very strong phansie; which alone is able to raise spirits, and of all spirits, those especially, that have most power of the wit; that is, the purest, and most abstract from materiality" (206–208). Casaubon distinguishes eight types of enthusiasm: contemplative or philosophical, rhetorical, poetical, precatory or supplicatory, musical, martial, erotical, mechanical. These eight are all "natural," whereas the power of divination is supernatural, as are all other kinds of religious enthusiasm.

tures his *Imitation of Christ* so that its final stage is the treatise on the sacrament of Communion. Inversely, damnation is reversion from Christ.

Comus, which moves toward the baptismal sacrament of its penultimate scene, is a drama of initiation: the trial of the Lady and her brothers in the "heavenly footrace," where, beset by wandering paths and dark ways in the wood, they have to *pass through* error, in order to come home to their parents. We might call this action a rite of passage, at the end of which the children have "grown up," and now masters of Ludlow Castle along with their parents, can join the town revels.[19]

Another great Miltonic theme to appear here, almost full grown, is the theme of temptation. Comus is the poet's first great tempter. He is also a Dionysian theatre god, the child of two mythic impostors, Circe and Bacchus. In him Milton develops his equation of the actor as seducer and builds the ground plan of his dramatistic theology. Insofar as Comus tempts the Lady, he tries to transform her (his father had transformed the sailors in a Homeric Hymn, which line 48 recalls), so that we retain overtones of the Bacchus-Circe myth throughout the masque. Though somewhat indirectly, as Jayne has observed, the myths of Circe and Bacchus do color the drama of moral choice allotted to the Lady.[20] The

[19] See Wallace, "Milton's *Arcades*," *passim*, on the idea of spiritual pilgrimage and wandering; also Welsford, *The Court Masque*, 339, and the important Platonic interpretation of Sears Jayne, "The Subject of Milton's Ludlow *Mask*," in Diekhoff, *A Maske at Ludlow*, 172–173. Casaubon says, "The cause of natural *Enthusiasme* in point of *Prayer*, may be referred either to a *vehement* and continued *intention of the mind*, or to the power of language, or to the *natural temper* of the person" (*Treatise Concerning Enthusiasme*, 211). Clearly, then, there is a rhetoric of prayer.

[20] "The Subject of Milton's Ludlow *Mask*," in Diekhoff, *A Maske at Ludlow*, 166.

metamorphic principle controls the action, a point well made by Isabel MacCaffrey:

> The idea of metamorphosis expresses figuratively the choice offered to the soul in its journey through the wood of the world. Circe's victims, and Comus's, are "chang'd into some brutish form," their "foul disfigurement" signifying their abandonment to subhuman irrational pleasure. The alternative is eloquently described by the Elder Brother, who suggests that constancy in virtue, like abandonment of it, can alter "the outward shape"; instead of becoming the thrall of deathly powers, the body may be turned "by degrees to the soul's essence, Till all be made immortal." The virtuous maiden Sabrina, who "underwent a quick immortal change," dramatically embodies this principle, and also witnesses to the promise enunciated in the Epilogue. It is altogether fitting, therefore, that she should be invoked to "unlock the clasping charm" of Comus that imprisons the Lady's body, though not her mind and soul.[21]

The action of *Comus* shows that although the Lady can defeat Comus in argument (his rhetoric is simply "gay") and her brothers (representing on the Platonic level two branches of philosophy) can drive the villain away, neither she nor her brothers can restore her soul's essence, its power of motion. Enthroned in the enchanted palace, the Lady cannot move until Sabrina liberates her. The paradox of the Lady's state lies in the fact that to be free she must have and must show the power of movement, of change, and yet her greatest strength is the twin virtues of chastity and virginity. For, elusive as chastity and virginity may be, they can be said, at first, to be the power to remain unmoved, unseduced, unmetamorphosed, undeflowered, uninitiated, unchanged. For the virgin to remain chaste requires all these

[21] *Samson Agonistes and the Shorter Poems of Milton* (New York, 1966), xxiv.

kinds of stability. What drama then can be expected of such fixed and fixating virtue? One answer can be—and I believe it was one Milton learned from Spenser—that the Lady's virtue is a paradoxical stability. The paradox is inherent in the doublet of terms, chastity and virginity. Only the latter, the essence of the former, implies absolute stasis. Chastity, which joins in the sacred triad of faith, hope, and chastity (and therefore carries with it the outgoing forces of charity), can permit the freedom of movement and experiential trial, by which one learns to be inwardly pure. Chastity permits change as an aspect of experience, whose heroic model, in this case, must surely be Britomart, in Books III, IV, and V of *The Faerie Queene*. The action of *Comus* will also have to show that, as with other moral dilemmas, here too the genuine virtue is threatened by its demonic parody. Comus will become the enemy of humanizing change, however changeful his philosophy is made to sound, as Mutabilitie in the *Mutabilitie Cantos* would, by her triumph, have destroyed her own principle of being. The enchanter's changes, which are death-dealing like those of his mother, work by imprisoning the soul in a magical *raptio*.[22]

Against Comus the mimetic plot sets Thyrsis, the liberator, as much an artist as the man who played him, Henry Lawes. An uncanny aura is created by the fact that like the real prince playing himself as the mythic prince, the real musician plays his pastoral double. Thyrsis has a classical origin: he appears in Theocritus' Ecologue I and loses the singing contest in Virgil's Eclogue VII. But the irony of his name is deepened by a pun, since the *thyrse* is the Bacchic wand, as in the ancient Greek proverb, "Many are the worshipers of Bacchus, but few are the true bearers of the thyrse." The

[22] Jayne, "The Subject of Milton's Ludlow *Mask*," in Diekhoff, *A Maske at Ludlow*, 172.

name Thyrsis embeds an irony at the heart of the masque, although dramatically Thyrsis commands a magic that will undo—that is, unmask—the power of evil. Comus, the demonic parody of Dionysian virtue, only pretends to possess the power of benign transformation. Thyrsis, however, has this power. By invoking the water nymph, Thyrsis creates the paradoxical condition of change-without-change, of moving stability.

His music perfectly conveys such a paradox, because both harmony and melody may appear simultaneously to move and stand still. Music may provide the best metaphor for the idea that thought is the power of moving without motion.[23] If the revolution of the wheel is "perfect," music can convey this ideal movement "in place," and traditional thought will justify us in looking to music for the structure of a masque in which two magicians challenge each other for the crown of true, ideal, perfect mutability. For Comus' frozen vision Thyrsis will substitute the moving fixity of quiet, echoing song. Milton uses the night scene of his fable to create a resonant acoustical vault. In the dark forest even the beating of insect wings can be heard. The *Maske at Ludlow* is a study in listening.

The triumph of song

The triumph of song is the main thing that happens in *Comus*. Its consequences, besides the liberation of the Lady and the general homecoming which that permits, include two more purely technical effects. The first is an infusion of something like the impassioned feeling-tone of operatic recitative

---

[23] See J. A. Mazzeo, "St. Augustine's Rhetoric of Silence: Truth vs. Eloquence and Things vs. Signs," *Renaissance and Seventeenth-Century Studies* 1–28. On the iconography of listening in *Comus*, see John Demaray, *Milton and the Masque Tradition*, 132.

into Milton's prosody (though I believe this process had be-
gun earlier in his career). The second is the role that music's
triumph accords to the singer, a role played by a famous
musician, which provides a definitive instance of the Daedalian archetype. (In Caroline court circles Henry Lawes
occupied a privileged status rather like that, in Venice, of
Claudio Monteverdi.)

The Attendant Spirit, or Daemon, played by Lawes in a
costume he may six months earlier have worn in *Coelum
Britannicum*, presides over the redemption of enchantment.
In his role as guide and guardian (as pastor), he defends the
wandering children and brings them home. A development
of the Genius of the Wood in *Arcades*, he provides the
masque with a second *genius loci*, Sabrina, who plays Ariel to
his Prospero and completes his own larger role as *genius
loci*.[24] The Daemon brings information to the two brothers,
who might have saved their sister—having forgotten her in
the first place—had they been free of their own self-absorp-
tion, idle philosophizing and ineffectual fears. The Daemon
also gives them the first countermagic against Comus, the
gracious talismanic herb haemony, which permits them to
enter the enchanted palace-prison. Finally, he provides the
last victorious countermagic, in his successful invocation of
Sabrina. The Daemon is thus directly opposed to Comus in
the main spheres of thaumaturgy and incantation. The two
brothers cannot mobilize the kind of knowledge or power
that will defeat Comus, and they have a narcissistic self-im-

[24] See D. T. Starnes, "The Figure Genius in the Renaissance," in
Studies in the Renaissance, XI (1964), 234-244; and Geoffrey Hartman,
"False Themes and Gentle Minds," *Philological Quarterly*, XLVII
(1968), 55-68, especially 58-59, on *genius loci* in romantic tradition.
This essay, with others on the concept of genius and *genius loci*,
is reprinted in Hartman, *Beyond Formalism: Literary Essays, 1958-
1970* (New Haven, 1970).

portance which only grace could raise to the level of liberating energy.

The mimetic, magical, song-centered plot of the masque can now be summarized, roughly, as follows:

1. *The introduction and prologue* by the Attendant Spirit, in which the last thing we learn is that he will disguise himself as a shepherd who, "with his soft Pipe, and smooth-dittied Song"—a music animated by his "faith"—possesses Orphic powers.

2. *The antimasque dance and the opening soliloquy* of Comus, in which his revels are identified with the dances symbolic of natural processes, with the elements, and especially with the freedom of nighttime secrecy. When the dance is interrupted by the sound of the Lady's footsteps, Comus apostrophizes his own magic spells, hurled into the "spongy air, / Of power to cheat the eye with blear illusion, / And give it false presentments." This "magic dust" of false-seeming courtesy, flattery, and deceit permits the magus to put on his disguise, to compete with the Spirit. Comus becomes a villager instead of a shepherd, thus introducing the town-country polarity of pastoral.

3. *The Lady's soliloquy.* Alone, she thinks out the meaning of error, of wandering labyrinthine doubt, which the Wood both represents and induces, so that finally the physical body is far less endangered than is the mind. She speaks of "the labour of my thoughts," and the "thousand fantasies [which] begin to throng into my memory / Of calling shapes, and beck'ning shadows dire, / And airy tongues, that syllable men's names / On Sands, and Shores, and desert Wildernesses." She announces that three virtues guard her, seemingly under the aegis of "a strong siding champion Conscience": faith, hope, and chastity. Faith is "pure-eyed"— its possessor will see, will perceive, will think through, will

even investigate, simply because faith gives unimpeded vision. Hope is "white-handed," indicating purity primarily, but perhaps also an element of simple physicality in its natural function, which is to give, to hold, to touch, to sense with its human or divine hand. Chastity, most important of the three, is not only the particular surrogate here for charity— and thus for the greatest of the three theological virtues— but it is, or it has, "unblemish't form." "Form" is the remarkable key word, since chastity is a design, the divine principle which Spenser had celebrated in the third book of *The Faerie Queene*, in the myth of Adonis and his gardens. Indeed the "idea" of chastity is commanding enough to serve as a prime mover. Chastity is a final cause of the Lady's destiny, and the masque may be regarded as the demonstration of what follows, magically as well as logically, from this cause.

4. *The Lady's song*. The Lady sings in the hope that her voice will be heard as far away as possible, and thus she sings a responding tune to Echo, comparing her brothers to Narcissus. She promises Echo, if Echo will tell her where the brothers are, not merely an earthly reward—it would have to be one or both of the brothers, each a Narcissus—but beyond this, a reward in heaven, a "translating" to the skies which will wondrously confer "resounding grace to all Heav'ns Harmonies." [25] Exactly because she sings this song

[25] The musical form of "echo song" is not only popular throughout the baroque period, but its fundamental idea, of echo, also informs baroque polyphony. For the more linear polyphony of the High Renaissance is substituted a verticalized, harmonic polyphony, where the canonic imitation of voices is easier to hear. Echoes are acoustical reflections, and in music this form of song takes the place of a specifically visual mirroring, of the kind in Velásquez' *Las Meninas*. For echo devices in a more modern context see Ralph Freedman, *The Lyrical Novel: Studies in Hermann Hesse, André Gide, and Virginia Woolf* (Princeton, N.J., 1963). In musical terms, the echo song allows an equivalent of visual perspective, since the echo is usually produced

so perfectly, Comus, who has been listening, wonders, "Can any mortal mixture of Earth's mould / Breathe such Divine enchanting ravishment?" Hers must be a "holy rape." Comus has met his match, and her song establishes her as the first singer, the first Orphic voice, of the masque. The contest is drawn along those lines: of divine song versus demonic rhetoric and insidious machinery.

5. *The dialogue of Comus and the Lady.* This interchange initially betrays Comus' awareness that the Lady sings a "blest song," and his further sense that not even the siren music of his mother Circe's enchantments could compare with the Lady's ravishing melody. "Sure something holy lodges in that breast, / And with these raptures moves the vocal air / To testify his hidden residence," he says, and the truth is that he has perceived the true home of the soul, the locus of song, the "vocal air." Again the masque presents the problem of error and the evil chance—"dim darkness, and this heavy labyrinth" have led the Lady astray.

6. *The dialogue of the brothers.* By line 330 the scene is set for the ineffectual but charming debate between the two youthful brothers, which amounts to a demonstration that the Elder Brother, who philosophizes skeptically, is a champion of faith, the younger a champion of hope, though neither is "redeemed" in virtue, since neither can see beyond the narrow confines of oversimplified theories about the true way. The Elder Brother captures our attention because he gets the strong role of apologist for a magical chastity, a "hidden strength" (and the phrase is repeated thrice). In a passage that oddly recalls *Hamlet*, the Elder Brother acclaims

---

by an offstage singer or chorus. C. L. Barber, in " 'A Masque Presented at Ludlow Castle': The Masque as a Masque," in J. E. Summers, ed., *The Lyric and Dramatic Milton* (New York, 1965), has the best account of echo in *Comus*.

his sister's virginity as an instance of a power greater than any daemonic, faerie influence.[26] "Saintly chastity" is so "dear to Heaven" that it will strike the profane eye "with sudden adoration, and blank awe." We need to realize that what makes this speech work is not merely that it embodies a theory of chastity (over which scholars have debated, seeking its true sources), but more dramatically, it places the chastity of the Lady in open competition, open conflict with the magical spells of darkness and error and "brute violence." The Elder Brother at least perceives that evil magic would, if it could, reverse the metamorphic process of the soul's transfiguration. This transfiguration assumes a proper natural guardianship of the body, "the unpolluted temple of the mind," which is but the soul's "outward shape." What saves the chaste soul is its "oft converse with heav'nly habitants," which raises it and keeps it pure of "a degenerate and degraded state." This all might persuade completely, and the Younger Brother is much taken by it; and yet the Elder Brother is indulging in deception, as we learn from the delighted, naïve response he gets: "How charming is divine Philosophy!" Indeed so, if the term "charming" is given its true sense of magically binding. At that moment we are being prepared for the various ironies of the magic "charms" which the brothers will finally have to depend on, and which will not derive from philosophic creeds or sentiments of hope.

7. *The Spirit's entrance disguised as Thyrsis* allows the poet to reintroduce the uncanny tripling of the singing, composing, acting roles in the person of Henry Lawes. His account of the Lady's fate is varied and full of "enchanted

---

[26] I have in mind the line "A thousand liveried angels lackey her," (cf. "Goodnight, sweet prince . . ."), but the whole of the speech (ll. 418–475) recalls the iterative theme of contagion in *Hamlet*. Bush, in *PW*, 125, sees in the Younger Brother's response a possible reminiscence of *Love's Labour's Lost*, IV, iii, 342–343.

isles" and Circean witcheries and the like, but it climaxes
with the reminder that when she sings, hers is a voice "that
might create a soul / Under the ribs of Death." A second
time in the masque she is introduced in the role of singer,
here a "hapless Nightingale." The discovery of her "aidless"
doom elicits a revealing outburst from the Younger Brother.
Almost as if to cast doubt on the whole idea of philosophic
certainty and dogmatic pride, he blames his academically
learned and pedantic brother for showing misplaced, half-
tried faith, a travesty of genuine faith: "Alone, and helpless!
is this the confidence / You gave me Brother?" Still the elder
believes in the power of virtue against malice or sorcery, and
he swears he will drag "that damn'd Magician" around "by
the curls," just as if he had come from a reading of the *Iliad*.
A second time his junior admires him (this time his courage
and "bold Emprise," the virtues of the epic hero), but as the
one who anticipates difficulties and always hopes for the best,
the Younger Brother observes that they will need better
weapons than the faith of "divine philosophy" and its false
confidence.

Magic again becomes the central issue as the Spirit recalls
(in Wordsworthian style, curiously) how the shepherd lad
had given him the drug, haemony, which enables entrance
into the enchanted palace, and then tells the two youths how
they are to undo the spell over the Lady. Like any professional magician, he describes the countermagic exactly;
performed exactly, the undoing rite will save her. They must
get the wand and smash the glass.

8. *Comus and the Lady* next debate the reasons for her
acceding to pleasure, in terms that show his libertinism and
her devotion to cosmic justice, to which he is a "traitor" and
"treasonous." "Hence with thy brewed enchantments" she
cries, and we know that he will not have his way with her.

His famous defense of pleasure is indeed "gay rhetoric," full of flourish and display, and yet beside the point insofar as it makes an irrelevant assumption about the Lady's virtue. It assumes that the only arguments for chastity worth considering are those of the Stoic philosophers and their sober ilk, whereas in fact the chastity of the Lady belongs to a higher realm.

To the magician's "gay rhetoric" the Lady makes a two-fold response. The first half of it is a refutation of the *sense* of Comus' theory of satiety, anticipating a celebrated "digression" in *Lycidas;* the Lady sets forth a goal of political economy, namely, that there should be a better distribution of wealth. Her reasoned attack on lust in the form of "swinish gluttony" treats the question of temperance as one of ideal order and right reason. She shows that Circe's magic metamorphoses symbolize the loss of the soul's balance. Demonic magic can therefore be undone by reason's force. It need not be fought by a countermagic, but by good sense. Only after she has paused and Milton has added a whole extra capping argument, answering her own question, "Shall I go on?" does the diatribe against Comus gain the ecstatic Orphic momentum of the masque itself. For in these climactic lines she says two things: first, that Comus errs because he is deaf, if not blind, or rather blind because deaf, since he would not listen to the utterance and explication of the doctrine of virginity; and second, that if she were to proclaim this doctrine, her "rapt spirits" would be kindled "to such a flame of sacred vehemence" that an Orphic sympathy would be established between her and even the dumb beasts and things of "brute Earth," "Till all thy magic structures rear'd so high / Were shatter'd into heaps o'er thy false head."

9. *The entrance of the brothers and the Spirit, with the invocation to Sabrina.* This concluding scene of the main action

raises the conflicts between spiritual and demonic magic to a yet higher level. Haemony has been the liberating drug, and now the song to Sabrina, with its appeal to the soul of poetry through the allusion to Meliboeus, the mythic Spenser, and the blessing of the water nymph when she appears, can break the final spell over the Lady. The prayer to Sabrina employs one form of magic, the spelling of sacred names—Oceanus, Neptune, Tethys, Nereus, Triton, Leucothea, and so on—but more important, it uses an "echo song" which, with its mirror refrain "Listen and save," creates a magic doubling. This recalls the Lady's first song, to Echo, as if reaffirming the primacy of song. Again, although Sabrina's benign thaumaturgy resembles nothing so much as a Christian rite of lustration, the whole dramatic effect of the rite is simply to meet the Spirit's request: "Goddess dear / We implore thy powerful hand / To undo the charmed band / Of true virgin here distrest, / Through the force, and through the wile / Of unblest enchanter vile." (This is the meter of "Mirror, mirror, on the wall.") The Spirit knows very well that the liberation of the Lady is a miracle, that it requires a *deus ex machina*, that it can only occur "while Heaven lends us grace." (Milton would accent the word "lends"; he is punning on the musical sense of "grace.")

10. *The final scene and songs.* The final moments are the masque movement proper, with its heavy insistence on the family, the home, the town, the castle, the rule of the Lord President. The final dance and song reveal the meaning of the prior action, and this is a meaning, summed up in the one word "fertility," which will be given its cosmic form in the last vision of the earthly paradise, the Spirit's epilogue. That epilogue presents a redeemed nature guarded by all sorts of beneficient triplicities, and opens out finally into the Spenserian mythos of the Garden of Adonis, with the attendant

marriage of Love and the Soul. Venus and Adonis, Cupid and Psyche, the earthly paradise—here as in Spenser they combine into a set of double meanings: the myth of fertility (whether in animal nature or human intercourse) and the myth of imaginative power (whether poetic, philosophic, dramatic, or musical creativity). The "garden of forms" is the ultimate, westernmost location of genius, and the rewritten text of the *Maske* transports the audience to the last encounter with the redeeming poetic genius. Song has triumphed over a diabolical magus and his spurious creativity, and the epiphany assures us that a specific voice has triumphed—the "second voice."

After the Italian manner, stilo recitativo

We have seen that transcendental forms are virtuosic displays. They are filled with ideas that are presented "in terms of" other ideas or other things, and yet allegory is not necessarily the consequence thereof. One explanation for the lack of allegory (though the potential for allegorical significance still remains) may be that the inner transcendence of the typical transcendental form is not the conversion of image into idea, of concrete detail into abstract theme, of symbol into significance. That would be allegory. Here, on the contrary, transcendence works by the conversion of one medium into another, and the audience never leaves the plane of medial transformations. A given dance does not primarily convert to an allegorical significance derived from the motions of that dance; rather, the dance converts to a song, which may convert to a speech, which converts to a scene shift. Each medium "mediates," not a transcendent meaning, but another medium. This convertibility of means is based finally on the function of masking itself. The mask is the transcendental device that entertains but finally rejects a complete shift into allegory. Behind each mask there is only another mask—a mystery that fascinated the major poets of the Renaissance (and that has recurred powerfully in modern postnaturalist theatre).

In such terms as these we can begin to assess the famed "music" of Milton's verse. That music only partially arises from the poetic iconography of music, the *musica speculativa*. Such iconographies occur naturally in this poetry but do not provide its inner life. We have to look deeper, undeterred by the uncertainty of our definitions. The musicality of Milton's verse is more fundamental than the sonorous effect of certain meters, rhythms, vocables, pitch stresses, and the like. They are its *consequences*, oddly enough, not its cause. The music of such verse resides in a doubleness of utterance. This doubleness Eliot "overheard" in the uncanny voicing of certain Shakespearean speeches; it is brought about by the covert presence of the "second voice." The sonorous *Doppelgänger* works in Shakespeare without music in the technical sense. But the history of music shows another specific means by which this magic doubling of voices can occur: the musical medium known as recitative.[27] Here words and music coexist in a medial mirroring of each other. Most commonly, music becomes the double of the text it sets. Sometimes—most notably, in Wagner—the words become the double of the music. For Wagner the Schopenhauerian value of music (and his own talents) demanded this reversal of the procedures set down by early Italian opera composers.

[27] On recitative, see for a general, brief treatment, besides Blume, *Renaissance and Baroque Music*, Claude Palisca, *Baroque Music* (Englewood Cliffs, N.J., 1968), 28–53, 118 (on the drier style of Roman opera recitative), 161–168. On the discovery of expressive means in early opera, see the Norton Lectures of Leo Schrade, *Tragedy in the Art of Music* (Cambridge, Mass., 1964), 67–69, *et passim*. Milton knew Roman opera firsthand, but not before his Italian journey of 1638–1639.

Since there is no written musical score to accompany the blank verse and the dialogue couplets of *Comus*, its recitative must be an imagined doubling, experienced by the viewer or reader in the absence of melody. Precisely this imaginative effect is the "higher" yield of the transcendental form of *Comus*. The work transcends, as it were, in form and medium as well as in content. The musical background of Milton's effort in the *Maske* will illuminate the ways in which the poet could respond to developments in opera and song. A lively debate among scholars seems to suggest that recitative and its expressiveness are a Miltonic goal. Stylistically *Comus* stretches its genre beyond common bounds by giving more than usual range and rhetorical fullness to the speeches in blank verse. Blank verse had been used in innumerable masques, and in every case its effect had been magniloquent. One of the most perfect cases of this eloquence and grand style is an earlier one, the oration of Paris in Act IV of George Peele's *The Arraignment of Paris*. There, amidst the machinery and pageantry and artifice of a masque-drama, Paris suddenly brings the work *rhetorically* to life by the simple expedient of talking (unlike the other characters) in blank verse. The occurrence of this meter in *Comus*, so often noticed, has this effect: the work becomes declamatory. Blank verse in the public theatre is the vocal norm; in the masque it marks a leap to public address, almost as if suddenly one found oneself at the Globe or Fortune, free from the closed atmosphere of the Banqueting Hall or Gray's Inn.

The chief originality in *Comus*, therefore, is immensely physical, a matter of meter. Barber would align style with the thematic interests of the work, which "presents the possibility of a destructive release, and meets it by another sort of release, the release of imagination carried by rhythm out and up to other objects of love. This alternative release is in its way physical, and so can work to counter that which Comus offers. For poetry and song *are* physical, the whole body engaged in the rhythms of articulation, envisagement centered in physical utterance." [28] Two directions may be taken by the poet attempting this utterance. Wilfrid Mellers has argued that "as soon as the masque recognizes the reality of conflict it ceases to be a vision of order as it is or might be and tends toward drama—whether it be poetic drama or the drama in music that came to be called opera." [29]

These two tendencies, toward poetic or toward musical drama, together characterize the Miltonic achievement. Mellers himself regrets the "tendency toward operatic manner" in *Comus,* whereas Gretchen Finney has shown that, since operatic parallels between the *Catena d'Adone* (1626) and *Comus* are suggestive in relating the *Maske* to Milton's intense musical interests, we should explore the operatic aspects of *Comus* without any prejudice against the dramatic wedding of words and music.[30] It is not unlikely that Milton exploited the new Orphic voice of Italian opera, a form which he was shortly to meet firsthand, in Rome.

Critics have delighted to note that Milton and Lawes were personally very close, that Lawes arranged for Milton's passport when he went abroad to Italy, that Lawes sufficiently liked Milton's work in *Arcades* to ask him for a larger work celebrating the Lord President's installation at Ludlow Castle. But few have asked what style of music Lawes supplied, or

[28] " 'A Masque Presented at Ludlow Castle,' " 60.

[29] *Harmonious Meeting* (New York, 1965), 166.

[30] Finney, "*Comus: Dramma per musica*," in *Musical Backgrounds,* 175–194. For the conditions of production of *Comus,* see Willa M. Evans, *Henry Lawes,* 90–109. The *Comus* music is reproduced in A. J. Sabol, *Songs and Dances for the Stuart Masque* (Providence, 1959), with a useful Introduction. Sabol says, "Most of the songs for this masque may best be described as musical recitations in which the nicest balance is maintained with exquisite taste between declamation and melody" (15).

further, what its aesthetic implications are, or the yet more intriguing question: What would have been the general stylistic influence of a man like Lawes upon his friend and poetical admirer? To some of these questions we can give tentative answers. First of all, whatever we may say about Lawes's music, its technical innovations met with Milton's approval, since he later even exaggerated Lawes's claim to have invented the new expressive words-and-music technique of declamation and scansion. "They were not, as Milton in Sonnet XIII states, the invention of one man, Henry Lawes. William Lawes, John Wilson, Simon Ives, Charles Coleman, John Gamble and many others were setting verse in precisely the same manner at precisely the same time. All were subject to new styles emanating from the humanistic revivals in France and Italy." [31] Even so, Milton made his claim for Lawes's "tunefull and well-measur'd song" which taught English music "how to span / Words with just note and accent, not to scan / With Midas eares, committing short and long." That he was wrong to claim Lawes's priority of invention is a minor point, merely proof that he admired the sort of music which survives from Lawes's compositions for *Comus*. This music belongs unreservedly to the main stream of operatic tradition, emanating from Italy, and we are therefore committed to examine the interaction of words and music on an operatic plane if we are to grasp the importance of *Comus* to the fate of the masque tradition in England.

Here a methodological problem arises: the need to differentiate between medium and style. I am not seeking to show that Milton was a frustrated opera librettist, or that for *Comus* Lawes wrote a greater bulk of music than the five extant songs. True, he may have written and performed

[31] E. A. J. Honigman, ed., *Milton's Sonnets* (London and New York, 1966), 127.

more music for *Comus*. But the point is rather that *Comus* reflects a stylistic climate, supported by the Platonic cast of its themes. The influence of *musica practica* on the speculative music of the *Maske* will appear finally as a stylistic tendency. The voicing, the coloration, the metrics, the iconography seek a declamatory style, perhaps referable, in the last analysis, to concepts of rhythm and expression. The *Maske* therefore need not adopt a strictly practical music for its medium. Mannerist or not, it adopts a certain musical manner. Modern musicologists agree on the main quality of Lawes's style. Of his songs for *Comus*, Manfred Bukofzer says that they are "typical examples of the early baroque continuo song. They are quasi-recitatives characterized by incisive marking of the rhyme, frequent and sudden cadences, discontinuous rhythm, and an erratically moving bass. The melody is carried forward mainly by the prosody of verse fragments. The musical rhythm is, however, not derived from the regular meter of the verse, but is achieved by emphatic words or phrases." The essence of such a *recitativo* style, Bukofzer observes, is "the affective intensification of the word" [32]—precisely what gives Monteverdi's invention its amazing theatrical presence. Thurston Dart finds this intensification coming into English practice from "the kind of impassioned singing prescribed by Caccini." [33] The style puts a new emphasis on the verbal text. In line with the possibly artistocratic bias of the Italian import, Lawes's arioso style— with a rhythm following speech inflection rather than a fixed musical metric and a freedom that leads to *recitativo* style— frequently sets poems which are intellectually complex but not emotionally declamatory. "The majority of Lawes's set-

[32] *Music of the Baroque Era*, 185.
[33] *Interpretation of Music* (London and New York, 1954), 122.

tings of Carew are through-composed (i.e., arioso-style); and in all of them the music serves to point the verbal rhythm of the poem to underline the shifts in the argument." [34]

Mellers adds that this style is not strongly operatic. Here we reach the point at which we need to consider the inner drive of *Comus:* Is it toward or away from opera? That is, can the Milton-Lawes combination successfully marry the two media of word and song into an operatic mixture? Our answer may require a definition of opera as one kind of hybrid art or another. In framing any definition we would enter the confused debate over opera which has plagued all its more serious critics since its invention by Peri and Monteverdi around the year 1600—or to give an English date, 1617, since "rare Laniere" (Nicholas Lanier, 1588–1666)

[34] Mellers, *Harmonious Meeting*, 115. John T. Shawcross, in "Henry Lawes's Settings of Songs for Milton's 'Comus,'" *Journal of the Rutgers University Library*, XXVIII (1964), 22–28, shows that Lawes was concerned with "the accommodation of music to text," to the extent that he "was not averse to changing music even some years later than the original composition in order to achieve accord with a changed text" (27). More important, "The form of the mask and the music employed to greet the Earl of Bridgewater at his inauguration as Lord President of Wales are not certain despite the discussions offered over the years which assume such certainty. . . . We see that the extant music, at best, only approximates the earliest songs and is probably incomplete. . . . Perhaps most directly significant as conclusion from this study of the songs, however, is the underscoring of Milton's frequent changing of text and apparent lack of satisfaction with his earlier work. When he goes so far as to alter that which has been set to music, music being an integral part of a mask, we may be assured that his approach to this mask (now really poem rather than dramatic work) and its thesis had altered in some way." One simple reason for increased complication in the developed text, as analyzed by Shawcross, may be that once the original performance had been given, the authors were free to create an ideal form. As Willa Evans remarks, "Lawes may well have breathed a sigh of relief when Lady Alice came to the end of her measures" (*Henry Lawes*, 104).

created "the first English opera" in his collaboration with Jonson, producing *Lovers Made Men* in that year. "The whole Masque was sung (after the Italian manner) *Stylo recitativo*, by Master Nicholas Lanier; who ordered and made both the Scene, and the Musicke." [35] The purer Italianate singing style was apparently known to the English theatre from the beginning of the century, shortly after its invention; if it failed to catch on, it was not for lack of official recognition. On the other hand, it was some time before the accepted masterpiece of Purcell, *Dido and Aeneas*, introduced sung recitative into the theatre in a work of major stature.

Perhaps a bias against what was achieved by Lanier and others will result if we accept the views of Mellers, who holds that the English mode is a compromise between the lyric and the dramatic. Speaking of Lawes and his settings of poems by Carew, one of his favorite song writers, Mellers says:

We do not find here, as we do in Dowland, a poem metamorphosed into lyricism: nor, as later in Purcell, a poem that becomes musical drama. We find a musically unobtrusive setting that exaggerates the manner in which a reciter would declaim the poem before an initiated audience. By giving relatively long notes to the important words Lawes clarifies the complicated syntax; at the same time he underlines the conceits, exhibits them for polite applause. The musical rhythm is not a natural speech rhythm; but it is a reciter's rhythm: that of an orator who is trying to "get over" difficult language to an audience, and to impress that audience with his verbal ingenuity. In all these songs the music is the servant of the poetry in a manner that is remote from Dowland, or even Campion.

In these settings of Carew we remain outside the fully operatic use of arioso, and Mellers, in opposition to Bukofzer and others, concludes that "the harmony supports the voice;

35 H. and S., VII, 454.

but it does not attempt to intensify the words' meaning." [36] Any movement into opera represented by the production of *Comus* in 1634 would have required the poet and composer to use the recitative style in full confidence that its use would, as with Monteverdi, intensify the verbal and emotive line with every device of musical pressure. Yet Mellers grants only that Lawes and Milton were experimenting. "Despite its magnificent poetry," says Mellers, "*Comus* is unsatisfactory as an 'entertainment' because it falls between the conventions of poetic drama and of opera. Although it contains a dramatic conflict, it does not become poetic drama because it does not create the illusion of actuality. . . . In a superficial sense, the music seems to be more operatic than the music in Campion's masques, because it is conceived as more or less continuous arioso, with vocal lines that follow speech inflexion. The effect of this arioso, however, tends—here, as in Lawes's songs—to be narrative rather than dramatic, because there is little interpenetration of speech-inflected melody with harmonic tension, controlled by a latent dance rhythm." Mellers makes the more general point, which suggests an uncertain experimental climate, that "in the seventeenth century, compromise between musical and dramatic conventions did not work. The artist could, like Shakespeare, put all the action, the 'Becoming,' into poetic drama and use music negatively to reinforce the drama; or he could, as Purcell was to do later, make the music become dramatic action, thereby creating opera. But masque is not opera, and a confusion of genres is bad for either." [37] John Hollander takes a similar view: "We must class the masque as a thing very much apart from the opera, and perhaps not a real predecessor at all." [38] On the

[36] *Harmonious Meeting*, 115.   [37] *Ibid.*, 166, 167.
[38] *The Untuning of the Sky* (Princeton, 1961), 192. Demaray (*Milton and the Masque Tradition*, 145–146) argues from such points

other hand, Donald Grout states that "as in France opera grew out of the ballet, so in England it was rooted in the masque." [39] Grout's view need not, in fact, conflict so heartily with the Hollander's, if we are careful to ask what is meant when each critic uses the term "opera." If the term means a work entirely sung, "through-composed," then masque and opera must always remain genres very much apart. But suppose we broaden the definition to include works like *The Magic Flute* or *The Abduction from the Seraglio*—singspiels —then the term will cover even certain masques. Conversely, John Blow's little opera, *Venus and Adonis* (1680 or later), was called by its composer a "masque." If, besides *Dido and Aeneas,* we (as did his contemporaries) include Purcell's *King Arthur* and *The Fairy Queen* or *The Indian Queen* among his operas, we shall have admitted that with him, for whatever reasons of public taste and personal inclination, the musical theatre remained very much under the influence of masque. Owing perhaps to the prestige and classical status of the *dramma per musica,* this affinity between English opera and masque is rejected by various critics. In any event, as long as we define our terms, we are in no great trouble over the lineage of masque, but we must note that it is complex and even uncertain in direction. By opening up the term "operatic" as used in connection with Milton, we can characterize a poet whose belief in his own verse was so strong that he could, if he wanted, write an opera without music—*opera senza musica.* The strictly musical definition of opera yields to the *modal* characteristic of early opera: however it divides

---

that we should discount Gretchen Finney's view of *Comus* as *dramma per musica.* Edward Dent, however, in *Foundations of English Opera* (Cambridge, 1928), 39, holds that English opera largely developed out of the masques.

[39] *A Short History of Opera* (2d ed.; New York, 1965), I, 135.

up the units and whole forms of musical declamation, opera employs the intense inflectional drama of recitative.

The operatic relations of *Comus* thus remain ambiguous. This is so not least because in the Elizabethan and Jacobean theatre, as Albert Cook, following M. C. Bradbrook, has recently argued more broadly, "the recitative convention holds through all the fluidity of action and extravagance or inwardness of statement." [40] Characters in this tradition speak their thoughts, reciting ideas and feelings, while "the language of the play . . . *recites* the action." Modern drama, by contrast, tends to achieve expressive articulation through gesture, through silence, through various devices by which "the language *uncovers* the action." [41] Certainly, the openness of the rhetoric in public theatre suggests the musician's *recitativo*. Doubtless the recitative style of prosody, of unaccompanied, unsung words, would have been impossible had not the Elizabethans perfected the art of blank verse, which carried the recitation sonorously enough to do without music. Perhaps because English blank verse is such a powerful vehicle, there was never any real need to perfect the Italianate device of *stilo recitativo*, in the strict sense. The versifiers already had enough merely verbal music at command.

Yet the Italian example was not lost on Milton, if his praises of Lawes and Leonora Baroni mean anything. He could take the Italianate stylistic perhaps as an extreme to which, through mere verse, it might not be possible or even desirable

[40] Albert S. Cook, "Language and Action in the Drama," *College English*, Oct. 1966, 15–16 (reprinted in Cook, *Prisms* [Bloomington, Ind., 1967]); M. C. Bradbrook, *Themes and Conventions in Elizabethan Tragedy* (Cambridge, 1960), and *English Dramatic Form: A History of Its Development* (London, 1965).

[41] Cook, "Language and Action in the Drama," *College English*, Oct. 1966, 15, 18.

to attain. The excess has been perfectly described by Joseph Kerman, who thus depicts Monteverdian *recitativo:*

Music . . . should imitate the accents of passionate speech as best represented by the grand, exaggerated rhetoric of a great actor. Music should follow the cadence and thus the moving implication of the individual word, with little heed to the phrase, the sentence, or even the total feeling. The result was recitative, tumbling emotion, a continuing heart-cry, undistanced, "the naked human voice" behind the measured voice of the poet. Its magnificence and immediacy stem exactly from its impulsive nature, from its lack of forming control.[42]

This style was beyond the powers of Henry Lawes, though for an Englishman, subject to the pressures of conservative English taste, he went as far in the direction of the tumbling Italian ideal as any composer of his time—and with results that Milton went out of his way to praise and perhaps to invoke when they collaborated on *Comus.* The new art was that of Monteverdi, who had, as Kerman says, "a perfect genius for declamation; words formed themselves musically for him."

Thyrsis: The Orphic persona

Orpheus had been a central character in Campion's *The Lords Maske* (1613) where he served a purpose rather similar to the Daemon's purpose in *Comus.*[43] Both figures command the powers of song and can summon the agents of perfect incantation. But while the singing magician is the happier version of Orpheus, he has another, less happy side, in line with other myths of the culture bringer. Besides "building the lofty rime" he can suffer the Orphic death, and

[42] *Opera as Drama* (New York, 1956), 30.
[43] *The Lords Maske* includes the figure of Entheus, or Poetic Fury, whom Orpheus (l. 84) identifies with Phoebus Apollo.

Adonis-like, become the sacrificial victim whose highest parallel is Christ—a similitude Milton draws upon for *Lycidas*, which he significantly designates a monody. The Orphic persona thus has a double valence, which complicates and deepens his use for the utterance of the poet's "second voice." In commenting on the importance of the Orphic legend for Virgilian creativity, Berger has stressed the phrase from the *Aeneid*, Book IV, describing the loss of Euridice: *Orpheus respexit* ("Orpheus looked back"). "Here *respicere* means to look back unguardedly, in longing, toward the object of love. The poet must learn to look back at the beloved past without destroying its life, or his own happiness and control. *Respicere* can also mean to look back, in the sense of *reflecting on*, or, to look again, in the sense of re-vising." [44] In *Comus* we find a parallel situation: here the "looking back" is conveyed, as we shall see, in sonorous form, in the resonating mirror of the echo song. In both cases we are dealing with a deep irony in the culture bringer's passion. What he values is never to be directly his, since to possess the loved object would be to destroy it; it can only be his if it is reflected, recreated, resonated. The Orphic design is, in this light, a myth of resonance. Fulfillment is an echo.

The mystery of repetition is the secret of the Virgilian *respicere*. Kierkegaard asked, Is repetition possible? The myth of Orpheus embodies one set of answers to that question. It is thus significant that Orpheus was the hero of heroes for early opera, that most expressive art form. John Arthos has recently argued for an affinity between Monteverdi's operatic work and *Samson Agonistes*.[45] Gretchen Finney has shown

[44] *Berger*, "Archaism, Vision, and Revision," 32.
[45] *Milton and the Italian Cities* (London, 1968), Part II, "Milton and Monteverdi," 129–206. See also Arthos, *On "A Mask Presented at Ludlow Castle"* (Ann Arbor, Mich., 1954).

operatic analogies between *Comus* and the *Catena d'Adone*.[46] These parallels are haunting chiefly because in the Orphic aspect of Thyrsis, Milton seems to be projecting a mythic meaning that was strongly projected by the first operas. Kerman has described their mythic basis:

The myth of Orpheus, furthermore, deals with man specifically as artist, and one is drawn inevitably to see in it, mirrored with a kind of proleptic vision, the peculiar problems of the opera composer. Initially Orpheus is the supreme lyric artist. In the classic view he is the ideal of the prize-winning *kitharista*—or, in Christian allegory, the evangelical psalmist who charmed the melancholy Saul. To the fourteenth century, he is the minstrel who exacts his boon from the Fairy King; to the sixteenth, perhaps, the madrigalist; to the nineteenth, proud Walther who persuades the German pedants. The eighteenth century painted him, tremulously, as the amiable singer of Metastasio's faint verses who entranced the King of Spain. But for Orpheus the lyric singer, the crisis of life becomes the crisis of his lyric art: art must now move into action, on to the tragic stage of life. It is a sublime attempt. Can its symbolic boldness have escaped the musicians of 1600, seeking new power in the stronger forms of drama? Orpheus' new triumph is to fashion the lament that harrows hell out of his own great sorrowing emotion—this too they must have specially marked, wrestling as they were with new emotional means, harrowing, dangerous to manage. But the fundamental conflict of the myth transcends that time and this medium, and extends to every artist. It is the problem of emotion and its control, the summoning of feeling to an intensity and communicability and form which the action of life heeds and death provisionally respects. All this Orpheus as artist achieves. But as man he cannot shape his emotions to Pluto's shrewd decree; face to face with the situation, he looks back, and fails. Life and art are not necessarily one.

[46] *Musical Backgrounds*, 175–194.

Kerman goes on to show that the mythic failure of Orpheus is by no means clear or self-evident in its significance. Yet the failure is a great operatic crux. "To be sure, this 'problem of control' is an abstraction; few artists, and certainly not Monteverdi or Gluck, have drawn so clean and scientific an issue. Nor did Orpheus, in the simple, unelaborated myth. It is the dramatist's task to clarify the issue for Orpheus." [47] And we can say, with Milton in mind, it is the masque maker's task to clarify the Orphic failure by treating the masque as "defense and resource."

Barber has said that if *Comus* fails, "it fails by a failure of rhythm . . . mere vehemence, mere assertion . . . and where our imagination is allowed to rest on the merely literal or merely intellectual contest, the defense of chastity lacks the final cogency of pleasure." Barber finds this vehemence in Comus himself—perhaps according to Milton's design. Barber would seem to support the view of song as liberating spell: "It is notable that the images which suggest a benign sexual release refer to song." [48] Milton has accorded success to his benign magician, the Attendant Spirit. But evidence of the Attendant Spirit's power is not apparent in a mere reading of his imagery. We have to scan his rhythms, and besides, we have to make use of our surviving musical manuscripts of *Comus* in order to discover the metrical style Milton and Lawes together created. For here will be the antidote to all false vehemence and spurious assertiveness. To restate Barber's question, the masque has to achieve the natural grace of its own chosen *metron*. Compared with the use of verse and music, the use of dance is minimal, even negligible.

[47] *Opera as Drama*, 27–28.

[48] " 'A Mask Presented at Ludlow Castle,' " in Summers, ed., *The Lyric and Dramatic Milton*, 65. This essay is reprinted in Diekhoff, *A Maske at Ludlow*, with an interesting response to questions which Summers had posed in the earlier book.

It may even be misleading to suggest that *Comus* has much in common with the earlier dance-drama of the typical court masques. Unlike them, *Comus* could be presented without dances—a loss which would obliterate many earlier masques —although the spectacle and the meaning do in fact profit, in due measure, from the two dances that Milton did allow. Whereas the earlier models, Jonsonian especially, carried a weight of meaning in their dances and spectacle, Milton's work has displaced this burden and given it to the imagery of the speeches and the recitative music of their declamation.

Seeking the source of this "musical" style in the mythography of the work, we would associate expressivity with the Orphic voice. Orpheus sings in suffering. The music he makes is not instrumental: in *Ad Patrem*, Milton praises to his father the true Orphic bard (the *vates*), who sang at ancient festal occasions. He asks: "In brief, of what use is the idle modulation of the voice if it lacks words and sense and rhythmical speech? That kind of music suits woodland singers, not Orpheus, who by his song, not his lyre, held back rivers, gave ears to the oak trees, and by his singing drew tears from the shades of the dead. Such fame he owes to song" (ll. 50–55). This distinction Ficino had made.

In his treatise on divine madness, he states that the human soul acquires through the ears a memory of that divine music which is found first in the eternal mind of God, and second, in the order and movements of the heavens. There is also a twofold imitation of that divine music among men, a lower one through voices and instruments, and a higher one through verse and metre. The former kind is called vulgar music, whereas the latter is called by Plato serious music and poetry.[49]

Milton was to espouse the higher music in his own works,

[49] P. O. Kristeller, *Renaissance Thought*, II, 157–158.

where he forged "willing chains and sweet captivity." *At a Vacation Exercise* makes perfectly clear the equation in Milton's mind between music and the verse of his native language, which remains independent of any strictly musical accompaniment. Even when he praises the singing of Leonora Baroni, the great Roman singer, he does so in terms that place the standard of beauty in a celestial frame. God or the Holy Ghost, he tells her, "moves with secret power in your throat —moves with power, and graciously teaches mortal hearts how they can insensibly become accustomed to immortal sounds. But, if God is all things and interpenetrates all, in you alone he speaks, and in silence holds all else" (ll. 5–10). The second epigram to Baroni confers on her the power of reanimating the dead Pentheus, the archetypal victim of maenadic bacchic rage. To give Pentheus life is to make harmony the means of salvation. Milton imagines this sublime sacrificial act in ambivalent terms, for it was Orpheus whom the maenads tore to pieces.

Perhaps only in *Samson Agonistes* and its choral inventions did Milton control the full flood of this ambivalence. There the Orphic voice is committed equally to salvation and self-destruction. An unwitting yet half-chosen suicide rewards the singer who descends into the underworld. It is not clear how much of a sense of this descent in left in *Samson Agonistes;* this is a skewed myth, but Samson's doom elicits pure out-cries. Samson is the ultimate Orphic hero; his blindness drives him into a totally auditory world of hearing and speaking. As for persona, it is not unwarranted to question the parallels between the hero and his poet. The choice of Samson as tragic voice, for all its risk of dramatizing the stasis of tragic energy rather than its motions, is still the most daring of Milton's choices. Now he can fully utter the drama of an entangled self-consciousness; now it is proper for the hero to be in part the poet himself, and equally proper for the poet to voice his absolute command of the poetic medium. The final twist in this triumph of a rational self-awareness (and its mystery) is the invention of the Chorus, for this Chorus is planned on the principle of echo, to give resonance—to provide a resonating surface and mirror—to the second voice of the poet.

The particulars of every Miltonic work differ, but common to them all is a penchant for enclosed vastness. That the poet understood his own will to encompass may be seen throughout his writings, since he is generally so conscious of what, as a writer, he is attempting. No better example could be given than the encomium upon Cromwell in *The Second Defence of the People of England*, where, expanding on a traditional rhetorical topic, Milton uses the terminology of enclosure and expansion:

It is not possible for me in the narrow limits in which I circumscribe myself on this occasion, to enumerate the many towns which he has taken, the many battles which he has won. The whole surface of the British empire has been the scene of his exploits, and the theatre of his triumphs; which alone would furnish ample materials for a history, and want a copiousness of narration not inferior to the magnitude and diversity of the transactions.[50]

Later, observing that "the title of king was unworthy the transcendent majesty of your character," Milton defines the problem of naming the surpassing glory: "Actions such as yours surpass, not only the bounds of our admiration, but our titles; and, like the points of the pyramids, which are lost in the clouds, they soar above the possibilities of titular com-

[50] *Selected Prose*, ed. Hughes, 349. See also Douglas Bush *et al.*, eds., *Complete Prose Works of John Milton* (New Haven and London, 1966), IV, 668.

mendation." Cromwell had to let himself be called Lord
Protector because it was "expedient, that the highest pitch of
virtue should be circumscribed within the bounds of some
human appellation." In *Tetrachordon*, Milton describes the
practical problem of "the abundance of argument that presses
to bee utter'd, and the suspense of judgement what to choose,
and how in the multitude of reason, to be not tedious." [51]
It is the trial of superabundance, of genius conscious that it
generates.

Johnson was right. It was in Milton's character always to
choose subjects "on which too much could not be said, on
which he might tire his fancy without censure of extravagance." Inheriting a large literary capital, Milton put this
imagistic wealth to work. The capitalistic analogy is hardly
a metaphor here. Milton treats literary tradition like an entre-
preneur, investing one work in another, continuously making
"mergers." This parodistic takeover particularly colors the
Ovidian elements of *Comus*, which show that myth is a currency convertible from one generation to another. Comus the
seducer replays Leander's sermons of love to Hero. Suddenly,
the poem of *Hero and Leander* rises like an apparition, staring
Comus in the face. We shall need to speculate further on this
mirroring.

Then, too, Milton has the power of extreme concentration.
He holds a whole tradition of exegesis suspended in the little
speech on haemony, where Thyrsis knowingly refers to "that
Moly / Which Hermes once to wise Ulysses gave." It was to
this moly that the Stoic philosopher Cleanthes applied an
early allegorical gloss, perhaps about 200 B.C. (and in trans-
cribing Cleanthes' view, Apollonius the Sophist made what
may be the earliest use of the term *allegoria*): "Cleanthes the
philosopher says that Reason is indicated allegorically, by

[51] *Complete Prose Works*, II, 614.

which the impulses and passions are mollified." [52] Haemony is more than moly, as scholars have labored to show. It acts magically in the framework of a dramatic action. But it has the effect of a *logical* power as well. It is entangled in a kind of witchcraft, the verbal spell, for as Milton would know from the *Remedia Amoris*, Ovid had said: "If anyone thinks that the beneficial herbs of Haemonia and the arts of magic can avail, let him take his own risk. That is the old way of witchcraft; my patron Apollo gives harmless aid in sacred songs." One can no longer tell if haemony is a drug or a word. *Comus* is full of such terms. Extravaganza without extravagance results. The richness of commentary on the *Maske* itself suggests that wealth is one aim of transcendental form.

[52] Quoted by R. P. C. Hanson, *Allegory and Event* (London, 1959), 37, from *The Fragments of Zeno and Cleanthes*, ed. A. C. Pearson, (London, 1891).

6   *The Bound Man*

Milton, the religious and the political man, writes more or less continuously about imprisonment. Religious origins of such a theme are many and deep in the Christian context, especially when Christianity veers toward dualism, so that the soul is conceived as imprisoned in the body, the spirit buried in matter. A generalized fear of imprisonment is furthermore a natural response during civil war; by poetic justice the poet himself was incarcerated, though soon released, after the Restoration.

A darker prison had closed round him, earlier in life. By the winter of 1651–1652, when Milton was in his forty-third year, he had gone completely blind. This physical annihilation of one sense may have led him to insist on the phenomenon of loss, which, by a mysterious inversion, becomes the point of exit into a larger freedom that "shoots invisible virtue even to the deep." *Paradise Lost* builds its cosmic scope with all the greater clarity and force for having originated in the perceptual void. The "universal blank / Of nature's works" implies a death, and its paradoxical turn backwards into life is Christian enough. To be reborn, one must first die. Yet even before his physical loss of sight Milton had envisioned something like it. In *Comus* the Lady is imprisoned and, with her brothers, who are lost in the wood of error, she is "from the cheerful ways of men / Cut off." Comus the magician is a pagan devil, but Milton seems always to have sensed that his God also is a kind of gaoler, benign enough, he assumed or sought to prove. For if one eternal prison is hell, the other is paradise.

The themes of prison life and death are held in balance by a regulative myth, which reveals a link between service and servitude. True verses, we shall see, are the benign imprisonment. The idea comes very quickly to Milton. His first sonnet, "O nightingale, that on yon bloomy spray," praises a binding service to the double ideals of poetry and love. The weightless armor of the angels in the *Nativity Ode* makes it light work for them to "sit in order serviceable." *At a Vacation Exercise*, dealing directly with the poet's vocation, records the heroic songs sung at King Alcinous' feast, "While sad Ulysses' soul and all the rest / Are held with his melodious harmony / In willing chains and sweet captivitie." The notes of the musical scale ("in perfect diapason") of *At a Solemn Music* are a great chain of being which, like the prelapsarian "fair music that all creatures made," is broken at the Fall. In *Arcades* this original music can be revived; it is a happy instrument of love, "such sweet compulsion doth in music lie." The "immortal verse" of *L'Allegro* leads "many a winding bout / Of linked sweetness long drawn out." Here the myth of Orpheus and Euridice leads directly to thoughts of imprisonment, but the poem sustains a paradoxical, ambivalent view of the powers of poetry, "Untwisting all the chains that tie / The hidden soul of harmony." Milton's phrase for the poetic power, "the melting voice," suggests something of the feel this paradox had for him, and in *Il Penseroso*, when the religious music dissolves the poet into ecstasies, the theme of melting recurs. Verse must be as easy as melting, and as responsive to a kind of heat. In *Paradise Lost* the muse nightly visits the poet and "inspires / Easy my unpremeditated verse." In the invocation to light poetry feeds on thoughts "that voluntary move / Harmonious numbers."

The poet imagines and tells us that his prosodic method sets him free. In a prefatory note on "The Verse," Milton observes that in *Paradise Lost* "this neglect then of rhyme so little is to be taken for a defect, though it may seem so perhaps to vulgar readers, that it is rather to be esteemed an example set, the first in English, of ancient liberty recovered to heroic poem from the troublesome and modern bondage of rhyming." Ben Jonson, in *A Fit of Rhyme against Rhyme*, had called rhyme "the rack of finest wits" and a "tyrant." Yet Ben continued to rhyme. Milton had written with exquisite freedom in the rhyming mode. The aesthetics of rhyme thus appear complicated by the problem of magnitude, for it seems clear that Milton at least avoided rhyme in his longest works. In that revealing critical exercise, Andrew Marvell's prefatory poem *On "Paradise Lost,"* one of the great rhymers praises Milton for abandoning the allurements of "tinkling rhyme." Tagged verses would be "vulgar."

> I too transported by the mode offend,
> And while I meant to praise thee must commend.
> Thy verse created like thy theme sublime,
> In number, weight, and measure, needs not rhyme.

Marvell suggests a correlation between the lack of rhyming closure and the "work so infinite," a work that could be spanned truly only if the texture of the verse was syntactically free.[1] For Milton, he seems to hold, it was structurally necessary to avoid "the jingling sound of like endings."

[1] Marvell's poem was prefixed to the second edition (1674); it is here quoted from *PW*, 210.

This avoidance opened up a felicitous path toward larger syntactic unions. It left the field open to the use of half-rhymes, off-rhymes, but far more important, to assonance of every kind. Assonance in fact conspires to give *Paradise Lost* its own covert kind of rhyming texture. These buried reflections of sounds are deliberately not "the jingling sound of like endings." Assonance works cryptically, yet it is audible to the trained ear, and on the acoustic level forms the basis of the sound structure of the whole vast transcendental form. Whereas end-stopped lines written in couplets tend to reflect only each other—and thus stop the reader's or listener's mind from engaging the poem on a more subliminal level, beyond couplets—the Miltonic paragraph manifestly carries the mind forward, and backward, in vast soaring motions. By avoiding strong devices of closure, such as end rhymes, Milton increases the power of internal rhyme through assonance, so that there is perhaps no large poem in the English language with more feeling of rhyme than *Paradise Lost*. And this happens all because the poet has thrown off the "modern bondage of rhyming."

The principle of echo

Such retrospective innovation belongs to a larger purpose, which I shall call "the principle of echo." Echo is a principle in Milton (and in authors he influences deeply) because it gives structure to his work. Thus his use of assonantal mirroring gives to *Paradise Lost* the structure of a language that continuously reaffirms its own order through each mirrored recollection of itself. During the Renaissance, to be sure, the myth of Echo plays a structural role—we could call it a "syntactic myth," along with its companion myth, of Narcissus. Much labor would go into the demonstration of all the echoing effects throughout a poem like *Paradise Lost*, but the reader, once alerted to the epic's cryptic rhyme, will find and hear it easily enough.

The poetry in *Comus* suggests another aspect of echo. Here the myth is invoked directly. The Lady addresses the nymph Echo and specifically recalls her myth. We can state its principle as follows: an echo is the phonic recollection of a sign, "air" echoing "impair," in such a way that the structural implications of that sign, as well as its immediate meaning are present to the mind. An echo in this kind of formulation brings back the logical connections of things as well as their particular sense. Verbal echo comes to be a metamorphosing technique, by which the meaning of a present context is altered through its phonic reflection of another whole context. An echo, like a visual reflection, is subject to perspective.

Thus, to begin with the Lady's appeal to Echo in *Comus*, she calls for help to an Echo that, as Carey observes, does not reply to her: "The Lady's loneliness is enhanced because, unusually, no echo replies."[2] In fact, this is the crux of the masque, for her liberation must await such a reply, and she

[2] John Carey and Alastair Fowler, eds., *The Poems of John Milton* (London, 1968), 188. Carey notes echo scenes in William Browne's *Inner Temple Masque;* Jonson's *Cynthia's Revels;* and John Webster's *Duchess of Malfi.* The "airy shell" of line 230, while mainly meaning the vault of the sky, implies also that the vehicle of air may reflect or resonate sound. Echo further suggests a theatrical "shell," or natural temple, which may be provided by the forest. Thus Sir Philip Sidney writes: "Is not every *eccho* [of Arcadian sounds] a perfect Musicke? and these fresh and delightfull brookes how slowly they slide away, as loth to leave the company of so many things united in perfection? and with how sweete a murmure they lament their forced departure? Certainelie, certainely, cosin, it must needes be that some Goddesse enhabiteth this Region, who is the soule of this soile" *The Countess of Pembrokes Arcadia,* in *Works,* ed. Albert Feuillerat [Cambridge, 1912], I, 57). Cf. *At a Solemn Music:* "That we on earth with undiscording voice / May rightly answer that melodious noise" (ll. 17–18).

will eventually get it. Meanwhile Milton has established the metaphysics of his comedy, the problem being that if an echo answers the Lady, the Lady will hear the reflection of her own voice. By the same token, her appeal enunciates the idea of the difference between the narcissistic self and the alien other. The Lady appeals to a heavenly harmony, asking to be freed from her own echo chamber, but that appeal also will have to await response from a providential friend. Carey observes that the final line of her song—"And give resounding grace to all heaven's harmonies"—"is the only alexandrine in *Comus*, mimicking the lengthening of heaven's song by echo." It may also suggest that the true and final echo will not come along for a while.

The larger dramatic result of the song is the reminder that the Lady begins alone, trapped in the structure of her own thought. She may promise transfiguration to the nymph Echo, but in the song reveals that her brothers are two likenesses of Narcissus; if they are, then she may be like Echo, the acoustical, female Narcissus. Grace finally does resound, of course, and the musical pun is physically rendered by the closure of the Spirit's final song. Lawes composed his songs so that, without precise musical duplication, the song to Echo and the Spirit's song to Sabrina are echoes of each other, since the falling interval of a fifth in the Lady's "Sweet Echo" is doubled by an identical falling fifth, more cadential to be sure, in the phrase "listen and save." If then the right sort of magic generally defeats the wrong, as the benign song defeats an evil enchantment, and if this process is broadly the redemption of magic itself, then the Lady's song to Echo is itself redeemed by its benign double, the echo song to Sabrina. On this level magic works mimetically, as a force in the dramatic conflict between two magicians—two inspired speakers—with the Lady and her brothers "immanacl'd" somewhere between the poles of Comus and the guardian daemon.

The principle of echo, however, is subliminal rather than open and mimetic.[3] It works in the semiological domain half-way between morphemes and phonemes. It is on this cryptic level that echo is most powerful, and most significant for the later stages of Milton's poetic career. Consider the fact that *Comus* is so "indebted" to earlier poems that it might be called, not just a transcendental form, but a transcendental

[3] The sort of echo scene one finds in Samuel Daniel's *Ulysses and the Siren*, ll. 348 ff., or in Jonson's *Pan's Anniversarie*, ll. 205 ff., is a reminder that echo can reach the level of prophetic vision. Thus, in *Pan's Anniversarie*, Jonson calls Echo "the truest Oracle on ground." This subject has been studied by Marie Desport, in *L'Incantation Virgilienne: Virgile et Orphée* (Bordeaux, 1952), particularly ch. ii, "Importance poétique de l'Echo." In Miss Desport's study of the terms associated with echo, she shows the variety of pulsing, striking, sounding, answering, intoning terms which are prefixed by the Latin *re* (67–75). Most interesting, for the masque, is a term she studies in some detail, *ingeminare* ("to redouble as if by twinning"). Resonance is magic doubling of sound, as the pastoral song divided by two shepherds is a magical incantation. Echo is almost an obsession with Renaissance poets, as it had been with the Latin poets: e.g., Jonson, *Oberon*, l. 11, "He wound his cornet and thought himself answered, but was deceived by the echo"; ll. 298–308 (echo song by "two Fays"); *Masque of Beautie*, 281–292 (echo song); Browne, *Inner Temple Masque*, ll. 33–34, "The last two lines were repeated, as from a grove near, by a full chorus"; l. 145, "What sound our echoes day and night?"; Thomas Campion, *The Lord Hayes Masque*, l. 162, "So eccoes Zephyrus the friend of love" (referring to the myth of Zephyrus, the sweet western wind, that leads eventually to the romantic myth of the aeolian harp); ll. 380 ff., a complex echo song "of transformation"; ll. 250–288, a complex of echo effects in a repeated invocation to "Powerful Jove" which mirrors the continuous theme here of Orphic doubling, by which Orpheus' music "Helps to induce a courtly miracle" (l. 145); Davies, *Orchestra*, ll. 307–315, where the air's "prattling daughter," Echo, "dances to all voices she can hear." George Herbert's *Heaven* uses Echo in a structural way; cf. Richard Crashaw, *Music's Duel*, l. 92, where musical notes, "Fluttering wanton

pastiche. Echoes of Shakespeare's voice predominate, most obviously from *The Winter's Tale, Hamlet, Antony and Cleopatra, Macbeth, A Midsummer Night's Dream, Measure for Measure, The Tempest*—from so many and to such an extent that if Shakespeare alone were a source, we should wonder what Milton was up to. But there is also the spectral presence of Marlowe, Spenser, Sylvester, Drayton, Jonson, Peele, John Fletcher, and William Browne, among the more notable English authors; Tasso and Guarini among Italians; possibly the neo-Latin author of a *Comus*, Erycius Puteanus; and among the ancients, again more obviously, Homer, Virgil, Ovid, Horace, Aeschylus, and Euripides. But this is not all, since the mythographic texture recalls familiar encyclopedic sources for "pagan mysteries" and syncretistic combinations of Renaissance myth and theology—the sort of display the two brothers regale each other with as they wander about, two charming, helpless schoolboys on the edge of doom. Finally there is an infolded structure of Christian thought on the subject of the three Pauline virtues, faith, hope, and charity, and their variant (faith, hope, and chastity) enunciated by the Elder Brother.

The whole business is astonishing. With Spenser, who affords an instructive contrast, all attempts to drown the poet under a variorum of exegesis flow off the poet's back; the same is true of commentary on and annotation of *Comus*. But

---

shoales, and to the Sky / Wing'd with their owne wild Eccho's pratling fly"; Andrew Marvell, *Musicks Empire*, st. iii: "He [Jubal] called the *Ecchoes* from their sullen Cell." On echo in Milton and Continental poets, see Leo Spitzer, *Classical and Christian Ideas of World Harmony* (Baltimore, 1963), 102–106, 198–204; Hollander, *Untuning of the Sky*, 204, 229, 319–322, 350, 351, 366, and throughout, on musical *responses*. On echo effects in *Comus*, see J. T. Shawcross, "Henry Lawes's Settings of Songs for Milton's 'Comus,'" 22–28, especially 25: "The use of echoes can frequently be demonstrated, for example, between lines 18 and 1012."

as the commentary becomes more precise, more scholarly, it
seems oddly to fit the text better and better. Somehow Milton
courts exegetical overrefinement in *Comus*. Its verbal echoing
is a radical process, a going to the bottom of language. By
recollecting so many poets dead and gone, Milton revives
their voices and their ghostly persons. Verbal and literary
echoes here achieve a baroque extension of the etymological
domain, so that it covers, not merely linguistic roots in the
classical languages (with puns from Latin and Greek), but
closer, denser literary roots within the linguistic area of
English poetry.[4] *Comus* seems to have been written to prove
the coherence of this root structure.

A full annotation of *Comus* would lead to endless examples,
of which one, typical enough, will suffice. The Attendant

[4] K. K. Ruthven, "The Poet as Etymologist," *Critical Quarterly*, II,
No. 1 (1969), 9–38, presents the large picture of Renaissance poetic
etymologizing, which continues the encyclopedic tradition of Isidore
of Seville and suggests a renewed interest in Plato's *Cratylus*. Spenser
and Milton etymologize freely. Marino's *Adone* raises pastiche of
Dante to a kind of poetic root myth, which U. Limentani regards as
typical among the satiric poets who "flourished, without exception, in
the shadow of that Florentine court where Dante was worshipped as a
local glory" (*The Fortunes of Dante in Seventeenth-Century Italy*
[Cambridge, 1964], 9–10). The mannerist poet is fully committed to
his Hermetic literary thefts, whose art consists in knowing how to
steal. This *knowing how to steal* is not corruption of the texts of a
golden age, but their discontinuous renascence in a spirit of incantation. Theft here is a magical rite, as, for example, in the mannerism
of Stravinsky. In our own century this principle was developed by
Walter Benjamin in his preface, "The Task of the Translator,"
written for his own translation of Baudelaire, in *Illuminations*, ed.
Hannah Arendt, tr. Harry Zohn (New York, 1969), 69–82. Benjamin,
who wished to write books composed entirely of quotations, held that
translation is a largely syntactic event, "aiming at that single spot
where the echo is able to give, in its own language, the reverberation
of the work in the alien one." Benjamin understood language as a
kinship system animated by a cosmic web of intentionalities.

Spirit's opening soliloquy ends abruptly when he hears the tread "of hateful steps." He has just announced that he will take off his magic sky-blue robe "spun out of Iris' woof" and will disguise himself as a shepherd (thus for the first, but not the last, time in this masque introducing the act of impersonation, of masking, directly into the plot of the drama). The Spirit's transformations are magically easy, and having donned the shepherd's cloak, or perhaps having alerted the spectators that he will have donned it when he next returns to the stage, he must now disappear. "I must be viewless now," he says. The hateful enchanter is about to enter with his extravagantly visible "rout of monsters." Naturally the Spirit will be invisible, to begin his career as loyal guardian.

The English word "viewless" is first recorded by the *OED* in *Measure for Measure*, Act III, scene i. It occurs in the following dialogue between Isabella and Claudio:

> *Isabella.*   What says my brother?
> *Claudio.*   Death is a fearful thing.
> *Isabella.*   And shamed life a hateful.
> *Claudio.*   Ay, but to die, and go we know not where;
>   To lie in cold obstruction and to rot;
>   This sensible warm motion to become
>   A kneaded clod; and the delighted spirit
>   To bathe in fiery floods, or to reside
>   In thrilling region of thick-ribbed ice;
>   To be imprison'd in the viewless winds,
>   And blown with restless violence round about
>   The pendent world; or to be worse than worst
>   Of those that lawless and incertain thought
>   Imagine howling,—'tis too horrible.
>   The weariest and most loathed worldly life
>   That age, ache, penury and imprisonment
>   Can lay on nature, is a paradise
>   To what we fear of death.

And the conversation becomes more and more terrible, till Isabella says, "I'll pray a thousand prayers for thy death; / No word to save thee."

The already overburdened reader may doubt if the sort of verbal echo which seems tied to a unique original source, *Measure for Measure*, carries any weight beyond a shared concern with the terrors of death and the obligation of chastity. The "viewless winds" may be the natural prison of lost souls. But after we have observed such correlations and granted that others still are possible, is there anything significant in the echo itself? It seems very difficult to weigh the resonance of such an overlap of language. My own view is that the apparent disproportion of contexts, between *Comus* and *Measure for Measure*, fixes the deeper meaning of their being drawn together by Milton.

Milton does not use "viewless," among other borrowings, to get a particular meaning into his poem at this moment (though that does happen); instead, he uses it to bring the perspective of *Measure for Measure* into the poem at this point, so that we remember in both works the hovering presence of "th' invisible King, / Onely Omniscient." [5] Milton is then not borrowing or stealing the metaphysical term "viewless," but is acting as if Shakespeare had originally invented and used the word with the express prophetic intention that, later, a Milton could use it *again*.

"Viewless" resembles the "printless" of Sabrina's song, as she rises to enact the role of the *deus ex machina*:

> Whilst from off the waters fleet
> Thus I set my printless feet

[5] *Paradise Lost*, VII, 122–123. Maurice Merleau-Ponty develops his notion of the "intertwining" or chiasmus of the body's relation to the world in *The Visible and the Invisible*, tr. Alphonso Lingis (Evanston, Ill., 1968), 13–155.

> O'er the cowslip's velvet head,
> That bends not as I tread.   [ll. 896–899]

Water is the printless medium, to be sure, and the idea of imprinting is basic to traditional notions of prophetic typology, with its shadows and *impresas* of divine things. But the assertion of negativity here seems designed to unify the concerns of *Comus* in a rather particular way. Both "viewless" and "printless" suggest an entanglement or knottedness of opposites, activity and passivity. With "viewless," for example, it is not clear that the radical concept of *view* has the force of a noun or a verb, when combined with *less*. Is the viewless wind unseen, or unseeing? Is the printless foot an instance of the purest agency (activity) or reagency (passivity)? The ambiguity in these complex words is such that the reader or spectator is drawn to speculate, in a variety of directions, upon the nature of the visible and the invisible. More simply, one is led to think about that boundary condition which Merleau-Ponty would call "the limit between the body and the world." In his terms such figures as Sabrina embody an "intertwining" of the self and the world around the self. Such reciprocal interactions are perhaps dramatically sharpest when the actor's role deprives him of all easy and common forms of freedom. Sabrina is bound to the river. Claudio is imprisoned.

In the brief compass of Claudio's speech, three times within four lines Shakespeare uses the suffix *less*—"viewless," "restless," and "lawless"—and when Claudio's sister denounces him for his simple need to *live*, she calls him a beast and "faithless" coward. The suffix implies absolute deprivation, as when Milton applies it to the imprisoned Lady: "In stony fetters fixed, and motionless"; and when she is earlier called "helpless" and "aidless." But this absolute lack or loss of strength or virtue is not quite imposed from without. It inheres, rather, in the nature of postlapsarian selfhood.

Milton insists on the enforced solitude, the deprivation of society, which the Lady experiences as the victim of Comus, because the *Maske* is an attempt to present the conditions of true vision. This truth and this vision have an intimate connection with solitude. Comus separates the Lady from the dulling comfort that common society affords. When the Lady finds herself *alone*, she assumes the freedom of the solipsist, to see, and maintains her visionary hold of her Self by welcoming, while still alone, the forms or ideas of her guardian virtues: Faith (pure-eyed), Hope (white-handed, like Leucothea, the "white goddess" of the Spirit's invocation to Sabrina, and a reminder of the apostolic "hands" of the confirmation service), and finally, spotless Chastity: "And thou unblemished form of Chastity, / I see ye visibly, and now believe" (ll. 210–219).

Milton is searching for ways to express the paradoxes of moral perception, which here circle about the idea of form. To think of chastity as a form which the Lady can see "visibly" is to imagine the invisible to be so brightened that it can light its own way into visibility. At once the visible and the invisible become, in Merleau-Ponty's phrase, "deeply consonant" with each other. The spirit becomes the form of the body. The Attendant Spirit can assume the mantle of invisibility, because this viewlessness proves the absolute existence of his spirited nature, whose prime characteristic, paradoxically, is that it is invisible. Out of the simple fact that the Attendant Spirit is making a stage exit, Milton constructs the riddle that the most pragmatically unseeable beings—spirits —are those most perfectly formed, most capable of being seen "visibly," as the Lady says of the "unblemished form of

Chastity." The Attendant Spirit is completely free, to run or fly, and is in that sense also like the winds. Like the Genius of the Wood in *Arcades* he has the "chaste ears" of Pythagoras that could hear the music of the spheres, and thus his vision is parallel to a sort of audible audition (to restate the Lady's formula of visible vision). The word "viewless" has led to this intensified idea of a vision and audition that are so true that they have a complete consciousness of their own activity.

It is therefore significant that the source of "viewless" is *Measure for Measure*, a play concerned with the need for self-awareness in the act of judgment. "Viewless" as a verbal echo of *Measure for Measure* recalls the structure of that play as well as the particular use of the word in it. At the very least it appears that such echoes make literary memory an integral and integrating part of the Miltonic style. The recollection of "viewless" is structural, not accidental, and it is thus all the more extraordinary that in Milton's usage such devices seem effortless. The echo is an easy and yet precise remembering; it probably occurred to Milton as most ordinary memories occur to all of us, without strain. There is John Aubrey's account in the *Brief Lives*: "He had a very good Memorie; but I believe that his excellent Method of thinking and disposing did much to helpe his Memorie." It is at least possible that Aubrey was here referring to the Ramist system of "dialectical memory." [6] However Milton managed such feats of recall, they occur within his poem as if by magic. Microcosmically, they entrap the earlier context within the webbing of the present moment. Dissimilarities of particular reference enhance this effortless integration. In fact the process of such verbal echoing cannot occur unless the echo is a species of etymological affinity; each echo is a response

[6] Cf. Frances Yates, *The Art of Memory* (London, 1966).

joining word and root. As with the science of etymology, we are often beset by "false" or "popular" derivations, and these in turn may work in spite of a lack of genuine etymological connection. Punning upon both true and false etymologies, Milton is a traditionalist, the true son of Virgil the master of "secondary epic" style, and a worthy successor to another master of echo, Dante. The immediate inspiration was clearly Spenser, for whom echo is an essential prophetic device and who, in the Miltonic manner, is fascinated by the "disparity action" of his parallels, a characteristic which Berger aptly called "conspicuous irrelevance." [7] The technique allows the poet to have his cake and eat it, a proverb which, as George Herbert's poem on the problem, *The Size*, reminds us, is one definition of a transcendental form.

Chastity, virginity, and time

For a poet whose aim is to assimilate as much literature as possible and whose method is to employ the almost hermetic technique of verbal echo, the themes of chastity and virginity have peculiar advantages. Both themes, but chastity in particular, support the poet's sense of his own heroic vocation. Chastity provides a kind of built-in controlling irony, by which the semantic wealth of the poem (often under the surface, at the level of verbal echo) is set off against a virtue of restraint, temperance, continence, deprivation—the virtue of chastity. The virtue is implicit in the timbre of the Lady's song:

> At last a soft and solemn-breathing sound
> Rose like a steam of rich distilled perfumes,

[7] Harry Berger, Jr., *The Allegorical Temper: Vision and Reality in Book II of Spenser's "Faerie Queene"* (New Haven, 1957), chs. v, vi, 7. Cf. Richard Macksey and Gerald Kamber, " 'Negative Metaphor' and Proust's Rhetoric of Absence," in *Modern Language Notes*, Vol. 85, No. 6 (1970), 858–883.

> And stole upon the air, that even Silence
> Was took ere she was ware, and wished she might
> Deny her nature, and be never more
> Still to be so displaced.

This passage sets a level of delicacy from which Milton wishes us to reach out to the idea of the chaste. He is aware that chastity is a kind of action without acting. The chaste person has no mask.

Chastity has the further interest of including a way of *living* and loving in the world—thus Milton identifies chastity and charity—and this way is maximally free within the limits of a self-regulating nature. Thus Milton achieves a genuine impasse at the conclusion of the masque: the Lady cannot move, but Comus cannot possess her. She remains chaste in the palace of night, but the palace of night makes her chastity virtually irrelevant. Immured as she is, it is to no purpose to be chaste, since chastity implies acting in the world. She then falls back upon or allows the resurgence of another ideal, virginity, and to this she vehemently appeals. Her words do "shatter" Comus, and exactly when he feels and fears "her words set off by some superior power," the brothers rush in to perform the first half of her rescue, the smashing of the bacchic glass, the cantharus.[8] These preconditions fulfilled, the way is ready for the *deus ex machina*, which follows in due course, and the whole unwinds in comic festivity and mythic repose. But virginity was the source within the action for this arrival of the *deus*, and we need to ask how, besides its apparent connection with grace, virginity differs from chastity.

[8] See G. W. Elderkin, *Kantharos: Studies in Dionysiac and Kindred Cults* (Princeton, N.J., 1924). It may be that *kantharos* is at times in cult the name of the god Dionysus (88). Since the original contents of the cup are the blood of the god, it is possible for it to become the sacred calix, or chalice, of Christian rite (42).

Here the ages of the Egerton children may make a difference. We have to imagine that night of September 29, 1634.
The Earl's youngest daughter, Alice, who played the Lady
that in fact she was, was fifteen years old. She was, we might
say, perfectly marriageable. John, who treated the audience
and his younger brother to considerable doses of philosophy,
was eleven. Thomas, lagging a little behind in eloquence, was
nine. The poet plays upon their childhood. There was never
a more delicious absurdity than the Younger Brother's outburst:

> But O that hapless virgin our lost sister
> Where may she wander now, whither betake her
> From the chill dew, amongst rude burs and thistles?

Once one tunes in on this comedy one finds it everywhere. It
entices the critic away from grave doctrinal matters. Immediately the effect is a heightening of the innocence of the
children, along with a sense of their immaturity. Like an inspired tutor, the Elder Brother exclaims, " 'Tis chastity, my
brother, chastity." The repetition keys the tone, and it verges
upon farce. (Perhaps, as the remarks of Rhymer upon *Othello*
suggest, dramas of the absolutely pure lead in the direction
of the farcical.) At the same time, however, the children's
naïveté is a saving grace. Their sister enjoys her own special
grace, and its name is virginity.

Textual evidence suggests that in the original acting version of *Comus* there was a lighter emphasis on the idea of
virginity than we find in the published texts of the masque.
Both the Trinity and the Bridgewater manuscripts omit lines
779 to 806; that is, they lack the Lady's peroration on the
mystery of virginity. By adding this peroration, Milton develops the range of his fable and gives it a final framework.
For while in this fable virginity assumes chastity, chastity

does not require virginity. Virgin being transcends the chaste. In his final reworking of the text Milton suddenly throws the whole of the *Maske* into relief by clarifying this transcendence.

There are probably many ways in which to distinguish the chaste from the virginal, but here the most important distinction is that one can go on being chaste as long as one likes, but virginity (in its ideal essence, which is not to be confused with its merely physical aspect) suffers from entropy.[9] Virginity at fifteen is more perfect than virginity at fifty. Physically, of course, humans may remain virgins for life. But metaphysically the virgin state, which is defined by its beginning as an unspoiled oneness, seems to tend, as an idea, toward a virtual disorder. Virginity, like paradise, needs to be lost —preserved, it gradually loses its springlike nature. Virginity is a fountain from whose perfect source the stream can only move away into less limpid channels. Chastity, on the other hand, is a ritually present, continuously rededicated ordering of the self. It is a cyclical rhythm, by which one lives and,

---

[9] Metaphorically, insofar as "entropy" (among several senses) means the tendency of a system, including the universe, toward increasing disorder and inertness. In Neoplatonic terms, there is a premonition of the second law of thermodynamics, since "heat" is the force of the soul's will; see Sears Jayne, *John Colet and Marsilio Ficino* (Oxford, 1963), 62–65, on the relation of "the flame of love" (this "heat") to the Pauline triad. Jayne evolves the complex as follows:

charity	faith	hope
heat	light	unity
will	intellect	being
goodness	truth	power

This schema helps to account for the Lady's awareness of her peroration (ll. 792 ff.): "the uncontrolled worth / Of this pure cause would kindle my rapt spirits / To such a flame of sacred vehemence." She must resist the unvirginal heat of her raptus.

more important, loves. In *Comus* it is the double of charity and thus has no beginning or end. It is the perfect instance of Christian temperance for both Spenser and Milton, since they are able to conceive of "married chastity."

By contrast with this continuous recurrence of the life process, the state of virginity seems to imply temporal non-recurrence. The virgin is a person whose integrity, whose being as an undivided, unsplit self, as an *individuum*, authorizes the one-directional flow of historical time. One does not get a second chance at being a virgin. A loss of virginity is always perfect and in ritual custom is often celebrated as such. The bride thus "puts on perfection and a woman's name." Virginity is ceremonially praised for being an ideal inception. It may, for example, be said to be born or to begin on the date when the young woman or man is officially accepted into the community as capable and therefore desirable as a marriage partner, that is, as one who must lose virginity. In some cases this date will coincide with birth, in others with the onset of puberty, in others with a ceremonial initiation. The *Maske at Ludlow* is that initiation for the Lady and her brothers, and as such, just before the dances and the epilogue it "presents them to their father and mother."

If this account is substantially correct, it will follow that the "sage / and serious [and therefore Spenserian] doctrine of virginity" is Milton's doctrine of a true beginning. Like all beginnings, its generative aspect is mysterious. It is even absurd. It implies the arrow of time. The mythic guardian of music can choose to fly or run to his "Beds of hyacinth, and roses, / Where young Adonis oft reposes," but what will happen to the mortal Lady and her two mortal brothers? What has happened to their parents? Ironies deepen, like shadows over "all this tract that fronts the falling sun." And it is all done gracefully, with only the hint of tragedy.

The Lady's ecstasy

We are now in a better position to understand the enthusiasm of the Lady's harangue against Comus (ll. 756–799). The lines build to a grand climax, starting from an attack on the seducer himself and his false argument, proceeding to an assertion of a benign political economy (which ends with a reminder that we should be grateful to God, who, as *Paradise Lost* calls him, is the Nourisher),[10] then suddenly, at line 780, leaping into an ecstasy of rhetorical freedom. Praising and defending the "Sunclad power of Chastity" and the "sage / and serious doctrine of virginity," the Lady is transformed. She is suddenly overcome by her own rhetorical superiority over Comus. Her verbal magic is so powerful that she can now condescend to him: "Thou art not fit to hear thyself convinc'd." She envisions her voice and words as "a flame of sacred vehemence." As we have seen, it is an Orphic power ("dumb things would be mov'd to sympathize").

This is, strictly speaking, the moment of the Lady's recognition. She recognizes herself, in the act of recognizing Comus. In this moment she stands aside, or stands outside herself. The Lady, we could say in other terms, discovers here the

[10] The assimilation of food implies the assimilation of the godhead, as in Origen, *On First Principles*, tr. G. W. Butterworth, ed. Henri de Lubac (New York, 1966): "For as in this bodily life of ours we grew first of all bodily into that which we now are, the increase being supplied in our early years merely by a sufficiency of food, whereas after the process of growth has reached its limit we use food not in order to grow but as a means of preserving life within us; so too, I think that the mind, when it has come to perfection, still feeds on appropriate and suitable food in a measure which can neither admit of want nor of superfluity. But in all respects this food must be understood to be the contemplation and understanding of God" (153–154). In *Paradise Lost*, Milton calls this "intellectual food."

separate nature of her self. She has arranged this separation of her self from her surroundings and from all prior confused images she holds of her self, her destiny, her place in the world. In terms of the drama she discovers that to be alone in a forest or a dungeon is, in itself, a meaningless condition, as long as "alone" is understood only from the point of view of an external observer. If her getting lost and being left alone were chiefly to be judged by someone, let us say, standing on a high hill looking down into the forest, counting bodies, even that observation would deny significance to the fact of the Lady's solitude. To give only one aspect of this insignificance, such an observer could not know if the Lady "wished to be alone" or not. Of course what transfers meaning to this scene is the way in which the Lady herself interprets her actions, and she does not fully "find herself" as an interpreter until this peroration. Once carried along by its momentum, however, she comes upon the hidden truth of her selfhood, which is the shocking, even scandalous fact that she is not one with her captor or her brothers or any other man, but that they are *others*. She had been a "cryptic individual," a person unaware of the degree to which she was a person, a person whose personality was hidden cryptically from the only one who really needed to uncover that personality, that is, from herself.

This philosophical gaming with self and other may help to resolve the traditional crux of *Comus* criticism. Chastity and virginity in the *Maske* differ with regard to the self. If chastity is a stylistic virtue and virginity an absolute physical and metaphysical fact, the two occupy different places in the biography of the individual. If both then differ temporally, chastity may be said to lead to an awareness of the world outside oneself, while virginity leads to an interior knowledge of one's inner life. This difference between what might be called the opposed "directions" of the two virtues may now be stated somewhat more abstractly.

Assuming that the Lady possesses both virtues (strengths), her chastity then affirms the transcendent existence of the other; but her virginity affirms the transcendent existence of her self. Further, we can hold that her virginity affirms the transcendent existence of her immanent self, or more briefly, her own "immanent transcendence." This is apparent in the way the Lady perorates: she first separates the other in her paean to chastity, and then separates her self in the paean to virginity, which turns out to be an encomium of her own rhetorical powers, of powers indwelling in her through the fact of her intactness. She has learned that to be a virgin really means to be chaste for herself, not in another's eyes, but in her own. This chastity-for-oneself is the definition of an ideal "virgin territory" which the self occupies, while the heroine examines her passions and appetites, i.e., in affairs of the heart. She has been forced into a border situation and has found, through verbal magic, what country is marked out by her encounter with Comus. The dramatic shape of the *Maske* is thus akin to that of certain other plays of seduction, where the aim of the seducer is to get a lady to cross a line from which there can be no retreat (an absolute one-wayness that gives pathos, for example, to the exploits of Don Juan).

The roles of the Lady and Comus could be acted so as to suggest that it is she who would seduce him, but to a virtuous life. Their interplay is a drama of persuasive rhetorics. Because the Lady has for the first time discovered or uncovered her cryptic self, she can luxuriate in her selfhood. Her confident joy is expansive and transcendent to the degree that she has found words to express her intact virgin state as a metaphysical essence. Her body has become for her an ideal form, with ideal values, fully existent. For her there can be no void. Did no one in that September audience speculate on the character of the Lady Alice? We should not mistake the comic feeling of the entertainment. It was an affirmation of a community, as is usual with such masques. One likes to think that some petty scandal, universally disbelieved but somehow still circulating, attended the *Maske at Ludlow*. If there was one, we have no record of it. One cultural difference from our times needs to be stressed: the probability that for this audience physical sexuality possessed all the mythographic overtones necessary for an immediate shift into the realm of the "pagan mystery," which would tend to deflect the critical gaze of the ironist. Furthermore, the easy extravagance of the language and the comedy of it all, with the hapless brothers and the paradoxical Ariadne figure of the Lady, would allay any embarrassment in the great hall of Ludlow Castle. (In this sense *Comus*, like other early works of Milton, continues the tonal tradition of metaphysical wit.) Instead of a shudder at discussing such a tabooed subject in public, or the Widow of Windsor's "We are not amused," we get a manifest display of anthropological rhetoric. For the Lady, being a virgin is a public virtue, validated by a kinship system that matters a good deal more than her bodily state. As in most Old Comedy, the element of social structure is prominent in *Comus*, and it permits the poet to talk easily about the prohibition of license. Milton, I suspect, was not uninterested in this customary restriction upon the young growing up in a highly structured kinship system. But here he is after a more basic structure; he wants to find out and validate the grounds on which a person possesses his own voice. This discovering role he gives to the Lady. His theme permits him to impute to the Lady an absolute formal clarity of being (her "virginity"), which she realizes gradually, through speech, and then uses to ground her own dream of personality.

The mere fact that physical virginity is so trivial gives it astonishing metaphysical force, as *Paradise Lost* shows with the triviality of the forbidden fruit.[11] And, oddly, this force comes from the structuralist implications of virginity; the loss of virginity is like a breakdown in universal logic; to be unchaste to make an error in drawing a single implication. In the highest sense, therefore, *Comus* performs the office of the traditional masque, in that it asserts the logical coherence of society by representing dreams of reason.

To prefer virginity over chastity is to prefer dynastic integrity over moral decorum. But it is also to assert that in this highly structured noble society of the Egertons, moral decorum cannot lead anywhere without the dynastic system. So the *Maske* makes a public exhibition and encourages a public acceptance of the Lady's happy destiny, which is that she discover herself in a sacrament of initiation into womanhood. Let us emphasize here, not the secondary marvel of chaste womanhood, but the primary and prior marvel of self-discovery. The Lady is transformed in the course of the *Maske* from a cryptic individual into a revealed person, who knows herself and therefore can be known by others, who knows the other and can therefore know herself.

[11] One of Empson's points in "All in *Paradise Lost*," in *The Structure of Complex Words*, 101. Empson's great work is, from one angle, the analysis of what I am calling the "principle of echo." A word like "honest" almost literally *echoes* through *Othello*, as it echoes other works and usages outside the play. But as a principle, echo in the present essay leads generally to incantation and magic symbolism, which is not true in every Empsonian case (e.g., Pope's use of "wit" in the *Essay on Criticism*). Empson perhaps stresses the intellectual and structural aspects of echo, while I try to stress the emotive and dynamic aspects; both stresses should interact.

Typological repetition

Suppose then that *Comus* never mentioned virginity. The *Maske* would not be the same, but it would be appropriate, interesting, and no doubt successful as an entertainment. And yet Milton is making a dramatic distinction between the two virtues of chastity and virginity, which follows from their relation to time and temperance. The demand "Be chaste" will be met by a continual vigilance and rededication of powers. The metaphysical resource of this rededication is the Platonic anamnesis, the "recollection" that opens the eye of the mind to the eternal idea of a thing, thereby giving a perfect intellectual plan to follow. According to a Platonic format, to reach back or up into this intellectual realm requires the discipline of the mind.[12] Within the Christian framework it requires an Augustinian training of the memory, which makes the mind present to itself. For Augustine, notably, the memory is identified with the father, and readers of the *Confessions* and the *De Trinitate* will remember that, as a modern scholar puts it, memory is "a psychological focus through which conversion is initiated, reformation gained out of time and multiplicity." [13] Augustine himself simply said that memory is the entire width and depth of the mind which learns how to know itself and how to direct its will toward the right kind of love. This last typically Augustinian reference to love recurs in the Miltonic alteration of the Pauline triad, to comprise faith, hope, and chastity, for a powerful

[12] See the series of essays of Harry Berger, referred to in his "Archaism, Vision, and Revision"; also his "Pico and Neoplatonist Idealism: Philosophy as Escape," *Centennial Review*, XIII (1969), 38–83.

[13] G. B. Ladner, *The Idea of Reform: Its Impact on Christian Thought and Action in the Age of the Fathers* (New York, 1967), 202.

verbal echo brings the two cardinal ideas of chastity and charity together as the final reflection of each other.

Another reason may be given for associating chastity and recollection. Seen in the larger perspective of ethnology and anthropology, the Platonic doctrine of anamnesis appears, as Eliade and others have shown, to point to the stratum of human thought that is *strictly* archetypal. Anamnesis includes the intellectual recapturing of those ideal forms that resist the flux of time and mutability. Platonic thought generally betrays the most acute anguish and attentiveness in its reaction to human mortality. But one residual effect of the metaphysical doctrine of anamnesis has been a tendency, among poets at least, to harmonize the metaphysical doctrine with those more primitive archetypal myths that revolve around the eternal return. Spenser makes a useful Renaissance example, for while his poetry breathes the Platonic view of the purity and beauty of "intellectual love," it simultaneously presents the most vigorous mythography of human and natural fertility. The seasonal myth is every bit as strong as the metaphysical eternal return. And Milton reflects this inheritance in *Comus*. Chastity is the guarantee that temperance will rule the seasons of love and procreative power.

Virginity is not in the same sense a procreative virtue. Yet it holds a higher place. This superiority forces us to think about it differently. Anamnesis will not define the metaphysic of virginity. But a notion advanced by Kierkegaard,[14] and familiar in the older traditions of prophetic typology—the idea of "repetition"—will account for the temporal aspect of the Lady's virginity. To be chaste she needed only to remember, to recollect the archetype of the virtue. But to sustain the

[14] Søren Kierkegaard, *Repetition: An Essay in Experimental Psychology*, tr. and ed. Walter Lowrie (Princeton, N.J., 1941; repr. New York, 1964).

more brittle state of virginity it would not be enough to work toward continuous rededications and eternal returns of the springtime of the body. Virginity, once lost, would induce despair, were the loss not capable of a restoration in the absurdist terms Kierkegaard proposed.

His idea of repetition is so simple as to seem useful only in a farce, and his examples in the half-fictional treatise, *Repetition*, are at first weird and humorous. He attempts, for example, to "repeat" a former journey to Berlin, with comically disastrous consequences. His question, seemingly clear on the surface, was, Is repetition possible? Can something happen twice? Can you hear the same sound twice? When you say, "I saw him again in Philadelphia," what have you said? This seems to be a variant on the philosophical puzzle as to what is meant by the term "same," but here a temporal factor has even further complicated the problem. Kierkegaard gives farcical instances of what he has in mind, but he clearly wants to think about repetition on a more serious plane, for his final example is the repetition of the blessings of Job. Job, who had lost everything, once again found everything, and even more than he had lost. The blessings of Job, in Kierkegaard's formulation, were doubled. That is, the later blessings were "the double" of the earlier. They were the repetition of those earlier blessings. They were their echo.

The Kierkegaardian notion of a repeated act or situation has at least two aspects that illuminate what Milton is doing in *Comus*. On the one hand there is a literary mystery, a mystery of pure diachronic sequence, the sort of thing Jorge Borges implies in his story "Pierre Menard, Author of the *Quixote*," where two identical passages appear face to face, the one written by Cervantes, the other produced independently by Menard.[15] Ironically, Borges calls the repetition a

15 In *Ficciones*, ed. Anthony Kerrigan (New York, 1962).

"revelation," and we can perhaps say that he is most interested in the fact that although events may never duplicate each other, the words used to name them may be repeated, and in literature at least there is no theoretical barrier to an exact "repetition."

Another and more Miltonic idea of repetition in Kierkegaard's sense would seem to be the traditional theory of biblical typology, or the repetition of persons and events according to a basic identity, by a prophetic leap from the Old Testament to the New Testament. Unlike the doubling of signs that allegory demands, where a thing or a person stands for an abstraction, here one person stands for another person —Joshua stands for Jesus, for example. This historicity of typological symbolism has been much commented upon. The mode is forward-looking and prophetic in the most radical sense. The prefiguration of New Testament events by those of the Old Testament provides the historical structure for the prophetic tradition upon which Christianity, as a temporal system, is built. Thus, to the extent that *Comus* introduces the higher virtue of virginity in order to add this temporal dimension to the fable, it gives the sort of typological perspective which any orthodox Christian of Milton's time would accept without question. Milton himself would have been more than usually disposed to think typologically.

His mythic use of Sabrina does give this temporality to an otherwise nontemporal collision between Comus and the Lady. For Sabrina and the Lady are related to each other, not only through recollection, but more importantly through repetition. The Lady can continuously refine and refind her chastity. But she can be guaranteed the continued possession of her virginity only because Sabrina intercedes for her. The Lady and Sabrina share the repetition almost equally: both

are assaulted, both are saved; both have been changed by
events, both have been saved in their essentially unchanged
purity; both have been threatened with death, both have in
effect been made immortal.[16] By introducing the legend of
virginity as an old tale of local history, Milton gives an immediately typological coloring to the salvation of the Lady.
She and Sabrina are doubles, not just archetypally, but also
"historically." In the treatise on *Repetition*, Kierkegaard holds
that the philosopher must ground the "interest" of metaphysics in the novelty and the antiescapist character of repetition. He speaks of repetition—of our command of it—as
"the task of freedom." This he believes on the ground mainly
that without basing life on the possibility that events could be
doubled, repeated, echoed, shadowed—and he uses all these
terms—man could not avoid mere chaos and noise. Without
repetition no constructive forming of life would be possible,
and no intelligent and emotively sound choice of action
would have a chance of success. The avowedly miraculous
aspect of repetition does not disturb Kierkegaard, for he must

[16] Insofar as Kierkegaard's *Fear and Trembling* analyzes sacrifice
and utterance, it relates closely to *Comus*. One might compare the
Lady with his ideal tragic hero, who "like every other man is not
deprived of the power of speech, can at the instant of his culmination
utter a few words, perhaps a few appropriate words, but the question is whether it is appropriate for him to utter them. If the significance
of his life consists in an outward act, then he has nothing to say, since all
he says is essentially chatter whereby he only weakens the impression
he makes, whereas the ceremonial of tragedy requires that he perform
his task in silence, whether this consists in action or in suffering. . . .
On the other hand, if the significance of a hero's life is in the direction of spirit, then the lack of a rejoinder would weaken the impression he makes. What he has to say is not a few appropriate words,
a little piece of declamation, but the significance of his rejoinder is
that in the decisive moment he carries himself through" (tr. Walter
Lowrie [New York, 1954], 125).

believe in it if only for its absurdity. I am not trying to turn Milton into Kierkegaard.[17] Yet there is a Puritan affinity of thought that occurs the moment *Comus* shifts to the higher plane of the Lady's ecstatic peroration on the virgin state. In any event Milton would agree with Kierkegaard that "the true repetition is eternity," and he might add that virginity is the earthly double of this eternal stability. On the other hand, the particular interest of such a repetitious rather than recollective ideal is its human, earthly, moral context. History, typology, repetition—they are tied to the most local and time-bound of myths. Here it is the myth of Sabrina, whose actual river—the Severn—seems to flow in the poem with the water of life. She pours that water, which is an eternally flowing, englobed, complete substance and at the same time is an emblem of the virgin's intact state. Sabrina sprinkles wholeness on the Lady, and she is set free. The repetition occurs for Sabrina, because she and the Lady have become one, sharing a baptismal rite; it occurs for the Lady in the same sense. If we fail to believe this mystery, Milton may be content that we believe something more common:

[17] *Repetition*, like other works of Kierkegaard, is much concerned with the theatre as the framing scene of personality, personation, discovery, reversal. Here the idea of theatre is to be understood as the primary metaphor for mind. The word *theatrum* is pregnant with meanings for Christian theology, a fact which has confused arguments about the existence of actual theatres in earlier times (see Dino Bigongiari, "Were There Theatres in the Twelfth and Thirteenth Centuries?" in *Essays on Dante and Medieval Culture* [Florence, 1964], 157). Modern thought on the mind, beginning at least with Hume, uses the idea of a theatre for analyzing temporal flow: "The mind is a kind of a theatre, where several perceptions successively make their appearance; pass, re-pass, glide away, and mingle in an infinite variety of postures and situations" (David Hume, *A Treatise of Human Nature*, quoted by Aron Gurwitsch, "William James's Theory of the 'Transitive Parts' of the Stream of Consciousness," in *Studies in Phenomenology and Psychology* (Evanston, Ill., 1966), 306.

that while for the Lady this is a true repetition, as for true believers miracles are simply facts, for us her miracle can be virtually miraculous. The poet will be content with the "art" of a Prospero, whose "great globe itself" is a virtual miracle and whose alchemy is the human imitation of an other-worldly condition of absolute wonder. Like the refrain of an old ballad, the Lady's rescue carries wondrous, if deliberately dumb, conviction.

To manage this repetition, with its acceptance—one might even say its creation—of time and temporal passage, the *deus ex machina* must be divided in two, so that the brothers and their counsel or Thyrsis may save the "lower" virtue, chastity, while Sabrina and her psychopomp, the Daemon, may rescue the "higher" virtue, virginity. The first rescue resides fully in the realm of magical spells and their reversal, and it affirms the metaphysical principle of Platonic recollection. The second rises higher because, as a repetition, it is achieved through what amounts to a prophetic structure: the whole process of the invocation to Sabrina, her epiphany, her baptismal participation, her reciprocal exchange of place with the Lady (*"Sabrina descends, and the Lady rises out of her seat"*), her departure, and the promise of reward given her by the Spirit. Structure has the higher function, particular charms and particular insights into human nature and psychology the lower. For Milton, although he wants in this virtuoso performance to force his reader beyond the confines of drama as fact, into drama as mystery and metaphysic, must come across, as we say, with a hard dramatic action. This hardness he can, and does, learn from the lighter masques of his masters. He is led to the myth of sacrifice. He discovers the dramatic form implied by his metaphysical interests. *Comus* is a comedy of sacrifice, whose structural form we can more easily grasp if we contrast it with its double, the tragedy of sacrifice. We may speak of the Lady as Northrop Frye has spoken of certain tragic heroes.

Because the heroic is above the normal limits of experience, it also suggests something infinite imprisoned in the finite. This something may be morally either good or bad, for the worst of men may still be a hero if he is an individual, but being so great an individual he seems constantly on the point of being swept into titanic forces he cannot control. The fact that an infinite energy is driving towards death in tragedy means that the impetus of tragedy is *sacrificial*. Sacrifice expresses the principle that in human life the infinite takes the same direction as the finite.[18]

In those tragedies of Shakespeare that seem most sacrificial, plays like *Othello*, *Lear*, or *Antony and Cleopatra*, there is clearly enough amplitude of character and action to convey this entrapment of the infinite in the finite. Such, comically, is the effect of the *Maske at Ludlow*.

Ricercare on a theme of atonement

The end of *Comus*, as the masque was transcribed for the 1637 edition and then substantially copied for the 1645, is remarkable from the formal point of view. From lines 975 to 1010 the Attendant Spirit's epilogue presents a mythological *tableau vivant*. The effect of tableau is common in masque-making, but its usual method is staged presentation, by which the scene, costume, and statuesque dance visually render what here Milton has compressed into the verbal medium. The technical reason is obvious: it was convenient at Ludlow Castle not to attempt such elaborate staging. Even the visual chiasmus of the Lady rising as Sabrina descends could be staged with extreme simplicity, since its idea far outweighs its

---

[18] *Fools of Time: Studies in Shakespearean Tragedy* (Toronto, 1967), 5.

physical splendor, despite the probability that a director could seize on it for brilliant spectacular purposes. Yet we have seen before that in *Comus* the poet took advantage of limited facilities. The suppression of spectacle leaves words free to hold the listener. To the virtuoso it is important that the Spirit have the last word.

Had Milton omitted the Spirit's tableau, or relocated it in the manner of the Bridgewater Manuscript, his masque would have ended on a much more didactic plane, like *Pleasure Reconciled to Virtue*, whose fourth song the Spirit's last lines recall, with their image of Heaven stooping to aid earth-bound Virtue. Such final songs are typically spare of imagery, in line with their valedictorian purpose, whereas the Spirit's final tableau is a debonair revelation of Elysium. The Spirit charms the ear, pours languor on the eyes, and when he says his task is "smoothly done," we believe him. Like the ecphrasis of a classical poem, lines 975 to 1010 leave the reader suspended in an imaginary space. Perhaps then the *Maske* intends to move toward this suspension, which may recall Prospero's farewell to the revels of *The Tempest*.[19] The tableau, by im-

---

[19] The difference between *Comus* and the Shakespearean masque is somewhat like that between the two meanings of "reflexion," as given in Pierre Thévanaz, *What Is Phenomenology?* ed. J. M. Edie (Chicago, 1962), 114: "Either *reflect* means to project onto a new level, and then it is the movement by which the subject, starting from a sort of original unity which cannot be grasped as such, tries to grasp itself by dissociating itself, by dividing itself or by doubling back on itself, by multiplying itself. This reflexion, by means of a centrifugal motion and by successive regressions, gradually reaches a state of greater expansion and proliferation around the original central point, a play of infinite reflections. [This I should call Shakespearean reflexion.] Or *reflect* means to concentrate oneself, to go from multiplicity towards unity by a centripetal motion. The subject thus moves from a state of dispersion or distraction; he turns to himself, he collects himself, simplifies himself and concentrates himself at his center. By an ascesis or by stripping himself (by 'reduction,'

mobilizing time and movement, comes to represent the motion of epiphany itself, the movement of a polyphonic music.

It is no doubt systematically significant that in recent years two major theorists of myth, Northrop Frye and Claude Lévi-Strauss, have persistently recurred to the analogy between mythmaking and musical form. Music and "the musical," we have seen, played a systematic part in Milton's career, and this could not have happened except as an aspect of the Miltonic demand upon myth.[20] Here in *Comus* the demand is simpler than it was later to be, in the epics or in *Samson*. But the musical analogy will be as revealing to us as it was seminal to Milton.

The *Maske at Ludlow* is a ricercare, a figure searching out

Lagneau would say), he rediscovers his immediacy, his immediation to himself, his coincidence with himself." Is this not the movement of Milton's consciousness, which ends, centered and ascetically "reduced" in *Samson Agonistes?*

[20] Frye, *Anatomy of Criticism;* Claude Lévi-Strauss, *Le Cru et le cuit* (Paris, 1964). The point is perhaps supported by Donald Davie, "Syntax and Music in *Paradise Lost,*" in *The Living Milton,* ed. Frank Kermode (London, 1963), 83–84, where although Davie will not allow the "music" of the poem to be "a structural principle, as it is in the invocation to Light, leading on the reader's lively interest from line to line," on the other hand the music "is a matter of vocal colouring and skillul resonance, leading only the voice and the ear." My view would be that voice and ear are typologically so full of *sense*, in *Paradise Lost,* as elsewhere with Milton, that "only the voice and the ear" are of very great significance. Robert Beum, in his article "So Much Gravity and Ease," provides suport for the present argument for a principle of echo. Observing that in Italian, "the language itself rhymes," Beum then shows that through assonance and alliteration Milton gets one effect of rhyme: linkage. "What one thinks of first is the power of these acoustic repetitions to augment unity of impression by binding together phonologically groups of lines that form a close semantic bond" (*Language and Style in Milton,* ed. R. D. Emma and J. T. Shawcross [New York, 1967], 354).

its thematic implications, on the theme of atonement. The musical search has its themes and harmonic structures—chastity, virginity, temperance, pleasure, and so on—and the *Maske* arrives at a final, festal, Hesperidean tapestry because all along it weaves that tapestry. Atonement, the supernatural mode of community, is the transcendental theme of the *Maske* when we experience it as an ensemble. The theme has various values in post-Reformation theology, one of which suggests an adjustment of what has been said about *Comus* and *Measure for Measure:* their thematic link is not their shared concern with chastity and justice, but with chastity and the living process of justification. Justice as an ideal is a hermetic exercise in perfect form; but as a human creation and human enterprise it is scarcely perfect. Man simply errs, for a thousand reasons, and there seems to be no way to lead him to do what is completely right, rational, or even sensible, let alone what is kind. For one thing, who is certain what these words mean? Knowing this uncertainty and this intractability, the philosopher and the saint, from their apparently opposite corners of the room, have arrived at the sacramental construct of atonement as the means of "justification."

Whether the sacrificed Son of God ransoms the fallen Adam, or whether through a more perfect obedience Adam saves himself, there emerges with the Reformation a *contractual* sense of the atonement whereby someone, either the Savior or man himself, pays a debt to the Father. In these matters, to use two modern terms, Protestant thought is capitalist and oedipal. Such theology rejects the mediation by the gracious Virgin (and thus, incidentally, *Comus* might be read as a witty anti-Catholic tract, showing the incapacity of the Virgin to save herself or anyone else). But perhaps more significant to Milton at this stage of his career is the fact that a very deep interest in the legalistic, and specifically in the nature of contracts, had preoccupied Shakespeare (as perhaps it must interest all great tragic dramatists). Since a contract is one human means of imitating God, it typically forms the basis of *Measure for Measure*. Over this brittle study in *limpieza de sangre* there hovers the mystery of a justice embodied in a disembodied, absent, all-knowing, godlike ruler. Such dramas explore the idea of mediation.

In the court masque the protean figure of Daedalus had always mediated a justice of some kind, and this had led, following the antimasque, to a final state of reconciliation between powers. The masque typically would echo the Christian drama of Christ and the Dragon, Jesus and Satan, who fight to save or wreck the "king's peace" of the Father. The Son of Man, our only mediator and salvation, sets the divine pattern for the conciliatory Attendant Spirit in *Comus*. In *Measure for Measure* memories of the Eighty-fifth Psalm persist, with its reconciliation of the Four Daughters of God —Justice, Truth, Mercy, and Peace—and in that play, as in *Comus*, certain apparent artificialities of ritual fall into place and become natural, if we accept a liturgical purpose: both plays dramatize atonement in its original sense, as "at one-ment." [21]

[21] *OED* cites "To reconcile hymselfe and make an onement with god" (1533); "Having more regarde to their olde variaunce then their newe attonement" (1513); "There shall be now atonement of this strife" (1605); "Water is the proper atonement of the rage of fire; and that which changes a tempest into a calm, is its true atonement" (William Law, 1752). *OED* quotes from and glosses the important text Romans 5:11: "Our Lord Iesus Christ, by whome we have now received the atonement." Theologically, also, atonement applies to the redemptive work of Christ and the expiation of sin. On Milton and the doctrine of the atonement, see C. A. Patrides, *Milton and the Christian Tradition* (Oxford, 1966), 121–152. For a more general discussion, see E. O. James, *Sacrifice and Sacrament* (London, 1962).

A drama arrives at atonement when the characters come home. The Lady and her brothers enter their community (the ideal Ludlow, governed by their father, the Lord President) after wandering, getting lost, and being found, put on the track, and brought to their doorstep. This theme of homecoming is not unknown to pastoral poetry: Colin Clout came home again; in Marvell's poem *The Mower to the Glowworms* the speaker admits: "And I shall never find my home." In fact we could speak of a homecoming motif, in the musical sense.[22] The notion of home is highly structured. It serves to close off myths of quest, of marriage and covenant, of foundation and contract, where the end state is likely to be imagined as either a physical or metaphysical home. On a lower level home means physical shelter and dwelling (with the attendant idea of temporal extension, e.g., *dwell on an idea*). This is the level of Lear's first insight, in the storm. On a higher level home includes the family, with its warmth and kinship. On a yet higher level it connotes a range of sharings: first, as Husserl claimed, of "the commonness of Nature"—the sharing, we could say, permitted by common sense—and second, as Husserl might also say, the sharing of the openness and perspicuity of this nature, so that as members of an ideal community we become monads, ideal windows in a real landscape:

[22] Yet a motif, musically used, permits variant and metamorphosing shapes of the single idea. This is the supposition of Curtius, in his study of *topos*, in *European Literature in the Latin Middle Ages*, as it is in the practice of an author like Joyce, Thomas Mann, or Hesse. See Thomas Mann, *The Story of a Novel* (New York, 1961), on the method of *Doctor Faustus*, which besides being an almost perfect example of transcendental form, is also, significantly, structured on the myth of musical form and musical resonance, relying heavily on echo devices and finally including a character named Echo. Mann is the more interesting because he knew precisely what Faustian labor this transcendental form committed him to.

It is also clear that men become apperceivable only as finding Others and still more Others, not just in the realm of actuality but likewise in the realm of possibility, at their own pleasure. Openly endless Nature itself then becomes a Nature that includes an open plurality of men (conceived more generally, animalia), distributed one knows not how in infinite space, as subjects of possible intercommunion. To this community there naturally corresponds, in transcendental concreteness, a similarly open community of monads, which we designate as transcendental intersubjectivity.[23]

Husserl, in this intricate and not entirely open passage, suggests the limits of the ideal community, such as a masque might lead us to know. The masque has to risk the opening out of social structures. It must let the disorder flourish for a time. But the masque may then open up the eyes of the participant actors in a final scene. One assumes, without thinking, that here perception takes precedence over cognition, but perception itself is stretched beyond all common limits. The final tetrameters of *Comus* are full of piled-up imagery, like the strettos of a fugue; they project what Husserl called "a realm of endless accessibilities." At the close of the Spirit's epilogue all sorts of classical images—channels from material

[23] Husserl, *Cartesian Meditations* 120, 130. The reader, thinking here of Leibniz, may turn to Frye, *Anatomy of Criticism:* "In the anagogic phase, literature imitates the total dream of man, and so imitates the thought of human mind which is at the circumference and not at the center of its reality. . . . When we pass into anagogy, nature becomes, not the container, but the thing contained, and the archetypal universal symbols, the city, the garden, the quest, the marriage, are no longer the desirable forms that man constructs inside nature, but are themselves the forms of nature. Nature is now inside the mind of an infinite man who builds his cities out of the Milky Way. This is not reality, but it is the conceivable or imaginative limit of desire, which is infinite, eternal, and hence apocalyptic" (119). On the infinite mind as a magical formation, see also Cassirer, *Individual and the Cosmos*, 112, 122, 148–151, 169.

to spiritual reality—may be said to belong to the Lady. She possesses, and is possessed of, a certain freedom. That such a conclusion happens apparently only on the level of mythic elaboration, as in these final strettos, should alert us to the problem of "argument" in *Comus*. The *Maske* is making a mystery out of logical distinctions, the chief of which, dramatically at least, is the distinction between the two paired virgins, Sabrina and the Lady.

They are alike in the essential of virginity. They differ, not so much in the what or how of their stories, as in the when. This temporal difference may be what makes possible the dramatic use of Sabrina: because *once upon a time* she had left the domain of human time, she can now return from her "immortal change," to save the Lady, her double. The sacrificial doubling of the paired virgins follows the normal arrangement of a sacrificial drama, in which one victim (on a higher level) atones for another victim (on a lower). Such doubling seems to be necessary in sacrifice, but it also yields a metaphysical proof that a miraculous order of things prevails, according to the Kierkegaardian principle of "repetition." [24] Doubling implies not only a typological symmetry of two persons, two masks—which is mysterous enough in any case; it also leads to the belief that one of the doubles can flow into the other. Why not, after all, if they are echoes of each other? The double walks through the mirror into itself, like Alice.

On the other hand, the typical presence of the priest at the sacrifice, and the presence of the Attendant Spirit here, is functional, suggesting that the doubling alone is not enough for transcendence to occur. The Attendant Spirit is a mediating "third party" who adds something essential to the idea

[24] *Repetition*, 117. Cf. Paul de Man, "The Rhetoric of Temporality," in *Interpretation*, ed. Charles Singleton (Baltimore, 1968), 190.

of the sacred pair. He himself is the double, inverted, of the villain, and as such he would theoretically be part of his own sacrificial drama. But as an active person in the masque the Spirit seems to be associated with triplicities of all sorts: the three daughters of Hesperus; the three Graces; the three "rosie-boosom'd Howrs"; the triad of Adonis, Venus, and her son Cupid; and finally the more general triad-making power the Spirit himself enjoys, by which, when joined with any pair, he can add to theirs his own third voice. Edgar Wind's analysis of the triadic stance of the Graces has made us aware that such triplicities restore harmony to the conflict between unity and diversity, and then go beyond this restoration to something rather less strictly geometric. Alastair Fowler has shown how this triplication occurs in *The Faerie Queene*, where there are reminiscences of Orphic and Pythagorean doctrine.

Thus, early cosmogonies in the Pythagorean tradition commonly distinguished three stages of creation: (1) undifferentiated unity; (2) the separation out of two opposites to form the world order; and (3) the reunion of the opposites to generate life. This generative union of sundered opposites in the triad was often referred to as a marriage; so that the triad was the first of the so-called marriage numbers.[25]

The symbolism of numbers is not pure fiction. The child of two parents completes one kind of triad exemplifying generative harmony. Similarly, the self can be the child of one's double being.

The role of the priest is the management of an initiating trial, by which the "victim" of initiation enters into the domain of the triple mystery. Largely because the priest is there, the initiate emerges from trial *more* than she was before that trial. This "increase of selfhood" happens on at least two

[25] *Spenser and the Numbers of Time* (London, 1964), 19.

levels, the lower of which is socially useful, and the higher metaphysically necessary. The Lady ends her trial enjoying freedom on these two levels. The lower relates to the social structure called "reciprocity," a structure the initiate is enabled to escape from, through the help of the priestly shepherd. The higher level of freedom transcends social life and pertains to the soul and its immortal life. In principle one can reach the latter freedom through a perfection of the former. "Reciprocity" is the anthropologist's term for a general social system of mutual dependence, obligation, and even entrapment. "Briefly, the idea is that society is created and maintained through a complex network of exchanges—mainly of goods, women and language—between men, so that everyone is so dependent upon someone else for his vital needs that no escape from social life is possible." [26] Comus, in his defense of luxury, argues that nature is a vast reciprocating system, set up to serve such appetites as his; the imagery in lines 705 to 754 thus rather resembles that of the Shakespearean passage analogizing the state and a hive of bees (*Henry V*, I, ii), and in both cases reciprocity is the burden of the myth. Comus

[26] This and the following quotations from E. M. Mendelson are from "Initiation and the Paradox of Power: A Sociological Approach," in *Initiation*, ed. C. J. Bleeker (Leiden, 1965), 214–221. See also, in the same volume, S. G. F. Brandon, "The Significance of Time in Some Ancient Initiatory Rituals," 40–48. Mendelson is developing ideas launched by Claude Lévi-Strauss, for whose concept of diametric dualism, concentric dualism, and triadic organization, see his *Structural Anthropology*, tr. Claire Jacobson and B. G. Schoepf (New York, 1963), ch. viii. *Comus* could be analyzed as a familial drama of social structure, with Comus acting the role of the bad uncle, the Spirit acting the role of the good uncle. But Comus as a drama of spirit requires either a Neoplatonic analysis for its triadic imagery or a return, via Neoplatonism and Hermetic idea, to the gnostic or simply "Orphic" terminology. On the Orphic theology of triads, see G. R. S. Mead, *Orpheus* (London, 1965), ch. v, where the author discriminates seven triadic levels.

must attack the Lady's virginity, if not in fact, then as an idea, for it is impossible to insert that transcendental virtue into the bondage of natural reciprocity.

Yet before her trial the Lady is still a creature of that natural system. She must go through initiation, like Tamino and Tamina in *The Magic Flute*. Mendelson has argued:

The importance of initiation, in its broadest aspect, lies in that it offers a way out of reciprocity. The stress, in initiation, is always upon self-improvement, self-enhancement, self-completion: it is always something that is being *added* to the initiate and, if anything is subtracted from him by abstinence or sufferings, it is only a first stage so that something greater, more important, may ultimately be gained.

Various levels of transcendency in the methods of abstinence are possible: "The lower man will consider abstinence as a means of acquiring more power; only the higher man, the world-renouncer, will understand that abstention is an aim in itself." One is inevitably suspicious of such mystical goals, but if *The Magic Flute* is a legitimate parallel, we are entitled to find in *Comus* that, through the absolute perfection of the Lady's abstinence (which her brothers cannot share, busy as they are, eating berries), power is transformed into knowledge, and this gnostic truth obviates the need and the will for power. Such gnosticism may not be precisely Christian orthodoxy, but it is Miltonic enough, and it leads through and beyond the condition of grace, which is a state of unconditional weakness, as Christ taught in the Sermon on the Mount.

Paradoxically, although Christian meanings are strong throughout *Comus*, the *Maske* does not hesitate to draw the logical conclusion from the nature of its dramatic form, that all levels of initiation are not equal—as in *The Magic Flute* Papageno's initiation is not equal to that of Tamino—nor, it would seem, are all men, as potential initiates, equal. The fact of initiation leads to the thought that society must take a paradoxical view of human equality, on the one hand asserting it from the point of view of justice, on the other denying it as a fact of being. Equity, which plays such a powerful role in *The Magic Flute*, justifies this apparent lack of justice. It can also be invoked to justify the royal authority of the Lord President and his idealized daughter, the Lady. There is a sense in which only a royal figure, male or female, can be initiated at the highest level.

As Mendelson observes, "It is the king who normally commits what we might call 'crimes against reciprocity'; it is he who has more goods than anyone else and more women and it is he, where incest is committed, who usually commits it." Remembering then the overt parallel between the Lady and a crowned prince (she finally rules Comus and has to be saved by Sabrina only because the wand of Comus, his scepter, is not taken from him when the two brothers, her knights, rush in), we are less surprised by the insistence on her temporary exile from human company and comfort.

The king must be outside society to a certain extent in that he has to serve as a link between it and para-social forces. Thus everything happens as if the king is self-reciprocating: he renders a cult to himself, he marries his own blood, his goods are so taboo that no one inferior can touch them; he is imprisoned in a kind of self-sufficient solitude of which we get echoes as late as in Shakespeare and which is the most exalted characteristic of the ideal initiate.

The Lady's chief goods are her integrity of soul and body, while, reaching out beyond philosophical discourse into the magic of "para-social forces," she finds herself almost alone in the realm of spirit. Her baptismal entry into knowledge reverses the Oriental formula applied to initiatory success:

"The self itself explodes into nonself"; here the nonself explodes in a flame of sacred vehemence into self. A production of *Comus* would have to convey the royalty and separateness of the Lady through her demeanor. The delicacy of Sabrina's invocation and song may obscure the parallel necessity that she too be rendered as royally as possible. One can mistake the sense of the stage direction, "Sabrina rises, attended by water-nymphs, and sings," for her spectacular entourage seems to be inappropriate to her simple maidenhood. In the mind's eye she may appear girlish and maidenly, and nowadays her name may even suggest a Nabokovian nymphet. Such a conception will destroy the dramatic illusion of a true sacrifice.

Sabrina is a goddess, and though strictly a nymph, she is the presiding deity of a great river. She localizes the Severn as a divine power whose history is legend. She is here a typological figure, possessing the freedom of water itself, which means, in religious terms, the freedom conferred by baptism. She belongs to that select company of gods, associated with water, whose habit is to metamorphose themselves after the fashion of Proteus.[27]

Michael Drayton apostrophizes Sabrina's divinity in the fifth book of *Polyolbion*, just before recounting the birth of the mythic British prophet Merlin. Through local lore, if not through such a literary source, the higher legend of Sabrina would have been familiar enough to the audience at Ludlow, and from it they would have been led to expect what Milton also gave them, a regal apparition. Drayton's Sabrina is appropriately regal:

> Now *Sabrine*, as a Queene, miraculouslie faire,
> Is absolutelie plac't in her Empiriall Chaire

[27] Simone Viarre, *L'Image et la pensée dans les "Metamorphoses" d'Ovide* (Paris, 1964), 341.

Of Chrystall richlie wrought, that gloriously did shine,
Her Grace becomming well, a creature so Divine:
And as her God-like self, so glorious was her Throne,
In which himselfe to sit great Neptune had been knowne.

This goddess, Drayton tells us, had learned the arts of prophecy and had been given the privilege and duty of adjudicating
quarrels between warring waters. In her rule of all "this
mightie rout" she is the divinized River Severn, whose name,
Sabrina, is the one used in the old maps, where she appears
wearing her coronet, as in the map for Drayton's 1612 *Polyolbion*. What Lévi-Strauss would call the natural "hyperbole"
of myth appears in the fact that although Sabrina had, in Spenser's account and in Geoffrey of Monmouth's version, been
the victim of a royal scandal, she has at last assumed the rank
and title of a queen in her own right. Thus, because Sabrina's
epiphany in *Comus* is splendid, we may easily forget the
tragedy that underlies her coronation, her murder by a mythical "terrible mother," the jealous Guendolen, who is actually
Sabrina's stepmother. One implication to draw from the myth
of Sabrina would be that absolute purity is the female defense
against the fury of the terrible mother, and further that the
maiden would not be chaste, unless it were politic to be so.
Another is the deeper and more tragic reading, that even perfect virginity in her daughter does not satisfy this frustrated
mother who, having lost her own virginity, finds herself the
complete victim of fate. For her virginity is the name for
whatever is capable of being absolutely lost. Her rage answers
the fatal injustice. It also answers the more personal loss of a
virginity that guarantees to the female her value within the
social system of reciprocity. Milton follows the typically folk-
loric "displacement," in which the role of the enraged mother
is played by a stepmother, which tones down the most fearful
implications.

Milton's alterations from sources in Geoffrey of Monmouth and Spenser (or even Drayton) decrease the sense that Sabrina is the victim of personal envy and increase the weight of her sacrificial innocence. In Geoffrey, Guendolen has Sabrina drowned; here the maiden leaps into the flood. The voluntary leap is the original, etiological authorization for Sabrina's present gentleness; what she once gave freely—her life—she can give again, "if she be right invoked in warbled song." In fact the conclusion of the *Maske* places the Lady in a rather strictly ordered sacrificial structure. Sabrina, for example, shares the essentially tractable nature of the traditional victim described in the classic essay of Hubert and Mauss: "Above all it must be persuaded to allow itself to be sacrificed peaceably, for the welfare of men, and not to take vengeance once it is dead." [28] Not much is left here of the propitiatory ritual, but the Spirit's invocation serves such a purpose, while his promises of "full tribute" to her, after she has saved the Lady, place the sacred seal upon the liberation of the sacrificial spirit. Through Sabrina the Spirit has linked sacred and profane worlds. Sabrina is not destroyed in the present tense of the drama, because, like Christ, she had been destroyed and reborn in its past tense. Thus the Spirit, like the priest at Mass, re-enacts her death and resurrection in his report of the old legend (ll. 823–857), while the drama of the masque as a whole plays out roughly this same action through the experience of the Lady.

There is in fact far more genuine violence in *Comus* than in the typical collision of masque and antimasque, so that the manner of ending the *Maske* requires much skill. While the ending of *Comus* is full of submerged themes and mythic motifs reintroduced in a final coda, its chief dramatic aim is

[28] Henri Hubert and Marcel Mauss, *Sacrifice: Its Nature and Function*, tr. W. D. Halls (Chicago, 1964), 30.

the propitiatory calming of a sacrificial storm. Hubert and Mauss studied such calming as a stylized form of "exit." Typically, the priest removes his robe and returns to the sanctuary, "in order not to spread abroad the consecration." Often the utensils and accoutrements of the ceremony are washed and put away. Survivals of such customs appear in the Christian Mass, since the Communion chalice (here parodied by the cantharus of Comus) is washed and the priest washes his hands, after which the ceremonial cycle is over and the priest pronounces the words of dismissal: *Ite, missa est*. The closing ritual is the reverse image of the opening one; exit is parallel to entry. "The faithful and the priest are liberated, just as they had been prepared at the beginning of the ceremony." [29] Milton, following orthodox lore, confounds priest and faithful with the transformation of human agent (Thyrsis) into divine agent (the Spirit).

Comus is not unusual in its insistence on the vertical axis of human-divine transcendence. Hubert and Mauss speak of the

[29] *Ibid.*, 97. See also R. Money-Kyrle, *The Meaning of Sacrifice* (London, 1930), 178–180, on Hubert and Mauss. Note the curious parallel in Hubert and Mauss with what Edward Said says about origins: "The central fact of primitivism is not just its precedence, but its unobjecting assent to its own originality" (*"ABECEDARIUM CULTURAE:* Structuralism, Absence, Writing," to appear in *Tri-Quarterly*). In line with this, in Thomas Mann's *Doctor Faustus*, the Devil, in dialogue with Adrian Leverkühn as they are about to make their pact says: "A genuine inspiration, immediate, absolute, unquestioned, ravishing, where there is no choice, no tinkering, no possible improvement; where all is as a sacred mandate, a visitation received by the possessed one with faltering and stumbling step, with shudders of awe from head to foot, with tears of joy blinding his eyes: no, that is not possible with God, who leaves the understanding too much to do. It comes but from the devil, the true master and giver of such rapture" (tr. H. T. Lowe-Porter [New York, 1963], 237). In chapters xliv and xlv of *Doctor Faustus*, Mann creates the sacrificial persona of his nephew, Frido, to whom he gives the fictitious name of

priest, at sacrifice, "rising progressively into the religious sphere," where he "attains a culminating point, whence he descends again into the profane." [30] Roger Wilkenfield, in his rich analysis of the various transformations permitted by the "hinge" of *Comus*, has shown that the *Maske* rests on a complex structure of verticalities, and observes that "in his epilogue, the Spirit recalls and reinforces all that has happened, and reinterprets preceding events in the new light of the various vertical levels of the sky." As Wilkenfield notes, "the masque ends with a final emphasis on the vertical motif: 'Heaven itself would stoop'; the action of the masque has shown Heaven stooping in the form of a 'rising' Sabrina, and this paradox returns us to the opening lines of the masque and the sense they convey of heaven's bourne." [31] *Comus*, in these terms, is a rare ceremonial. A dramatic fiction, it permits Milton to use, instead of a priest, a daemon, who descends momentarily to "the smoke and stir of this dim spot, / Which men call earth." The earthbound "priest" of the *Maske* is then, not the Spirit, but the malign magician, Comus. This arrangement at once complicates the drama and any account we might wish to make of it. But verticality seems thereby to have become even more insistent than in a drama where the priest is human to start with, and subsequently "rises" to a transcendent place. One cannot doubt the rightness of Wilkenfield's stress on the stage direction "the Lady set in an

---

Nepomuk—"Nepo, as his family called him, or 'Echo' as ever since he began to prattle he had called himself" (461). In the novel Mann kills Echo. On the deeper implication of this fictitious name, see *The Story of a Novel*, 146, 153, 211 and 224.

[30] *Sacrifice*, 47.

[31] "The Seat at the Center: An Interpretation of *Comus*," in *Critical Essays on Milton from ELH* (Baltimore, 1969), 149, 150. This collection also reprints essays on *Comus* by Richard Neuse and Gale H. Carrithers.

enchanted Chair to whom he offers his Glass, which she puts by, and goes about to rise."

And yet there is a horizontal countercurrent, which is of cardinal importance to the poet. The verse is continually and in endless variety of form and texture subverting the metaphors of vertical movement upward to heaven, downward to hell. Verse is horizontal. The Lady's song to Echo promises the nymph that, if she helps, she will be "translated to the skies." Echoes are an earthly phenomenon, like their nymph. Echo is the guardian spirit of the passage of sound through space, and her principle of being thus permits the poet to create what Hubert and Mauss call the "continuous movement" of sacrificial ceremony. Echo guarantees the "rhythm of recurrence" of that narrative mode which underlies the "drama in epic style." [32] Verbal echo channels language on a verbal plane.

The *Maske* seeks a modality of flow, symbolized in the final epiphany by Sabrina's "sliding chariot." But the verse of the *Maske* is not a symbol. The verse, we might say, is real. Its elemental fullness need not be psychoanalyzed as the spirit of permeation. The verse is the poetic means by which the immanent, in the paradox of transcendental form, achieves an "immanent transcendence." For while ideas rise up like perfume from the themes a poem projects, the poem itself can remain "horizontal," as an event in human and terrestrial time. To this end the transcendental form possesses and is possessed by easy energy, unimpeded virtuosity, the ordering of massed detail by a magical suspension of organizational difficulties, so that all seems to hang together. There is a sublime empty-headedness about this whole enterprise, and it is in marked contrast with the more restrained, wittier, sharper, more

[32] This is the rhythm identified as epic in Frye, *Anatomy of Criticism*, 251–262.

modest aims of works that do not seek such virtuosity—a life by Isaac Walton, for example.

There is also a haunted atmosphere, for works like *Comus* are haunted by the past of language—after Shakespeare, a past too rich with ghostly affinities for any but the most daring poet. A meditation upon his sources led Milton to rediscover the verbal flux. At the same time he was led to the fact that poetic language is a kinship system, through whose structure myths and legends remain typologically alive in different ages. Words mirror the mutability of human life. Thus when the daughters of Nereus save Sabrina, dropping ambrosial oils "through the porch and inlet of each sense" to save her, their medicinal care is the inversion of a famous poisoning. The Spirit echoes the Ghost of Hamlet's father, who thus accused Claudius: "And in the porches of mine ears did pour / The leperous distilment." Such reversals are of the very essence of mystery as a verbal phenomenon.

The pun, the verbal double, must be a linguistic ghost, while echo would enchain the verbal wit that leads to madness, containing puns within a sequential prosodic system. In a larger perspective images of metamorphosis depend upon the verbal phenomenon of punning, and because echoes propagate in waves, a flowingness seems to inhere in the metamorphic process.[33] The change from one state to another (Sabrina alive, Sabrina dead, Sabrina alive) is, when looked at, a discontinuous break. But Milton and poets like him are determined to show that something persists *through* the change and break. *Implicitness* is the quality of this persisting

[33] The meditation *On Virginity* of Gregory of Nyssa envisions purity as a marriage of rivers: "If we could collect these wandering and widely scattered channels into one single stream, we would have a full and compact waterflow which would be useful for the many needs of life' (*From Glory to Glory*, ed. Jean Daniélou, tr. Herbert Musurillo [New York, 1961], 103).

element. Dramatically, the implicit resources of a myth or a phrase are maintained by the poet close to the surface of his play, but are always held just below that surface. In *Comus* the most important instance of subsurface implication is the use of the myth of Circe. Throughout the *Maske*, Milton suppresses the myth of the terrible mother. "Who knows not Circe, daughter of the sun?" [34] The continuous allusions keep Circe subliminal, while her child by Bacchus must take all the responsibility for actions that (we can imagine) he learned from his own mother. The inseparable bond between Dionysus and the mother, analyzed archetypally in *The Bacchae*, refers us to ideas of creative and destructive power. Milton seems particularly willing to plant sinister Circean traces in his fable because they concern his own vocation and its need for a chaste pursuit of craft. Comus, child of Circe, is a false virtuoso whose "gay rhetoric" is the maddened freedom of ecstasy without form. He is one of the Dionysian archetypes of ancient myth, the Loosener. His engulfing appetites are the demonic parody of transcendental virtue. In contrast with the

[34] The almost cavalier tone of the question averts our attention from the inner meaning. Consider, as a gloss upon the Miltonic treatment of chastity in the *Maske*, "Of Christian Charity," in *The Rule and Exercises of Holy Living* (1650), where Jeremy Taylor provides "remedies against uncleanness," to guide young virgins in the paths of purity. He warns the virgin and the chaste woman to "*fly from all occasions*, temptations, loosenesses of company, Balls and Revellings indecent mixtures of wanton dancings, idle talk, private society with strange women, starings upon a beauteous face, the company of women that are singers, amorous gestures, garish and wanton dressings, feasts and liberty, banquets and perfumes, wine and strong drinks, which are made to persecute chastity; some of these being the very Prologues to lust, and the most innocent of them being but like condited or pickled Mushrooms, which if carefully corrected, and seldom tasted, may be harmless, but can never do good: Ever remembering that it is easier to die for chastity than to live with it."

shepherd, he gorges himself on language. And this imbalance he learns from his mother. Yet Milton is withholding much of the direct narrative content of the myth of Circe, and it is this withheld content that fills the interior spaces of the myth of Comus, Thyrsis, the Lady, her brothers, and Sabrina. Circean myth is present in *Comus* as a tacit dimension. Sabrina had suffered a "quick immortal change," and in a way this is the perfect reduction of the *Maske* to its elemental source. The pun on "quick" points to a liveliness—that is, a continuity in change—as much as to a lightening speed. This pun can distract us from another, deeper one, on the inwardness of change. The process of metamorphosis here resembles that of musical modulation.[35] The *im* of "immortal" is a

[35] In Thomas Mann's *Doctor Faustus*, Adrian Leverkühn says: "There is something very odd indeed about this music of yours. A manifestations of the highest energy—not at all abstract, but without an object, energy in a void, in pure ether—where else in the universe does such a thing appear? We Germans have taken over from philosophy the expression 'in itself,' we use it every day without much idea of the metaphysical. But here you have it, such music is energy itself, yet not as idea, rather in its actuality. I call your attention to the fact that that is almost the definition of God. *Imitatio Dei* —I am surprised that it is not forbidden. Perhaps it is" (78). Martin Heidegger states the same metaphysical problem in another way: he will seek to reverse the main trend of philosophy by which thought has focused on "entities-within-the-world" (mostly natural objects), and instead will go back to "the phenomenon of the world" itself (*Being and Time*, 133). This enterprise is the philosophical parallel to the composer's and poet's search for transcendental forms. For the Renaissance the philosophy of "aroundness" finds an aesthetic parallel in what Panofsky has called the "redefinition of idea." Thus Federico Zuccari, in *L'Idea de' pittori, scultori ed architetti* (1607), by assuming a *disegno interno* or "inner design" as the creative form-impulse—the "idea"—gives the artist the transcendent power of rivaling God and allows him "to bring forth a new intelligible cosmos" and "to compete with Nature." See Erwin Panofsky, *Idea: A Concept in Art History*, tr. Joseph J. S. Peake (Columbia, S.C., 1968), 85–95.

privative, a negating prefix, whose obvious effect of undoing the mortal state is the primary sense of the words here. But a verbal echo that began early in the *Maske* and that comes to a climax in the Spirit's invocation to Sabrina, the acoustical mirroring of negation by immanence, here makes "immortal" a kind of "antithetical primal word." The reader will notice (and the audience would have been unknowingly affected by the fact) that between lines 823 and 857, where the Attendant Spirit recounts the myth of Sabrina, he uses the word "in" or a parallel verbal form at least a dozen times, an average of once every three lines (not counting the endings of words like "urchin" and "virgin"). For example, Nereus saves Sabrina while letting his daughters "imbathe" her "in nectared lavers strewed with asphodel." One need not press further the acoustical force of assonance on the letter *i*, in words like "river" and "still," in order to recall from elsewhere in the *Maske* a phenomenon of inwardness, signaled by words like "imbrutes," "immured," "immanacl'd," and the like.

The phenomenon demands an explanation, and to a degree the concept of a transcendental form, in which ideas, instead of exploding, turn inward, can be adduced for the purpose. But what, more directly, is the sense of this play on being *in* or *into* or *inside?* The simplest answer is in a way the deepest, it seems to me. "In" is the opposite of "out," and such antitheses have been a very English interest for many centuries; Nancy Mitford's U and nonU apply as much to the England of 1634 as to that of our time. It is a curious piece of grotesque realism that at the very moment when King Lear imagines that he and Cordelia will become God's spies, he remembers the courtly fashion of knowing "who's in, who's out." In the terms of *Comus* the initiate is brought into society and, imprisoned thereby or not, is now "on the inside."

But Milton is not the kind of poet who is only concerned with the externals of social integration. A fuller level of interiority for him is that which comes from the mythographic suppression of the explicit patterns of human behavior—a suppression he practices in his use of Circe. Such denials of the explicit lead to an immersionist vision. Here at least inwardness is a condition of flowing, immersion a state of rebirth.

The idea of sacred drowning is functional; that is, it actually provides the dramatic action, in one way or another, in a poetic genre which has great literary influence on *Comus*. Strictly in the family of masque, *Comus* is half the child of the English Ovidian "minor epic," the epyllion, in which often a hero or heroine is assaulted by a friendly or unfriendly seducer.[36] The defense of chastity is one of the essential themes in such poems, and it leads to a poetry of mellifluous ease. It provides, for the period, the archetypal dramatic structures, reversal and discovery, in their mathematic form. The two greatest dramatists of the time—Shakespeare in *Venus and Adonis*, and Marlowe in *Hero and Leander*—are masters of the epyllion, and that is no accident. Even the ruminative Drayton almost climbed into drama when he wrote his exquisite Ovidian experiment, *Endimion and Phoebe*. In all such poetry there is a tendency to cover up the graver and more tragic values of myth, restoring them to the level of the implicit, and it is this secret-sharing that Milton introduces from the epyllion into his masque.

The other and final aspect of inwardness in the "quick immortal change" is more cosmic. If it is true that the *felix culpa* originates and then governs the providential destiny of Christian man, it will be working here, no less than in *Paradise*

[36] As described by Hallett Smith, *Elizabethan Poetry* (Ann Arbor, Mich., 1968), 116–125.

Lost. Before Newton, the concept of the Fall conferred concentric unity on the universe. Things, like man, fell inward because there was nothing else they could do. They had to fall, homeward, into the center. Things were not thought to be universally attracted in every direction; they were subject to the simple mythographic axis of verticality. The fall of man was a metaphysical vertigo. Because man stood up, to become man, myth was arranged first under a vertical heading. One effect of this myth of standing upright was a tremendous, sublimely simple coherence. Adam's standing up was a silent utterance, needing no words with which to affirm. A secular lyrist, Sir Walter Ralegh, could say that man, however rich in love, is poor in words. Sir Philip Sidney could hold that the true poet "nothing affirmeth," because he counted on the silent affirmation of human verticality.

But even in man's erectness tragic pride was realized, as Milton demonstrated in his myth of the towering Satan. *Paradise Lost* is built upon the most massive symmetries and mysteries of narrative structure, all of which turn upon the *answering* role of Christ the Redeemer.

> O goodness infinite, goodness immense!
> That all this good of evil shall produce,
> And evil turn to good; more wonderful
> Than that which by creation first brought forth
> Light out of darkness!   [XII, 469–473]

Darkness is the mother of light. Silence is the mother of sound. What is inward must in some deeper sense always be what is negative, as what is immortal must be what is held *in* death. Milton built his symphonic defense of free speech, the *Areopagitica*, out of this riddle. Dark and night too are the times of procreation. Like *Paradise Lost*, the *Maske at Ludlow* has to make a connection between the creative and the

answering redemptive act. Conceived as atonements, "at one-
ments," these acts overlap each other. The poet's act of atonement, itself a response, is a search for response. The audience
may answer. It may not be inert. The dramatic action may
flow into the audience, "through the porch and inlet of each
sense." Echo fixes the limits of response, for when we call out,
we are answered by our own voices only. When we look
outward, we discover our own image. The poem reaches out,
into its own vitals. In this sense atonement leads to an immanent transcendence. Atonement leads us back into this
"impossible pig of a world," and to this end enlists the ritual
forms of sacrifice. Atonement holds nothing valuable in any
other world. Our interest, which atonement demands we accept for what it is, must then be confined to what is and what
can be, to "the facts of life." The stimulus for atonement is
always the uncertainty of survival.

Perhaps then Sabrina is the listener. She rises to the invocation of the Logos, the Attendant Spirit, for he is the shepherd
of the cosmos and of the individual soul. She is the song
responsive to his prayer. She expresses the spirit indwelling in
the Attendant Spirit. When, like a nurse, she has blessed the
Lady, she pre-empts the place of speech, and the Lady says
not a word—not because the Spirit will not let her, but because it is not logical for her to speak. To speak would be to
return to the wasteland of loss. Sabrina *has* spoken. She is the
Amen of *Comus*. Now the Lady can meet her parents, with
her brothers, as if for the first time. For the first time she has
experienced her own presence.

The revels begin. The Attendant Spirit leads them. Sabrina
steps from her metaphysical car and with the others she
dances, till all are exhausted. At the appropriate moment the
revels "now are ended." Everyone is still while the Spirit—
the music master—sings his closing lines. He describes Ely-

sium. All assent, without thinking. Inwardly they applaud their own good luck. The general sense of leisure is complete. The children are laughing. The Lord President advances to congratulate Comus on his "gay rhetoric," and as the two go out together, the guests prepare to leave the great hall to the silence of its darkened tapestries.

A Note on Blake's
Illustrations for Comus

Among the numerous illustrators of the poems of Milton, William Blake is remarkable in that he is a major poet. Perhaps because Blake was both poet and painter, his illustrations do more than decorate the texts they accompany—they comment on the written word. The pictorial critique presumes the authority of the literal text. As Marcia Pointon observes, in *Milton and English Art,* "no illustrator more closely follows Milton's pattern of idea and image and few are so precise in following details of the text." [1] This faithfulness to the text is everywhere apparent in the two sets of illustrations for *Comus,* in which Blake makes revealing changes from the first to the second set. The first series of eight drawings was finished about 1801; it was done for a patron recommended by the sculptor John Flaxman, a certain Reverend Thomas. This series is now in the collection of the Huntington Library in San Marino, California. In the following notes I shall refer to it as the H-series. The later set, produced sometime between 1805 and 1810 for Blake's regular patron, Thomas Butts, is

[1] Toronto, 1970, p. 138.

253

now in the Boston Museum of Fine Arts. I shall hereafter refer to it as the B-series.

Various elements in both H and B suggest that Blake wished to reveal the uniqueness of *Comus*. Whereas most illustrators of *Comus* are content to extract the merely scenic interest of the work, Blake follows its inner iconographic flow of ideas. His pictorial style, especially in B, has affinities with music and the dance, and these affinities, though difficult to define, are an aspect of a larger interpretive purpose, namely a reading of *Comus* as a transcendental form.

Perhaps the most important critical development, from H to B, is the increased sense in B of an elusive but nevertheless pervasive "interiority" of image. The *Maske at Ludlow* itself builds an iconography of inwardness, playing on the word "in," and in like manner the second series of pictures appears to undercut the grossly theatrical energies of the first series, replacing them by a quieter, more flowing interpretation of the drama. Various technical changes lead to this effect of an apparently effortless virtuosity: the generally more delicate modeling and subtle placement of the figures within each frame, the heightened lambency of the water-color tones throughout the second series, the greater articulation of the middle ground in each picture of B, the contemplative style which in B replaces the assertive, declamatory style of H.

Such overall changes of approach are not necessarily improvements—not all readers will prefer B to H. But it may be fair to say that, just as we have found Milton's *Comus* going beyond the focused theatrical splendor of the usual court masque, so here Blake's second series of illustrations advances from a theatricality in the first series to a more interior, more flowing drama in the second.

The theatrical, with its strong emphasis on dramatic gesture

and sharp visual contrasts of dark and light, gives way to the
musical, with figured gesture and a sense of echoing, inter-
nally resonating symbols. In the H-series, for example, the
opening scene shows Comus' rout in rough gesticulation,
whereas the B-series stylizes the torches and hands into elegant and balanced configuration.

Blake's second series is openly more musical than his first,
to the degree that in B the actors adopt more dancelike, less
agonistic postures than in H. The increased choreographic
control and containment in B create a heightened impression
of "speculative music," which we have found to be a medium
of transcendental forms in general. Throughout B, Blake
seems to have given more attention to the gracefulness of pos-
ture. In the fifth scene, for example, the Lady's hands rest on
her knees, instead of being crossed over her breast, as in H.
This repose of arm and hand suggests an openness—a constancy—which is absent in the more theatrical gesture of
defense which Blake had earlier given to her. (The change
from a sign of the cross to the resting hands follows the
intent of the *Maske*, which would replace the magic of signs
and portents by the magic of calm motion, i.e., music.)
Generally speaking, in B there is a tendency to illuminate the
picture plane more powerfully through the figures of the
actors, which thus possess an iconic brilliance, while cor-
respondingly the picture is less dependent on the stagy lighting typical of the backgrounds in H. A model of this search
for iconic radiance would be the unexpected use of the rainbow, which in the seventh scene of series B repeats the crown
of light around Sabrina's head. While this rainbow, not
present in H, echoes line 83, recalling the Attendant Spirit's
robe spun from a rainbow, or echoes line 300 (the "colours
of the rainbow"), its immediate effect is an increase of radi-

ance, as if one were looking, not at, but through the picture. Such effects, while exceedingly difficult to define, still work upon the reader as ambience. This heightened coherence of ensemble is projected throughout series B, in the sense in which I have used Hofmannsthal's term "ensemble" to define "transcendental form."

Blake's Illustrations for Comus *in Eight Scenes*

Two Series

FROM THE

Henry E. Huntington Library and Art Gallery
San Marino, California

AND FROM THE

Museum of Fine Arts
Boston, Massachusetts

The scenes from the first series (Huntington) are on left-hand pages, and the same scenes from the second series (Boston) on the facing right-hand pages. Commentary on these pictures may be found in "A Note on Blake's Illustrations for *Comus*," page 253.

SCENE 1. Comus with His Revellers; the Lady Lost in the Wood

COMUS *enters with a Charming Rod in one hand, his Glass in the other;
with him a rout of Monsters, headed like sundry sorts of wild Beasts,
but otherwise like Men and Women, their Apparel glistering. They
come in making a riotous and unruly noise, with Torches in their hands.*

(Courtesy of the Museum of Fine Arts, Boston; gift
of Mrs. John L. Gardner and George N. Black, 1890)

COMUS. Meanwhile welcome Joy and Feast,
   Midnight shout and revelry,
   Tipsy dance and Jollity. . . .
   Run to your shrouds within these Brakes and Trees;
   Our number may affright: Some Virgin sure
   (For so I can distinguish by mine Art)
   Benighted in these Woods.

SCENE 2. Comus Disguised as a Shepherd Addresses the Lady

COMUS. Can any mortal mixture of Earth's mold
Breathe such Divine enchanting ravishment?
Sure something holy lodges in that breast,

(Courtesy of the Museum of Fine Arts, Boston; gift
of Mrs. John L. Gardner and George N. Black, 1890)

And with these raptures moves the vocal air
To testify his hidden residence;
. . . I'll speak to her,
And she shall be my Queen. Hail foreign wonder,
Whom certain these rough shades did never breed.

(Courtesy of the Henry E. Huntington Library and
Art Gallery)

SCENE 3. The Brothers Plucking Grapes

> COMUS. Two such I saw, what time the labor'd Ox
> In his loose traces from the furrow came,
> And the swink'd hedger at his Supper sat;
> I saw them under a green mantling vine
> That crawls along the side of yon small hill,

(Courtesy of the Museum of Fine Arts, Boston; gift
of Mrs. John L. Gardner and George N. Black, 1890)

Plucking ripe clusters from the tender shoots;
Their port was more than human, as they stood;
I took it for a faëry vision
Of some gay creatures of the element
That in the colours of the Rainbow live
And play i' th' plighted clouds.

SCENE 4. The Brothers Meet the Attendant Spirit in the Wood

> ELDER BROTHER. *Thyrsis?* Whose artful strains have oft delay'd
> The huddling brook to hear his madrigal,
> And sweeten'd every musk rose of the dale.
> How cam'st thou here good Swain? hath any ram
> Slipt from the fold, or young Kid lost his dam,
> Or straggling wether the pent flock forsook?
> How couldst thou find this dark sequester'd nook?

SPIRIT.   . . . a small unsightly root,
  But of divine effect . . .
  And yet more med'cinal is it than that *Moly*
  That *Hermes* once to wise *Ulysses* gave;
  . . . if you have this about you
  (As I will give you when we go) you may
  Boldly assault the necromancer's hall.

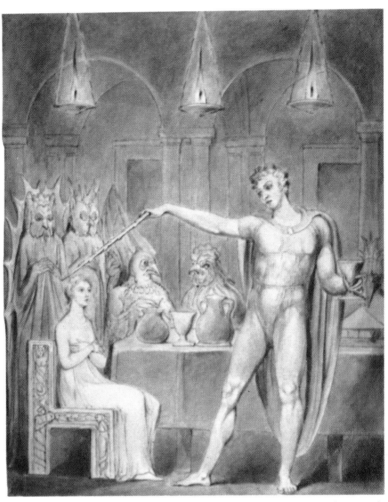

SCENE 5. The Magic Banquet

The Scene changes to a stately Palace set out with all manner of deliciousness; soft Music, Tables spread with all dainties. COMUS *appears with his rabble, and the* LADY *set in an enchanted Chair, to whom he offers his Glass, which she puts by, and goes about to rise.*

(Courtesy of the Museum of Fine Arts, Boston; gift
of Mrs. John L. Gardner and George N. Black, 1890)

Comus. Nay Lady, sit; if I but wave this wand,
  Your nerves are all chain'd up in Alabaster,
  And you a statue; or as *Daphne* was,
  Root-bound, that fled Apollo.

(Courtesy of the Henry E. Huntington Library and Art Gallery)

SCENE 6. The Brothers Driving out Comus

The Brothers rush in with Swords drawn, wrest his Glass out of his hand, and break it against the ground; his rout makes sign of resist-

(Courtesy of the Museum of Fine Arts, Boston; gift
of Mrs. John L. Gardner and George N. Black, 1890)

ance, but all are driven in.

SCENE 7. Sabrina Disenchanting the Lady

> SABRINA. Shepherd 'tis my office best
> To help ensnared chastity;
> Brightest Lady look on me,
> Thus I sprinkle on thy breast
> Drops that from my fountain pure
> I have kept of precious cure,

Thrice upon thy finger's tip,
Thrice upon thy rubied lip;
Next this marble venom'd seat
Smeared with gums of glutinous heat
I touch with chaste palms moist and cold.
Now the spell hath lost his hold.

(Courtesy of the Henry E. Huntington Library and
Art Gallery)

Scene 8. The Parents Welcome Their Children

> Spirit. Noble Lord, and Lady bright,
> I have brought ye new delight,
> Here behold so goodly grown
> Three fair branches of your own.
> Heav'n hath timely tri'd their youth,

(Courtesy of the Museum of Fine Arts, Boston; gift
of Mrs. John L. Gardner and George N. Black, 1890)

Their faith, their patience, and their truth,
And sent them here through hard assays
With a crown of deathless Praise,
   To triumph in victorious dance
O'er sensual Folly and Intemperance.

Index

The Transcendental Masque

Designed by R. E. Rosenbaum.
Composed by Vail-Ballou Press, Inc.,
in 11 point linotype Janson, 3 points leaded,
with display lines in Caslon Old Style 3371.
Printed letterpress from type by Vail-Ballou
on Warren's 1854 text, 60 pound basis,
with the Cornell University Press watermark.
Illustrations printed offset by Art Craft of Ithaca, Inc.
Bound by Vail-Ballou Press in Interlaken book cloth
and stamped in genuine gold.